The Soviet Bloc
and the Third World

The Soviet Bloc
and the Third World

The Political Economy
of East-South Relations

EDITED BY
Brigitte H. Schulz
and William W. Hansen

Westview Press
BOULDER, SAN FRANCISCO, & LONDON

Westview Special Studies on the Soviet Union and Eastern Europe

Published in 1989 in the United States of America by Westview Press, Inc., 5500 Central Avenue, Boulder, Colorado 80301, and in the United Kingdom by Westview Press, Inc., 13 Brunswick Centre, London, WC1N 1AF, England

Library of Congress Cataloging-in-Publication Data
The Soviet bloc and the Third World : the political economy of East
-South relations / edited by Brigitte H. Schulz and William W.
Hansen.
    p. cm.—(Westview special studies on the Soviet Union and
Eastern Europe)
  Includes bibliographies and index.
  ISBN 0-8133-7513-4
  1. Developing countries—Foreign relations—Europe, Eastern.
2. Europe, Eastern—Foreign relations—Developing countries.
3. Developing countries—Foreign economic relations—Europe,
Eastern. 4. Europe, Eastern—Foreign economic relations—Developing
countries. I. Schulz, Brigitte. II. Hansen, William.
III. Series.
D888.S65S63   1989
327.470172′4—dc19   89-30859
                                                              CIP

Printed and bound in the United States of America

The paper used in this publication meets the requirements of the American National Standard for Permanence of Paper for Printed Library Materials Z39.48-1984.

10   9   8   7   6   5   4   3   2

To the memories of
Billy Hansen, William's eldest son,
and Heinrich Kirch, Brigitte's father,
both of whom died during the preparation of this book

Contents

Acknowledgments

The editors would like to thank the various contributors for their willing cooperation and forthcoming attitude, no matter what the latest odd request (always accompanied by a "hurry-up" demand). We would like, in particular, to thank Peter Schulze, for recruiting several contributors, and Bill Graf, who at the last minute found Jokalee Vanderkop to translate Patrick Gutman's chapter over the Christmas holidays. Brigitte Schulz translated the chapter by Helmut Faulwetter.

Further thanks should go to the Westview Press staff, particularly Barbara Ellington, whose patience with us exceeded anything professionalism alone would dictate. Most of all, however, we would like to thank Erik Lausund, Brigitte's research assistant and student at Seattle University, who typed virtually the entire book at all hours of the day and night, including vacations and holidays. Without him, the completion of this project would have been impossible.

Brigitte H. Schulz
William W. Hansen

1

East-South Relations:
An Introduction

William W. Hansen

> *But if the designing of the future and the proclamation of ready made solutions*
> *for all time is not our affair, then we realize all the more clearly what we have*
> *to accomplish in the present—I am speaking of a* ruthless criticism of everything
> existing, *ruthless in two senses: The criticism must not be afraid of its own*
> *conclusions, nor of conflict with the powers that be.*
> —letter from Karl Marx to Arnold Ruge,
> September 1843

This volume deals with the nature of the relationship between the
countries of Eastern Europe and the Soviet Union and those of the so-
called Third World, within the context of a changing international division
of labor. This marks an important departure from the traditional focus
in both East and West on the ideological and strategic dimensions of
these relations within the framework of the East-West conflict. In the
Manichaean world that emerged after the Second World War the establishment of close ties between a developing country and the East
were seen by both sides in terms of relative gains or losses to the
respective bloc. Thus there existed a general agreement in both East
and West that the path of "socialist orientation" chosen by Angola and
Mozambique in the mid-seventies, for example, represented a significant
shift in the global balance of power in the direction of the East. In
earlier years this same attitude was reflected in analyses of countries
such as Laos, Vietnam, Cuba, Cambodia, Egypt, and Algeria, among
others. The South thus became the battlefield upon which the great
ideological and geopolitical struggles of our day were fought. This
attitude affected not only politicians but also scholars in both the East
and the West.

This volume marks a fundamental departure from the traditional view. Rather than focusing on the East's relations with the South within the context of superpower relations, contributors have analyzed the nature of these ties from the perspective of a changing global economy. Economic changes, most of the authors maintain, have forced fundamental and permanent adjustments in the East's Third World policies during the past decade. This assertion is not shared by all the contributors, some of whom are Eastern Europeans who tend to see their countries' activities in a somewhat less critical light than their Western colleagues.

Throughout the seventies and eighties important changes in the global economy led to a reevaluation of the East's foreign policy objectives *vis-à-vis* the Third World. Several interrelated phenomena were of concern to the socialist countries:

1. revolutionary developments in information technology had brought about fundamental changes in the production process of capitalist firms, not only in the West but also in the South;
2. the danger of the socialist countries becoming increasingly marginalized in the world economy due to the emergence of this technological revolution and of the so-called newly industrializing countries (NICs), who can produce at low labor costs while often employing state-of-the-art technology;
3. the continuing need to import expensive Western technology rather than being able to rely on internally generated innovation, thus requiring continuing hard currency earnings;
4. and a shrinking market for industrial goods in the West due to the non-competitiveness of most of the East's industrial products.

This volume shows that the emergence of Mikhail Gorbachev in the Soviet Union and the policies of *perestroika* associated with his leadership actually are grounded in economic developments that took place during the previous decade. Peter Schulze offers some background to the decline in the Soviet Union's international position, both politically and economically, over the last quarter-century. He points to the inability of the Soviet Union to develop new and advanced forms of production associated with the high-technology explosion in modern capitalist industry. More important, but clearly a consequence of this stagnant economic performance, has been the East's inability to create a separate political-economic mode outside the capitalist world economy. This, argues André Gunder Frank, necessarily led to the reintegration of the East into the global capitalist economy beginning in the seventies and intensifying in the eighties.

The East's inability to generate a socialist economic model also has had important consequences for the recently decolonized countries; i.e., it has failed to offer any kind of an alternative development program to the Third World. In fact, argues Frank in his chapter, the East is no longer interested in creating such an alternative. Forced by its own internal failures to intensify its foreign economic relations, the socialist bloc began borrowing heavily from the West in the seventies with the idea of exporting the resulting production there. However, the end of Western prosperity caused the buildup of an enormous debt in the East. The Western economic crisis was imported and added to the East's own already miserable performance. Abandoning its traditional argument that capitalism would inevitably collapse, the East hitched its economic wagon to a return to capitalist prosperity, thus eschewing any desire to revolutionize the existing global economic order.

As they have become more and more integrated into the existing capitalist division of labor, the socialist countries and their ruling classes have become embedded in, and supporters of, the international status quo. They have come to occupy what Frank calls an "intermediate" position in the world economy. The socialist countries import technology from the West in exchange for raw materials. They export inferior manufactured goods to the South, and in turn import raw materials from there. Often these primary commodities are then sold on the world market for hard currency, which is needed to repay Western debt. Having such an involvement with, and interest in, the status quo, it follows that the socialist countries also have a vested interest in Western recovery and maintenance of the system as it is.

If system maintenance has become one of the cornerstones of the East's foreign policy behavior, as some authors of this volume argue (Frank, Raffer, Schulze, Schulz), then relations with the South must also have undergone important shifts. The book seeks to address the question of how the East envisions that underdevelopment and economic dependence on the West will be overcome by postcolonial societies. To what extent are the socialist countries really interested in aiding in the independent economic growth of the South? Are they primarily interested in creating East-South structures of dependence? Is the building of socialism in the periphery of the global economy even a viable option under present circumstances? William Graf's chapter outlines the changing views of the East on these important questions.

Third World revolutions over the last forty years have been to varying degrees abject failures. Third World radicals have come to realize that they, too, must "fit into" the world system as it presently exists. This bitter lesson has recently been learned by the leadership of Angola and Mozambique, which tried in the immediate aftermath of their independence from Portugal to break all ties with the capitalist world economy. Their efforts were actually discouraged by the East, as both countries were refused admission into the CMEA and, thus, full partnership in the socialist community. International proletarian solidarity notwithstanding, the Eastern bloc was unwilling to embrace perceived economic liabilities when its own situation was so precarious. Winrich Kühne's chapter outlines how the FRELIMO government in Mozambique had to adjust its policies as a consequence of its experiences with the East, after coming to power in 1975.

With this general background, which stresses both the inability of the socialist countries to offer a viable alternative model to capitalist development and the East's growing dependence on the international capitalist economy, the book also deals more specifically with the precise nature of East-South economic ties. Three basic questions are addressed:

1. What is the nature of East-South trade? Do accusations of unequal exchange apply to this trade?
2. How important is this trade for the East, both in terms of imports and exports?
3. How should one assess the growing trend toward the export of complete plants from East to South; i.e., do they represent a special form of East-South economic cooperation or do they constitute a form of capital export?

The first question is answered in different ways by different contributors. Helmut Faulwetter, a well-known East German economist, argues in his chapter that trade between the socialist countries and the Third World is based on "mutually advantageous" relations. To another contributor, Austrian economist Kunibert Raffer, however, this insistence that the East's economic relations with the South cannot, by their very nature, be exploitative is simply a matter of faith that crumbles under the weight of existing empirical evidence.

The second question deals with the level of importance of imports from the South to the economies of the East. Istvan Dobozi, a Hungarian, argues that the East has consistently used the South to fill "supply gaps" for food and fuel in the socialist economies. The picture that emerges in his chapter is of a South that is important not only as a "dumping ground" for technologically inferior products in order to maximize hard currency earnings, but also as a supplier of various foods and raw materials. Brigitte Schulz's case study of East Germany's relations with sub-Saharan Africa outlines some of the mechanisms established to perpetuate these economic relations and essentially confirms Dobozi's findings.

The final question strikes at the heart of an article of "real socialist" faith: Lenin's theory of imperialism, particularly as it applies to the concept of the export of capital. Two Polish economists, Jan and Grazyna Monkiewicz, argue that an answer to the economic problems confronting both the East and the South might be partially addressed by a mutual investment of capital. They refer to this investment as a "form of cooperation" rather than as the "export of capital." Past opposition to capital export to the South is referred to as "ideological superstition" and "prejudice." The notion of profit is viewed by the Monkiewiczes as a necessary and proper by-product of the entire process.

But are such arguments ideologically motivated and designed to disguise CMEA capital exports, since direct investment would make the East the same as the West with regard to the South? Patrick Gutman argues that the creation of equity joint ventures is basically an acceptance of the notion of direct investment and that the export of complete plants is a disguised way of de-localizing and rationalizing particular production sectors through the export of the means of production. This suggests the potential for a transfer of value from the South to the East. Marx— and for obvious reasons Marxian categories are relevant here—clearly viewed the *means of production* as *capital;* the technical or organic composition of capital in his terms. Money, Marx asserted in Volume One of *Das Capital*, was only the original form of it. Thus, the distinction made between finance capital and the means of production does not disprove the notion that the East is able to extract surplus by exporting entire plants paid for through buy-back agreements of the resulting products. If this be the case, is the East just as imperialistic as the West, in the Leninist sense of imperialism?

Does the fact that these exported means of production are owned by the recipient country somehow make the investment qualitatively different from that of multinational corporations? If virtually total control over the resultant production, including the right to sell that production on the world market, remains in the hands not of the legal owner (i.e., the recipient country) but of the original exporters, how does this functionally differ from other forms of capital export? Gutman grapples with these important issues in his chapter.

The last section of the book presents several specific case studies of East-South relations. In looking at the Soviet Union's policies *vis-à-vis* Southern Africa, Winrich Kühne points out that this region is not very high on the Soviet list of priorities. Even in the Soviet Union there is a growing recognition that the East has been unable to provide a workable model for Third World development. This is a rather remarkable admission, given the fervor with which it had traditionally been believed that Leninism did provide such a guide. He concludes that the Soviet

Union will maintain its catechetical rhetoric with regard to the inevitability of the ultimate victory of its version of socialism, but that a more reasoned realism will govern its actual policies in the future.

The other two case studies focus on individual Eastern European countries: The German Democratic Republic (GDR) and Romania, occupying opposite ends of the spectrum in East-South relations. While the GDR has pursued a very orthodox Eastern line, Romania has pursued a more independent Third World policy and has even declared itself a developing country. Robin Remington argues that by pursuing this policy, Romania has created a dilemma. Its attempt to prevent itself from becoming a Soviet-CMEA "south" by pursuing a policy of independent development has pushed it farther toward the actual South. In part, says Remington, Romania identified itself as a developing country to deflect Soviet retaliation for its independent foreign policy. As its economic problems worsened, preventing it from expanding its influence in the Third World, it was urged by the Soviet Union and other CMEA countries to find alternatives, making it necessary for Romania to look to the South. Thus Romania's trade turnover with the Third World is much higher than other CMEA states and it is the only nation to operate at a trade deficit with them. The Monkiewiczes, in this regard, note that Romania is also the leading CMEA investor in the South.

If Romania represents one end of the CMEA spectrum in terms of economic performance, the GDR is its opposite—the economic success story of the East. In her chapter Brigitte Schulz focusses especially on the countries of "socialist orientation" in Africa to show the limits of East-South relations, even for a country as ideologically committed and relatively strong economically as the GDR.

The picture that emerges from this volume very much contradicts the notion of a Soviet bloc on the prowl in the Third World, seeking to gobble up every piece of real estate available. The East appears to entertain few illusions about the rapid, near-term spread of socialism. As most of the authors in this volume at least implicitly argue, what we are witnessing instead is an increasing incorporation of the East into the international division of labor, with the consequence of increasingly blurred distinctions between East and West as viewed from the South. If socialist construction is to take place in the South—and there are few left anywhere in the world who dream of the possibility of a rapid socialist transformation in the periphery—it will have to be done without the active aid of the socialist bloc. There is little evidence that the East actively seeks to alter the existing global order; on the contrary, it has become almost a full (if subordinate) partner in this order that was established and continues to be managed by the West. Should membership in the IMF and the World Bank follow, as is now anticipated by many members of the East bloc, this partnership at the expense of the South will become even more pronounced. The current process of "restructuring" in the East, particularly in the Soviet Union, is an attempt to develop a more streamlined, high-technology system of production able to satisfy the economic needs of the population. This does not include a radical restructuring of the international global economy in the direction of socialism. As discussed by various authors in this volume, in fact, it looks as though the trend is in the opposite direction.

2

The Socialist Countries in the World Economy: The East-South Dimension

André Gunder Frank

The real place and role of the socialist economies of the East in the world economy is ironical, indeed, if it is compared to their spokesmen's theoretical hopes and ideological claims. Just before he died, Joseph Stalin claimed in *The Economic Problems of Socialism* that by then there were two separate and different economic and social systems in the world, one capitalist and the other socialist. His successor, Nikita Khrushchev, belied part of this claim by inciting the Sino-Soviet split in the socialist "system," and he introduced "goulash communism" in the Soviet Union with the promise to "overtake and bury the United States" economically by 1980. The Soviet Union introduced timid economic reforms in the mid-1960s and some of its European allies, especially Hungary, introduced bold reforms in economic organization and policy. However, the hallmark of the latter was the increased role of market prices and increasing integration into the world market, including the progressive introduction of world market prices into the domestic economies of Eastern Europe. This applied especially to their trade among each other. The massive import of Western technology followed in the 1970s.

In 1971–72, all of the socialist economies of Eastern Europe, the Soviet Union, China, and North Korea decided vastly to increase their trade with the West and to enter into production agreements with the West; really to change the international division of productive labor. They would import technology from the West and use it to produce industrial commodities. They hoped to pay for Western technology in part with the export of raw materials, and in part with the export of manufactures that would be produced with this imported technology. Ironically, all the socialist economies and of course the capitalist ones as well (everyone in the world, if I may say so, except me and a half dozen others) were literally banking on the continued prosperity of the West. Many were still slow to realize it when the deep 1973–75 recession, the weak recovery from 1975–79, and the even deeper 1979–1982 recession showed that they had miscalculated. Socialist and Third World countries also had to increase their debts in order to cover these imports. The debt of the socialist countries increased from US$8 billion in 1971 to $80 billion in 1981; that of the Third World increased from US$100 billion in 1971 to $800 billion in 1981.

The socialist economies have come to a sort of intermediate position in the international division of labor. They import manufactures from the West and export primarily raw materials. To the South, however, they export manufactures of a lower quality and at a somewhat lower price. From them they import raw materials. Thus, with regard to the South, the East's position is analogous to its own with regard to the West. Moreover, the East generates a balance of payment surplus with the South and uses part of this to cover its balance of payments deficit with the West. More than 50 percent of Hungary's foreign trade is with the West; more than intra-CMEA. This has led to a crisis. As the crisis in the West has developed it has been imported into the socialist economies and added to the internal crises they already had. It is reflected most dramatically, of course, in Poland, which had a decrease in production of 2 percent in 1979, of 4 percent in 1980, of 14 percent in 1981, and of 12 percent in 1982; a total decline in production and national income of more than one quarter, leading to the political consequences (Solidarity, etc.) of which we know. Let me symbolically point out that the birth of Solidarity followed upon the strikes that came in the wake of the increase in the price of meat in August, 1980. This price increase was one of the austerity measures that the Polish government was obliged to take in order to meet the demands of the International Monetary Fund, Western banks, and so forth. Romania is in a nearly equal economic crisis. In Hungary in 1982 production also declined absolutely, as it did in Czechoslovakia. In the Soviet Union production stagnated in the early 1980s. For several years prior to 1982 the plan was not fulfilled, leading to the subsequent reduction of the targets for the following year, which in turn was also not fulfilled, leading once again to a target reduction for the forthcoming year, etc., until in 1982 the plan's growth target in the Soviet Union was the lowest since 1928, when comrade Stalin began the first five year economic plan. In general, in the socialist countries economic growth in each five year plan period was lower than in the previous one.

There is clearly a growth crisis in the socialist economies. The very serious question it raises is Lenin's *shto dielaet?*—what is to be done? Does one retreat to a more closed and more integrated intra-CMEA economy, or engage in a flight forward into further integration into the world capitalist economy? The answer is that only the second alternative is possible. Indeed, any more of the first also involves more of the second. The economic and political costs of trying to go backwards would be too immense and the only thing that can be done is to go further down the road that has already been taken; that of integration into the world capitalist market with the economic, social, and political consequences that this implies. When Stalin, just before he died, wrote about *The Economic Problems of Socialism,* he said that the law of value operates in one part of and not in another part of the socialist economy. However, he was referring to some sort of "socialist law of value." Yet not just some "socialist" law of value, but the law of value of the world capitalist economy operates in the socialist economies. This holds true not only for such an obvious case as Yugoslavia, but also increasingly for Eastern Europe as well as China. The plan is being increasingly abolished in China and market relations steadily reintroduced for all but the basic products; and of course the Chinese, let alone the East European, market is increasingly connected to the world capitalist market.

One might say, however, that the Soviet Union is relatively isolated, and this is true. However, the Soviet Union is connected to the world market through the East European economies. Consider the increasing dependence of the Soviet Union on manufactures imported from Eastern Europe, which are produced with technology imported from the West. Yugoslavia is an illustrative case in point. Technology was imported from the West with the thought that it could be paid for by exporting manufactures to the West. However, they were found not to be competitive. The reason that the trade between Yugoslavia and the Soviet Union has increased so much in the last few years is because the former is selling textiles to the Soviet Union, produced with machinery imported from the West, which cannot be sold in the West. In fact, there is here a possibility of some kind of a triangular relationship whereby Eastern Europe buys technology from the West and cannot pay for it. Consequently, it sells the products of the technology to the Soviet Union, which in turn exports gas and oil to the West in order to pay its bills and close the circle. There is a certain economic rationale to such an extension of already existing tendencies, but it would promote an extension of the political implications of further East-West trade as well.

Thus, it has turned out that the "independent" policies of "planned" goulash communism required the import of Western technology to ease the transition from extensive growth (stuffing more raw meat into the goulash sausage machine) to intensive growth (improving the productivity of the machine) in order to be able to produce and afford more goulash. Moreover, the import of this technology, and the imported technology itself, made the socialist East more and more dependent; not only technologically, but financially, economically, politically, socially, ideologically, and culturally on the capitalist West. The world capitalist economic crisis then exacerbated this dependence or its manifestations in the East. Western inflation and other manifestations of the crisis were imported wholesale. The Hungarian economist, A. Köves, points out, for example, with italic emphasis that ironically "the share of trade with the West grew in general also in the total trade of CMEA countries"; "the objective process of development demands that economic policy should give preference to export orientation at the expense of import substitution"; and "in other words, increased participation in the international division of labor, opening towards the world economy, was put on each CMEA country's agenda by the requirements of domestic social and economic development."[1] The requirement of this increased international participation is the strongest and has the most far-reaching domestic consequences precisely, and ironically, in the field in which the socialist economies were supposed to offer the most independent alternative and the strongest development policy; that is, technology. However, as it turns out, technological development and the development of technology are a subproduct of world economic development and the long cyclical process of capital accumulation on a world scale. Far from having escaped from this process through socialist planning, the socialist economies of the East turn out, ironically, to be integral parts and integrated processes of this world economic development. Moreover, although they have pulled ahead of many Third World countries, the advanced socialist economies still remain dependent upon, and increasingly behind, the most technologically advanced sectors of the capitalist world economy. Far from burying the United States by 1980, the Soviet Union has lagged further behind and is being outperformed by Japan. Ironically, the same planned command economy that promoted extensive growth now turns out to be a handicap in competing world wide through intensive growth with technological development. Indeed, some capitalist East Asian and also South American NICs (newly industrializing countries) have been outcompeting the socialist East European NICs and capturing their market share and more of industrial exports to the West.

All this suggests a serious observation. During the last crisis, when there was only one socialist country or, to coin a phrase, socialism in one country, there was still the policy and the hope that that country, and communist movements elsewhere in the world, would wish and try to use that crisis of capitalism to prevent its restructuring and the renewed recovery of capitalism on a stronger basis; such as then happened after the Second World War. In the present crisis, this is no longer the case. This is why, in spite of any arithmetic about communist party numbers and members, the crisis of communism is now vastly greater. Today there is not a single socialist country, not any communist party in power, out of power, or aspiring to power, which seriously proposes to use the crisis of capitalism to destroy capitalism, as Lenin had hoped. On the contrary, as Konstantin Chernenko said several years ago, there must be a revision of Khrushchev's 1960 CPSU program that contemplated the imminent demise of capitalism. Chernenko argued that communists must be realistic and recognize that capitalism is still very strong and that communists must take this into account. More than that, his predecessor by two, Leonid Brezhnev, noted that the crisis of capitalism deeply affects the Soviet Union because of its relationship with capitalism. Todor Zhivkov not so long ago declared that the crisis of capitalism affects the Bulgarian economy so deeply that he hopes that it will soon be over so that we can get back to business as usual. That is to say, socialists and communists now hope to do all they can to join the train of renewed capitalist recovery, and have abandoned any hope or effort that that train will soon derail. They want to get back on it and ride with it. That is a realistic assessment of the socialist economies and the communist movement. The real crisis—the danger and opportunity—and problem of socialists and communists is that they have no more program other than to help make a crisis-ridden world capitalism work better. The real challenge is to offer a plausible and effective alternative program which is at least as good, if not better, than that of the various competing new populist social movements (whose growing ability to mobilize people is itself a reflection of the failure of socialists and communists).

These tendencies have been further extended and accelerated in many ways under Gorbachev, as reflected in the Soviet Communist Party Program and 27th Congress in 1986, other Soviet political and scientific practice and pronouncements, and the actions, speeches, and writings of Mikhail Gorbachev himself. He never tires of explicitly emphasizing everybody's "integration" and "interdependence" in the world. Gorbachev's domestic economic *perestroika* reforms and the political *glasnost* liberalization necessary therefore testify to the unavoidable Soviet need to improve its capacity to compete in the world economy, which he says no one can any longer avoid. His diplomatic and strategic offensives are an extension of peaceful coexistence into the indefinite future and an implicit recognition that there is no further prospect of the even gradual replacement of capitalism by socialism in the foreseeable future.

He proposes strengthening the United Nations as an instrument of East-West, North-South, and other conflict resolution.

With regard to the Third World in particular, at the 1986 CPSU Congress Gorbachev and others all but eliminated references to Third World socialist orientation, which was distinguished as very different from, and not necessarily leading to, socialism. A Western observer writes:

> In rethinking their relationship to the Third World, the Soviets are engaged in a sweeping reevaluation of the appropriateness of the socialist model for developing societies, patterns of economic and political development, and the variety and vagaries of Third World aspirations. There is nothing "purely academic" about this endeavor; it has very real consequences. . . . Now some [Soviet] experts are arguing that an even more fundamental rethinking is in order—an admission that capitalism not only is but will remain the predominant system in the Third World. Such arguments go beyond what was set forth in the 1986 Party program, which only recognized that capitalism is not doomed but, on the contrary, has bright prospects. . . . The Soviets no longer seem to be claiming that socialism is the wave of the Third World's future, nor that capitalism, in these countries is a temporary transitional phase. And they are putting the Third World on notice that they no longer wish to finance the building of socialism in these countries.[2]

Other evidence suggests that the Soviet Union is downgrading its interests in Africa and in its own African Studies Institute (one of whose members at a conference in Zimbabwe relegated Southern Africa to the bottom of a list, behind a half dozen other regions more important to Soviet interests, as did an influential American Africanist for the USA). On the other hand, Foreign Minister Edvard Sheverdnaze's trips to Latin America and Asia and other evidence suggests that the Soviet Union is upgrading its commercial and political relations with major capitalist countries in the Third World. The Soviet Union and other socialist states recognize that they no longer offer an economic alternative for others to beat the capitalist world economy, and that they must do all they can just to join it themselves.

These observations raise further serious questions about North-South and East-West relations, and about the apparent and real relationships between these two sets of relations. In particular, it seems necessary to re-examine more objectively how real the options are either to build a new international economic order (NIEO), especially one based on alternative "socialist" North-South relations with the help of CMEA—or, failing that, to delink from the old international economic order and establish socialist relations on national or regional levels, or at least to pursue socialist oriented development (which is the new Soviet terminology for what they used to call non-capitalist development).

Any objective analysis soon reveals that North-South relations and Third World development have turned out to be far more the consequences (and subject to the limitations) of the cyclical course of world economic development than intentional political choice. Even the fifteen supposed Third World revolutions in the decade after 1974 have, in reality, done far less than their protagonists proposed, their supporters claimed, and their opponents feared. Despite the entrenchment of ideology in some capitals in the North and South, in reality ideology in the Third World has made far-reaching concessions to economic expediency.

The European and Japanese colonialism of the pre-war era was largely displaced by what some call US neocolonialism or neo-imperialism. The Americans said colonialism is bad, and everyone should open their markets to anyone. Free trade was a particularly attractive proposition for the Americans, of course, at the time when they were industrially dominant and could thereby penetrate the Third World markets of the old colonial powers. Britain had also been a free trader in the mid-nineteenth century when it was the industrial top dog. However, now the West Europeans and the Japanese have become the principal challengers to the United States in the previously American-dominated neocolonial Third World.

The last depression and the last war set the stage for substantial decolonization in the world. However, decolonization did not everywhere lead to the liberation that was anticipated, but led instead to neocolonialism in many parts of the Third World. National liberation became an important movement against colonialism in those regions. In neocolonial areas such as Latin America national liberation survived and, in some cases, grew, and continues to be an important political policy and movement. The reason is that accession to formal political independence is a long way from the achievement of real economic independence from the world economy, as bitter experience has taught many people to their chagrin. However, does the capture of state power by another class or coalition open the way to real political independence and economic development through national liberation and socialism, or at least socialist orientation?

In this regard, whatever else Washington and Moscow may disagree on, an important irony is that the one thing on which they do seem to agree is that this movement, which some call national liberation and others call the opposite, is advancing by leaps and bounds. Concretely, both Washington and Moscow count fourteen different countries in the Third World that in the decade after 1974 have become either socialist, or what the Soviet Union calls socialist-oriented; the Americans claim that they have fallen under Soviet domination. The Americans think this is a very bad thing and the Soviets think it is a very good thing; but both agree that this process has been taking place. The Soviet Union's position is that this process must be supported and promoted; the Americans want to contain it, and presently under President Ronald Reagan they even want to roll it back. The Kissinger Commission Report on Central America made it terribly clear that the issue in that area, in the eyes of the Reagan administration, is not North-South and not internal responses to internal problems, but in reality an East-West problem. There are very few other people who would agree with that point of view, which seems at odds with all the evidence.

Current American policy in Central America, and most specifically in Nicaragua, is forging a relation and some alliance between the Nicaraguan Sandinistas and the Soviet Union which would not exist were the Americans not pursuing such a policy. The same thing happened when Vietnam, after 1975, wanted immediate so-called normalization of relations with the Americans; diplomatic recognition, economic aid and foreign investment, especially in oil. It was the Americans who refused. The Americans responded negatively in part on their own hook, but in part because they were blackmailed into this policy by the Chinese. The Chinese said to the Americans in 1975 that the latter would have to choose between Beijing and Hanoi. The Americans chose Beijing and abandoned Vietnam to the Soviet embrace. The same process is now being repeated in Central America, although it is not done at the behest of the Chinese as with Vietnam.

However, the main irony in the Washington-Moscow agreement about the supposed pro-Soviet socialist/anti-American imperialist progress of totalitarianism/liberation is that much of this supposed progress/regress is belied by the facts. These fourteen cases are well-known; Socialist Vietnam, Laos, and Kampuchea in Indochina; the ex-Portuguese colonies of Angola, Mozambique, Guinea-Bissau, Cape Verde, and Sao Tomé, along with Zimbabwe and Ethiopia in Africa; the PR Yemen, Iran, and Afghanistan in West Asia; and Nicaragua in Central America. Grenada, before it was invaded by the United States, once made the total fifteen. However, first of all, the ones that have become socialist are not very many and their socialism has been, all things considered, a bit disappointing to the people and to their leadership, and to many elsewhere who supported the national liberation struggle, especially the very heroic struggle in Vietnam.

Secondly, what the Soviets call socialist orientation, the countries which are not yet socialist but supposedly on the road to it, are not travelling very far or very fast along that road. None of them have cut or even tried to cut their economic and political relations with the West, and those that went a little way along that road in the mid-seventies have stopped and backtracked during the eighties. A stellar example is that of Mozambique, which under very severe pressures—economic, political, military, and climatic—signed a pact with South Africa. David Rockefeller visited Mozambique to look at investment opportunities. Rockefeller already said some time ago, referring particularly to Angola, that a lot of places that call themselves Marxist are not really so, and even if they are, it does not matter as long as they are responsible and can be dealt with; that is to say, when it is possible to make money with them. Moreover, the main export of Angola is oil from Cabinda and that is guarded by the Cuban troops there. Most of the oil and Angola's diamonds and coffee, etc., are exported to the West. So another irony is that there has been really no attempt on the part of Angola to cut its ties with the West. Indeed, ironically, the Soviet Union has repeatedly insisted that Angola should not cut those ties because the Soviet Union does not want another Cuba there (although, also ironically, Cuba is helping defend the regimes in Angola and Ethiopia).

In Zimbabwe, which was also decolonized through protracted guerilla struggle, progress toward socialism or even away from dependence on the West, or indeed on South Africa, has not been any greater. Its prime minister, Robert Mugabe, has declared that he is not only a practicing Marxist, but also a practical one! So all of these regimes are well on the road to neocolonialism on the Kenyan or Ivory Coast models, though probably without the relative successes of these countries prior to their present crises. The other ex-Portuguese colonies, Guinea-Bissau, etc. are best left altogether unmentioned in this regard, other than to observe that the politically and ideologically most advanced socialist movement in Africa, which was led by Amilcar Cabral, has failed completely to build the kind of society he had envisioned and fought for. In each case, world economic realities negated national political illusions.

So, to begin with, these revolutions are not all that they are claimed to be, either by Moscow or by Washington. Then, in reckoning, no one seems ever to mention what has happened on the other side of the balance; first and foremost the Sino-Soviet split and then the de-Maoization of China. The Washington-Beijing-Tokyo axis has even caught up Ronald Reagan. Secondly, Egypt, Somalia, and then Grenada have changed sides. In Grenada, it happened with American military intervention; but the murder of Maurice Bishop certainly provided a pretext, at least in Fidel Castro's judgement. Moreover, we have to ask ourselves seriously, how many Grenadas (while Bishop was there) and Sandinista Nicaraguas does it take to counterbalance one China? Quite a few, to any balanced reckoning, which seems to be out of fashion in both

Washington and Moscow. So, on the one thing about which the Americans and the Soviets really agree, they are both wrong.

Particularly revealing in this regard are the experiences in Cuba and Fidel Castro's observations about revolutionary social change. In January, 1985, Castro reported that the top and middle Cuban leadership had undertaken a three-day intensive agonizing reappraisal of the Cuban economy and economic policy the previous November (as a result of which dozens of senior cadre were replaced).[3] He noted that the widely acclaimed Cuban welfare state, and especially the maintenance of its social services during periods of world economic recession, were only possible due to the generosity of Soviet aid. Henceforth, the same level of social services could no longer be maintained, and Cuban economic policy had to be changed radically. From then on, the first order of priority would have to be export promotion to hard currency (capitalist) areas. The next priority would be export promotion to socialist countries. The third priority would have to be import substituting production to save both hard and soft foreign exchange. The last priority would be to save the minimum necessary state welfare services. Everything else, including many other welfare services, would henceforth have to be sacrificed. Since then, Fidel Castro has had to announce several more notches of belt tightening.

Castro has recently also made revealing observations about revolution and social change elsewhere:

> Social change alone is not enough. . . . Marx himself always considered economic development to be a premise for socialism. . . . I tell you, a revolution in poverty is better than a system of exploitation, but you can't meet the enormous needs that have accumulated in all our countries—in Cuba, Bolivia, and Nicaragua—with social changes alone. . . . If you ask me what I think, I'll tell you. I'm a socialist above everything . . . but . . . the dumbest thing I could do in these statements would be to say that everything should be nationalized and socialized and begin to confiscate this, that, and the other. Not even the Nicaraguans do that. They have a radical revolution, but they have said "Well, let's advance the mixed economy and the pluralist system, which is what is needed in these circumstances."[4]

As a realist, in view of the dominance of the world economy and the present effects of the world economic crisis on the Third World, Castro now answers the question as to what he wishes, both as a revolutionary and a radical by saying,

> Do you know what I want? Right now, I sincerely believe that the cancellation of that [Third World] debt and the establishment of the new international

economic order is much more important than two, three, or four isolated revolutions. . . . I said without any hesitation, "It is preferable to achieve the new order immediately, so we'll all have the right to make social changes, than to have three or four revolutions . . . and I'm a radical."[5]

However, the position of Cuba and the revelations of Fidel Castro highlight a major additional problem for, and irony of, Third World development, socialism, North-South, and East-West relations. As titular head of the non-aligned movement (NAM) of Third World states from 1979 to 1982, Castro already experienced the failure of the new international economic order (NIEO) at first hand. The ideological roots of the NIEO had been planted at the founding of NAM at Bandung in 1955. The economic philosophy was developed at the Afro-Asian Economic Seminar in Algiers and the founding of the Group of 77 (now 125) countries and UNCTAD in Geneva in 1964. The political imperative of NIEO was supplied by the apparent success of OPEC and expressed at the NAM heads of state meeting in Algiers and the UN General Assembly resolutions in 1974. Countless negotiations followed for a decade to no avail. Finally, in 1983, all practical hopes for NIEO were buried in the sands of Cancun, Mexico by the failure of face-to-face dialogue of North-South presidents set up at the instance of the Brandt Commission (to which, symbolically, Fidel Castro was not invited at President Reagan's insistence). The NIEO, to which Fidel Castro seems to refer, has already proved to be a nonstarter and a pipe dream. The USSR never, never showed any enthusiasm for, and occasionally voted against, NIEO.

So is Castro calling for a new and different NIEO? In the above-cited interview and speech, he says that

> . . . as a Third World, developing socialist country, Cuba has already established a form of new international economic order with the rest of the socialist community. Without these foundations, our great and social successes . . . wouldn't have been possible. . . . If we hadn't established that New Order you (journalists) wouldn't be here now, and neither would I.[6]

Yet, in his speeches on the Cuban economy, Fidel already recognized that this new order could no longer be maintained without reversion to more trade with the capitalist countries and more domestic economic and social sacrifices even by Cuba. Of course, still less is any such new order an option for Nicaragua, Angola, Mozambique, and other "socialist-oriented" countries, as Castro himself recognizes when he names their revolutions and observes, "What happens when they occur: since we are totally dependent, they immediately blockade us; they grab the pygmies one by one when they rebel."[7]

However, the real problem of this dependence is not so much that the capitalists take advantage of it to blockade, or invade, as in Nicaragua and Grenada; but that economically the Third World pygmies, and, apparently, even its giants such as China, have nowhere else to go, and especially not to escape into a socialist new economic order. There exists no alternative "third way, non-capitalist" NIEO, and the socialist countries led by the Soviet Union, have failed to create even a second way, an alternative socialist NIEO. We will examine some of the limitations of the CMEA for the Soviet Union and Eastern Europe below.

For the Third World, the CMEA offers scarce options beyond some trade expansion, however, and certainly no alternative socialist world market or new international economic order with significantly different rules of the game. In fact, as we observed above, the socialist countries themselves are increasingly reintegrating into the same old international economic order of the world capitalist economy. This reintegration may or may not be due to the limitations or failures of economic planning in the Soviet Union and Eastern Europe, or China. However, even more and better economic planning in the CMEA would not offer wider or better opportunities for the Third World to participate in an alternative socialist world economy, as Romania has found to its great cost. Instead, the better the intra-CMEA planning, the more it excludes integration of additional outsiders who have only recently made political revolutions. More CMEA market integration offers the Third World wider trade options but with a division of labor and on price terms that are not significantly different from those in the remainder of the world capitalist economy.

The irony—and in the classical Greek sense, tragedy—is that, as Castro is forced to recognize, political revolutions, not to mention political rhetoric alone, offer scarce possibilities to escape from the world capitalist economy, which may only be politically denounced. In other words, much Third Worldist socialist rhetoric is just that, and no more. Ironically, political support from the Socialist East for liberation in the South violates the classical Marxist historical materialist maxim about the priority of the economic infrastructure over the political superstructure: The East has supported superstructural change in the South with words and sometimes arms, but without being able to offer the really necessary infrastructural support of an economic alternative. Marxist theory and practice has come full circle: from Marx's priority of (infrastructural) development of the forces of production—to Lenin's (superstructural) change in the relations of production—to Mao's cultural revolutionary change in consciousness—back to the classical Marxist infrastructural development of the forces of production, which is newly in vogue in the supply side West, East, and South.

Of course, this fact of life in the world economy also means that the anti-communist rhetoric, and anti-socialist or anti–Third Worldist military policies of some capitalists—especially of the Reagan administration— is little more than a Quixotic and illusionary right-wing response to left-wing political illusions. For without a viable economic alternative, which does not now exist even on the horizon, the political alternative of a socialist new order for the Third World has no real foundation. For the same reason, the conservative political opposition to this non-existent radical alternative has no sense; or at least not the one that is claimed for it by both right and left ideologues alike.

These observations, among others, suggest that much of the past East-West conflict, especially between Washington and Moscow, is a smokescreen cover for North-South conflicts. We have already observed that the East-West conflict is used by both Moscow and Washington to press harder bargains and even to avert blackmail against their respective allies. One of the areas in which Moscow, and especially Washington, do so is on North-South issues. The examples are legion of United States pressure on its European allies to back up, or at least condone, American policy; earlier in Vietnam and now in Central America, as well as constantly in the Middle East, on the supposed grounds of combatting a Soviet communist threat. The successful pressure by the conservative President Reagan on the socialist President, Francois Mitterrand of France, again to intervene militarily in Chad is another example.

However, the East-West conflict also provides a welcome, if unnecessary, pretext for United States and Soviet direct intervention in the Third World to further their own interests in the North-South conflict. The intervention of the United States in Central America under the Reagan administration is only the most recent example of a long list that stretches back to Grenada in 1983, Lebanon in 1983 (and in 1958); Vietnam, Laos, and Kampuchea; Chile from 1970 to 1973; Santa Domingo in 1965; and many other cases too numerous to mention. The argument is always the same, to combat or prevent Soviet communist intervention or takeover; and without this pretext, the American intervention would lack the necessary "legitimacy." Perhaps the most revealing aspect is that the Soviet communist bogeyman is used in Washington to drum up congressional and public support for ever larger military expenditures, the vast bulk of which are not for nuclear and other arms directed at the Soviet Union, but for conventional arms specifically designed for use in and against the Third World. The US Rapid Deployment Force is only the most conspicuous tip of the iceberg of this United States military capacity for direct intervention and other shows of force in the Third World. Without the convenient availability of the Soviet communist enemy, neither this American military expenditure nor its policy of intervention to keep the neocolonial Third World in line, and especially to keep the United States' backyard in Latin America subservient, could be politically justified.

Moreover, the maintenance of this capitalist economic neocolonialism on the part of the United States does not even require most of this kind of political intervention; for the dependent Third World countries have few real alternatives. The ones they have are largely closer economic and political relations with American rivals in Western Europe and Japan, as long as the Soviet Union and Eastern Europe remain unable to offer adequate trade and industrial alternatives. Of course, this means the continued use of East-West conflicts to intervene in intra-Western rivalries. The same East-West conflict, moreover, also plays a significant role in the domestic class struggle within each of the countries of the West and the South, where the supposed communist threat and the Soviet bogeyman are used to legitimate virtually any policies of the ruling classes and to strengthen their bargaining power against the interests of the majority of the people. Of course, the usefulness of the communist scare internally, then, exposes America's allies to its use against them by the United States abroad.

Is it any different in the East? Perhaps. However, there can be no denying that the allies of the Soviet Union are also under pressure to accept its foreign policies in the Third World in the name of combatting the common American-led imperialist enemy. Moreover, the Soviet intervention in Afghanistan was a clear case of defense or promotion of the interests of the Soviet Union, or its Russian ruling class, against the threat of a Muslim movement that might spread into Muslim areas of the Soviet Union itself. However, this threat was backed up by the United States and its Central Intelligence Agency, against which Soviet intervention is supposedly necessary. Soviet aid and trade in the Third World, much of which is often on terms that are no better than those of the West, is also justified by reference to the imperialist enemy. Soviet and allied social control at home and abroad, as was the case several years ago in Poland, is of course also fortified by reference to defense against imperialist subversion. So the East-West conflict is also used by the Soviet Union to promote Northeastern interests in the South and to defend the status quo in the East. The East-West conflict is useful for many purposes on both sides, most all of them detrimental to the Third World.

Conclusions

A number of conclusions are almost inescapable for Third World countries and liberation movements today. There may be scientific or political disputes about the evaluation of really existing socialism today; however, it is indisputable that both economically and politically the socialist countries are rapidly reintegrating in the world capitalist international division of labor and promoting peaceful coexistence between socialist and capitalist states. Moreover, with particular exceptions (like Cuba and Vietnam that prove the rule?), the socialist countries have failed to establish a division of labor and market as a viable *alternative* to the world capitalist one, either for themselves or even less for "noncapitalist development" "socialist oriented" progressive Third World countries and liberation movements.

Furthermore, the Chinese since the ascension of Deng Xiaoping and the Soviet Union since that of Mikhail Gorbachev have sought increasingly to disengage their foreign policy and foreign trade from (never all too great) solidarity relations with the Third World and have increasingly replaced these with commercial interests and relations with the capitalist world economy, particularly with the West but also with commercially selected parts of the South.

As mentioned above, Marxism has come full circle in praxis and theory, except that now any contradictions of this development with relations of production are postponed into the unforeseeable future—and for now it is time to play catch as catch can.

Thus the Chinese Premier Zhao Ziyang told the Thirteenth Party Congress:

> Whatever is conducive to the growth [of the productive forces] is in keeping with the fundamental interests of the people and is therefore needed by socialism and allowed to exist. . . . To believe that it is possible to jump over the primary stage of socialism, in which productive forces are to be developed, is to take a utopian position on this question and is the major cognitive root of Left mistakes.[8]

From an earlier Deng Xiaoping statement that it does not matter if a cat is black or white so long as it catches mice, Chinese orthodoxy has moved virtually to "anything that works is socialist," or more accurately promotes the development of primary socialism and the subsequent transition to real socialism, which China is now not scheduled to reach until the middle of the twenty-first century.

As for Soviet socialism, Mikhail Gorbachev has written,

We have seen the main issue—the growing tendency toward interdependence of the states of the world community. Such are the dialectics of present-day development. The world [is] contradictory, socially and politically diverse but nonetheless interconnected and integral. . . . We say with full responsibility, casting away the false considerations of "prestige," that all of us in the present-day world are coming to depend more and more on one another and are becoming increasingly necessary to one another.[9]

In his report to the Central Committee on the occasion of the 70th anniversary of the Revolution, Gorbachev concretized:

The reasons for this include the internationalism of world economic ties, the comprehensive scope of scientific and technological revolution, the essentially novel role played by the mass media, the state of the Earth's resources, the common environmental danger, and the crying social problems of the developing world which affect us all. . . . By making it possible for us to attain the world level in all major economic indicators, perestroika will enable our vast and wealthy country to become involved in the world division of labour and resources in a way never known before.[10]

With regard to the Third World, Gorbachev said on the same occasion that "the calls for severing historically shaped world economic ties are dangerous and offer no solution." He argues:

I have explained on many occasions that we do not pursue goals inimical to Western interests. We know how important the Middle East, Asia, Latin America, other Third World regions and also South Africa are for American and West European economies, in particular as raw material sources. To cut these links is the last thing we want to do, and we have no desire to provoke ruptures in historically formed, mutual economic interests.[11]

Instead, in his above cited 70th birthday of Soviet socialism speech, Gorbachev lauded the "colossal potentialities of the organizations [who] have a stake in the new world economic order" from the Non-Aligned Movement and the Organization of African Unity to ASEAN and the Organization of American States.

With regard to southern and South Africa, where popular hopes for socialism with close relations with the Soviet Union are perhaps highest, Gorbachev wrote that "the Soviet Union has no special interests in southern Africa."[12] Victor Goncharov, the Deputy Director of Moscow's Institute of African Studies, publicly explained further in the author's presence at a conference in Harare that southern Africa is at the bottom of the list of Soviet regional priorities:

We said at the conference that USA interests are minimal in the region, ours are even less in South Africa itself. This is why, from my point of view, there is a basis for cooperation for an acceptable settlement, acceptable to everybody. . . . The emotion of the past three years has given birth to hopes of a quick victory, but it will not be very quick. Maybe ten years, I say not less than ten years. Yes, I believe that in the end South Africa will become socialist, maybe not in 25 years, but in a century. . . . I am an optimist.[13]

In short, both objectively and subjectively speaking, really existing socialism offers scant realistic hopes for any real alternative solution to Third World problems today. The socialist economies offer the Third World no alternative escape, and their leaders condemn proposals to "stop the world, I want to get off" and de-link as illusory and dangerous. On the other hand, two other developments are gaining force and possibility. One is that more of the Third World (and some First and Second World) populations and regions may be increasingly marginalized or de-linked, or un-linked, against their will. The other is that both linked and un-linked populations are increasingly resorting to largely defensive social movements instead of, or at least in addition to, the more classical political liberation movements.

Long before Henry Kissinger coined the term "de-stabilization" for his policy of embargoing, isolating, and undermining the government of Salvador Allende in Chile from 1970 to 1973, the West sought to de-stabilize and de-link socialist and socialist oriented countries. Indeed, the economic isolation of, and embargoes against, Cuba, Vietnam, and Nicaragua were far more the political volition and doing of the West, and particularly the United States, than of their own designs. Cuba's number one demand during twenty-five years of revolution as been that the American embargo against it be lifted. Each progressive government or regime in its turn is threatened and blackmailed with economic isolation and political de-stabilization.

However, both the short run course of the present world economic crisis and the long run resource-saving, informatic-service society developments in the West now threaten to marginalize or de/un-link ever greater populations and regions, because they offer declining economic sources of profitable exploitation (in some cases after they had already been squeezed dry in earlier historical phases). Much of Africa, which is highly dependent on raw materials exports and where per capita incomes have declines by one fourth during the 1980s alone, seems to be a major case in point. It may be hoped that if Africans and others are increasingly marginalized economically, they may at least—through what used to be called benign neglect?—be left to their own political devices. These may include the domestic redistribution of political power and economic wealth, but they are not likely to provide for long term income benefits from economic isolation.

At the same time, people are organizing themselves into all kinds of social movements to serve their own immediate demands. A major reason is the popular perception of increasing foreign and domestic paralysis of states and governments in attending peoples' widespread economic needs and political and cultural desires (of both linked and un-linked populations). Although many of these demands cannot and will not ever be met, these social movements mobilize masses of people in their own pursuit. In so doing, they help to transform society through the promotion in praxis of active participatory democracy in civil and often political society and the dignification of the participating individuals. It is these social movements that today express and represent peoples' greatest hopes.

Notes

1. *Acta Oeconomica,* Vol. 21, No. 4, 1978, pp. 306, 302, and 301.

2. Elizabeth Kridl Valkenier, "New Soviet Thinking about the Third World," in *World Policy Journal,* Vol. 4, No. 4, Fall 1987, pp. 672, 664, 668.

3. *Granma,* 6 January 1985.

4. Interview in *Excelsior* of Mexico, and reprinted by *Editora Politica,* Havana, 1985.

5. *This is the Battle for Latin America's Real Independence,* Address given at the Fourth Congress of the Latin American Federation of Journalists, Havana, July 6, 1985, official Cuban translation.

6. *Ibid.*

7. *Excelsior* interview, *op. cit.*

8. Quoted by Stuart Schram in *IHJ Bulletin,* Tokyo, Vol. 8, No. 2, Spring 1988.

9. Mikhail Gorbachev, *Perestroika,* Harper and Row, New York: 1987, p. 137.

10. *Moscow News,* Supplement to No. 45, 1987.

11. Gorbachev, *Perestroika,* pp. 137, 178.

12. *Ibid.,* p. 188.

13. *Liberation,* Dar es Salaam, No. 10, March–April, 1988, pp. 4, 7.

3

The Theory of
the Non-Capitalist Road

William D. Graf

The general concept of *a* non-capitalist road to development (ncr) is
an analytical construct, produced by historical reality, to account for the
fact that Marxist-based revolutions in this century have not occurred at
the peak of a series of stages of socio-historical evolution leading through
the full development of the productive forces of advanced capitalism.
Lenin's notion of the "weak link" of capitalism, Trotsky's "law of combined
development," and Stalin's strategy of "socialism in one country" all
represent attempts to come to terms with, and indeed to rationalize and
prescribe, a revolutionary theory and strategy for undeveloped and
underdeveloped areas in the world capitalist system. The theory of *the*
Non-Capitalist Road (NCR), building upon but simultaneously transforming the ncr, has been formulated by Stalin's successors as a set of
prescriptions evolving over time for socialist-oriented development in
the "Third World." With all its variations and nuances—socialist orientation, the national liberation movement, the state of democratic
revolution, etc.—it has become something like a leitmotif in the official
thinking of the Soviet Union and the Peoples' Democracies in Eastern
Europe as a theoretical-ideological underpinning of policies, tasks and
prescriptions *for* the South; entirely analogous to the role of modernization
theories in the West. Also like the NCR, it represents an ideological
concession based on a realization that much of the Third World is not
(yet?) capable of rapid socialist transformation and that the world capitalist
system still functions in some measure as a dominant global force.

In this chapter,[1] I first attempt to "reconstruct" the theory of the
Non-Capitalist Road from a variety of complementary and occasionally
contradictory East European sources. This admittedly tenuous and, to
some extent, subjective endeavor is intended to clarify and elucidate the

premises and analytical-ideological core of the theory, which it necessarily simplifies without, one hopes, oversimplifying. An important aspect of this process is to achieve an adequate "periodization" of the evolution of the NCR, since locating it in a temporal and power-political context helps to impose some conceptual order on a number of ostensible inconsistencies and departures. The argument leads into a critical analysis of the functions, interests, and effects of the theory, its "fit" with Southern needs and conditions, and its correspondence with the wider complex of state-socialist policies and goals. Throughout, the method of analysis is that of immanent critique, which I take to mean as unbiased an examination as possible of the actual theory, based on its own content, values, and prescriptions. While this in no way is to advance a claim to objectivity, it does mean eschewing any attempt at *a priori* reasoning based on predetermined categories or ideological predispositions.[2] In other words, I will try to present the NCR on its own terms and criticize it within the framework of its proclaimed norms and goals.

The Need for Theory

During the two decades of socialism in one country, the Soviet experience of development was in itself a sufficient model of the non-capitalist road to development, and the Leninist theory of imperialism, revolution, and monopoly capitalism an adequate theoretical-ideological explanation for relations between the Soviet Union and the Third World. Before the Second World War, the Soviets' capacities were, apart from their leading role in the Communist International, necessarily directed toward domestic development and the creation of the material preconditions for the transition to socialism. Under the circumstances, Soviet prescriptions for overcoming underdevelopment amounted to vague recommendations for an international anti-imperialist front combined with emulation of the Soviet model: anti-capitalist revolution under the direction of a vanguard party, forced capital accumulation by the state, centralized economic planning and control, mass mobilization guided by democratic centralism, a cultural revolution (as part of the latter) to eliminate illiteracy and traditionalist attitudes, and a system of labor rationalization and intensification.

However, after 1945, the changed constellation of world political forces placed the Soviet Union squarely at the intersection of two fundamental historical-political movements: the East-West and North-South conflicts. The Soviets rapidly emerged from the period of relative isolation and underdevelopment into the role of hegemonic power in a world communist movement encompassing one-third of the world's population, including the "Third World" countries of China, North Korea, and North Viet

Nam. At the same time, the postwar period also produced a great variety of independence movements and national liberation fronts which, despite their diversity, were moving toward an anti-imperialist strategy in that their central goals could be realized only in opposition to the then prevailing system of direct colonialism.

Partly for reasons of ideological ossification, partly because of the material constraints of postwar reconstruction, but mainly inspired by the rapid and successful dissemination of the communist model, the Soviet Union under Stalin persevered in prescribing a Soviet-style non-capitalist road for the decolonizing countries. The assumption underlying this prescription was that "socialism" *had* now been achieved in the USSR, in record time and against imperialist opposition, and was therefore *a*, if not *the* sole, model suited to emulation. For Stalin, therefore, the bipolarity of the Cold War directly and unambiguously translated into North-South policy: either a country/party/movement was in the imperialist camp, in which case it was left more or less to its own devices; or it was in, or inclined towards, the socialist camp and thus deserving of Soviet support, aid, and protection from foreign capitalist powers, all of which however, for reasons already suggested, were relatively modest.

Stalin's successors, Khrushchev in particular, set out to expand Soviet influence in the South. The "arrival" of the Soviet Union as a superpower, its advances in scientific technology (nuclear weapons, Sputnik), the growth in number and size of communist movements world-wide, and the intensification of the decolonization process throughout the fifties made an increase in the Soviet presence in the South both desirable and feasible. Sometimes on an *ad hoc* basis, and sometimes by design, Khrushchev transformed the USSR—and in its train the Peoples' Democracies—into a principal actor in North-South relations, from 1953 trade agreements with India and Latin America to 1954 credits to Afghanistan, to the 1955 "B & K" tours up to the substantial aid programs granted to Indonesia and Egypt in 1956.

The ideological rationale surrounding these foreign policy incursions into the South was at once less consistent and more nuanced than had been the case under Stalin. On one level, Khrushchev's policy represented a revision of Stalin's bipolarity thesis. The new global orientation conceded that even those developing countries following a capitalist road were important to Soviet economic, political, or strategic interests, since their independence struggle objectively contained certain anti-imperialist tendencies. If such countries could be induced merely to remain neutral— perhaps even brought into a common anti-colonial front—this in itself would work to the advantage of the socialist camp, since this "would deny capitalist states the monopoly of influence in the Third World, contribute . . . to quickening a self-assertive consciousness among the less developed countries, and identify the USSR with the liberationist aspirations of these states."³ At this level, the means appropriate to the theory included relatively untied aid, assistance for mega-projects in the South (Aswan Dam) as visible evidence of Soviet largesse, and active support for Third World states in struggles against neocolonial powers (Egypt during the Suez crisis). At the same time, Soviet policies often tended more toward reinforcing friendly bourgeois regimes, even where these were involved in persecuting local communist revolutionaries. Thus even while Khrushchev in 1955 was praising Nehru's accomplishments, the CPI was engaged in a serious struggle with the Congress Party. The corresponding theoretical framework for a broad, anti-imperialist alliance between the socialist countries and Third World neutrals was formulated at the XXth Congress of the CPSU with the notion of a global "Zone of Peace"—an extension of the concept of peaceful co-existence enunciated there—comprising these areas.

However, on another level, Soviet policy toward the South was also frankly political. In some ways, in fact, Khrushchev's policy was more consistently and radically anti-imperialist than Soviet policy has been since, and the application of that policy clearly indicated that the ncr still dominated its prescriptions for overcoming underdevelopment. Aid and support were concentrated on Algeria, Iran, Ghana, Mali and, after 1958, Iraq, as well as Egypt—all states which, it was thought, were potential followers of the NCR and in any event had a strong anti-imperialist orientation. At this point, the two facets of Soviet strategy come together. Selective aid and moral support, coupled with an explicitly anti-imperialist propaganda campaign and a policy of economic competition with capitalism were aimed at nothing less than a fundamental shift in the postwar political status quo and the assertion of the Soviet position as chief articulator and main beneficiary of the revised world order.

In the heyday of Soviet self-confidence and expansion, these policies were relatively functional. However, the failure of the USSR to overtake the West in terms of living standards and scientific innovation, combined with its weakening hegemony over international communism—the growing Chinese challenge, uprisings in Poland and Hungary—soon forced the Soviet leadership back toward ideological orthodoxy. For instance, the central revolutionary role of the peasantry which Mao recognized, and the importance of guerilla warfare as advocated by Che Guevara and Ho Chi Minh, were negated by the Leninist adherence to the proletariat as the sole agent of anti-capitalist revolution. Soviet ideology thus began to depart in some measure from actual Third World conditions. Moreover, the *ad hoc* quality of Khrushchev's Southern policy left him open to charges of "adventurism" within. For one, he clearly overestimated the speed and efficiency with which socialism could be established, particularly in Africa. Promised revolutionary changes had not taken place, while the costs of supporting the non-capitalist roaders were mounting. Even where Soviet policy appeared to have been borne out, as in Cuba, the $1.5 million daily commitment of support was a substantial drain on Soviet resources.

By the early 1960s, Soviet policy was confronted by the paradox of how to retain hegemony within the nominally revolutionary world communist movement, while at the same time maintaining the global status quo of which it was rapidly becoming a central pillar. Attempts to resolve this paradox led directly to the formulation of the theory of the Non-Capitalist Road to development. The 1960 Moscow Conference of Communist and Workers' Parties transformed the ncr into the NCR, and the theory was further elaborated and refined at the October 1961 XXIInd Congress of the CPSU. By 1963, R.A. Ulyanovsky articulated the systematized doctrine as ". . . that stage of social and economic development . . . in which by noncapitalist means the necessary preconditions for the transition to the construction of socialism are created."[4]

Reconstruction of the Theory—Primacy of the Political

The transition to the NCR as a prescription for development during the 1960s and since has rightly been described as a shift in tactics, from the communist *offensive* to the communist *model*.[5] This concept is useful because it places the NCR into a context of "normalizing" East-West relations, intra-communist differences, and Soviet policy reverses in the Third World. With it, the "fit" between ideology and reality is a better one.

At the center of the NCR stands the concept of the *socialist world system* whose very existence promotes socialism in the South. "Like a shield [the socialist camp] protects the liberated countries from the imperialists' blows, provides them with an example and moral sustenance, is a huge source of enthusiasm and renders economic aid."[6] Thus, the socialist world system functions as an international proletarian avant-garde, as a reliable mentor and protector.[7] It is posited as the strongest and most determining of the three revolutionary currents in the contemporary world; the others, the international working class in the capitalist countries and the national liberation movements, stand together with international socialism in objective and subjective opposition to imperialism.

The presence of this progressive array of anti-imperialist forces suggests two important corollaries. *Explicitly* the revolutionary struggle is being increasingly internationalized: "Every revolutionary change in an individual country is today simultaneously an international factor. And vice-versa—the totality of international factors is expressed in the development of the socialist struggles of the individual countries."[8] Since this strong, progressive, socialist camp has forced decolonization, opposes neo-colonialism and exerts a magnet effect on countries striving for independence, it has also caused the advanced capitalist powers to band together in a defensive alliance under US hegemony. Nevertheless, these powers have been compelled to mitigate their classical forms of exploitation of the South and to seek new methods of imperialism, deployed collectively. Implicitly, therefore, the NCR also represents a substantial revision of Lenin's thesis that intra-imperialist rivalry is the primary contradiction in the world system.[9] Rather, the conflict between world socialism and world capitalism, particularly as it is enacted in the Third World, has emerged as the primary contradiction, and indeed, capitalist countries are continuously constrained to maintain a united front in the face of socialist solidarity. Hitherto, international contradictions of this magnitude have produced world wars; but technology too, especially arms technology, has progressed so far as to render global conflicts a zero-sum game. Even the imperialists have come to realize this. Besides, where wars do occur, socialism inevitably gains, as after World Wars I and II. Thus, capitalist-socialist rivalry in the South must be carried out within a context of peaceful competition, the outcome of which naturally favors the socialist camp.

It is this evolving world order that provides the preconditions for developing countries to follow an accelerated capitalist path to development. At this point, the theory becomes rather murky, not least of all due to the differentiated nature of the phenomenon with which it attempts to come to grips. Setting aside several nuances, three often overlapping types of non-capitalist roads can be discerned:

(1) Outright adaptation to, and emulation of the Soviet development model—the NCR—is on the political agenda at anytime, and remains the most desirable option for Third World countries. Such regimes *might* develop in countries where imperialism is forced to intervene directly (South Viet Nam) thus intensifying mass opposition under revolutionary leadership, or where for other reasons mass revolutionary enthusiasm is high (the Middle East, certain areas in Latin America).[10] Here, the Leninist concepts of the weak link of the capitalist system, the specificity of individual revolutionary situations, and the global nature of the anti-imperialist struggle are obviously still held to be valid. They apply in particular to the less developed "countries" at the periphery of the USSR itself (Mongolia, Uzbekistan, Kazakistan, Transcaucasia, the Soviet North and Far East, etc.) as well as isolated cases such as North Korea,

Viet Nam and (until the late 1950s) the People's Republic of China. A crucial factor is that the revolution should be led by the proletariat, which in Soviet theory is the one consistent revolutionary class on account of its social position and objective interests. The NCR model, updated and marginally revised in the seventies as the "State of Socialist Orientation," is the one consistent variant of state-socialist prescriptions for Southern development.[11]

However, the merit of the NCR as ideology, as suggested above, is its recognition that a Marxist-Leninist revolution, for a variety of reasons (differences in resource bases, pace of industrialization, constellation of class conflict and collaboration, etc.), is not imminent in large areas of the South. It therefore allows for two further possibilities, according to the respective scale of capitalist penetration and consequent level of class formation.[12]

(2) Underdeveloped countries characterized by a low degree of class differentiation in which a capitalist class may exist, but does not yet determine the direction and intensity of development. Such countries may *bypass* the stage of capitalism entirely and proceed directly to socialism via the NCR.

(3) Third World countries where capitalist development is underway and a capitalist class exists in a ruling coalition with other pre- or non-capitalist strata. In this case it is necessary to *break off* capitalist development before advancing through the NCR.

Since developing countries today mainly fall into categories (2) and (3), especially the latter, they are of special interest to any analysis of the NCR and its related theories. As these categories suggest, the NCR explains and justifies both the bypassing and acceleration of the classical Marxian developmental scheme—or at least the vulgar Marxist simplification of it—of a historical progression from feudalism via capitalism to socialism. In other words, it can be theoretically demonstrated:

> . . . not only that one formation necessarily develops through revolution into another formation and one socio-economic structure is transformed into another, but also that they coexist and interact, and that it is possible to bypass in part or in full a historically transcended and hence superfluous stage of development.[13]

Under what conditions can pre-capitalist or incipient capitalist countries at the world periphery embark on a non-capitalist path?

A provisional answer to this question must start from a negation. The NCR is nowhere defined as a distinct socio-economic formation somewhere between capitalism and feudalism, or between capitalism and socialism. It is, rather, a *transitional process* which, moreover, takes

place at a different pace and with different components from country
to country. Thus, there is no "formal" point of entry; countries may
simply be proclaimed to be, or not yet to be, on the NCR. For all that,
however, entry onto the NCR is first and foremost a political step. It
can only be taken by a *political* movement—a more or less progressive
élite coalition or other anti-imperialist grouping normally described as
the National Liberation Movement (NLM)—seizing state power and
establishing a State of National Democracy whose mission is to create
the political, socio-economic, material-technical, and cultural preconditions for a subsequent transition to socialism. In this sense, it is possible
to speak of the primacy of the political, or the inversion of base and
superstructure, since control of state power is the *sine qua non* to economic
development and with it the transformation of all other spheres of
society. This will become apparent in what follows.

The National Liberation Movement, whose task it is to capture state
power, varies considerably from country to country and reflects the
respective economic deformations brought about by colonialism and
neocolonialism. The merger of pre-capitalist forms of exploitation with
those of colonialism resulted in the export of any surplus these economies
produced and thus blocked the overall development of peripheral societies.
As a result, several different modes of production existed, and exist,
side by side with few organic linkages. Such heterogeneous, deformed,
multi-sectoral economies produced a similarly uncoordinated lumping
of social formations, from local-feudal and neocolonial-dependent groups
to national and comprador bourgeoisies and progressive socialist movements. Thus, the formation of a modern class structure has also been
blocked with no clearly profiled bourgeoisie or proletariat.[14] The challenge
to the NLM then, is to mobilize the progressive elements within this
social mosaic into a militant, aware, anti-imperialist force as a basis for
the State of National Democracy. Though the composition of the NLM
varies according to local conditions—and therefore cannot be dealt with
in detail here[15]—its universal foundation is seen as "new nationalism"
which, in an emergent nation seeking a development path to overcome
the socio-economic blockages just alluded to, is *ipso facto* anti-imperialist
and hence anti-capitalist. There is therefore a "congruence of interests"
between the industrialized socialist countries and the NLM, since both
are located on the same side of the global struggle against imperialism.
Both want continuing peaceful coexistence, need revolutionary changes,
and support proletarian internationalism.[16]

What distinguishes the National Liberation Revolution from Marxist-
Leninist social revolutions is primarily its class basis. Since the distorted
economic development of developing countries has not permitted the
growth of a numerically significant proletariat, and since the bourgeoisie

remains, in André Gunder Frank's telling coinage, a "lumpenbourgeoisie," the peasantry presents itself as a mass base for an anti-imperialist revolution. Numerically representing the overwhelming majority, not yet bourgeoisified (i.e. not owning the land it works), and mainly feudally organized or even living in communal arrangements, the peasantry has a strong *objective* interest in national independence. Their interests are complemented by those of the mass of urban dwellers, particularly artisans, small traders, semi-proletarianized strata and a large "pre-proletariat" of mainly uneducated first-generation city dwellers, whose elementary goals can only be realized in opposition to imperialism. Leadership of the NLM, however, will have to be assumed by classes who are *subjectively* conscious of the inhibiting effects of the international class struggle, in particular the "civilian and military revolutionary-democratic intelligentsia."[17] Again, the composition of this crucial group necessarily varies, but may take in the urban petit-bourgeoisie, the technocratic intelligentsia, state employees, semi-proletarians in the cities, some sectors among the better-off peasantry, and most workers.[18]

The theory attempts to take account of the limitations of this heterogeneous stratum but to preserve it as a leading force by positing at least two radicalizing forces working on it constantly. For one, its continued mass legitimation is provided by peasants and workers and merely to attempt to represent their interests is to be under permanent constraints toward more radical policies of redistribution and social justice. Second, the alliance, or at least cooperative arrangements with the socialist countries, furnishes ready access to the experience of scientific socialism as well as aid and advice at every stage. This assumed dynamic is an essential aspect of the entire NLM-NCR theory complex, since it does account for the non-existence of a large, militant proletariat, the relatively amorphous quality of class formation (and hence the low level of class struggle) and the necessity for a mass revolutionary basis to emerge after the revolution from out of the peculiar conditions of underdevelopment. This will be further dealt with presently.

Once the NLM has gained control of the National Democratic State, the Non-Capitalist Road to Development proceeds quasi-automatically, though subject to setbacks, reverses, or plateaux. The centerpiece of the national-democratic stage is the *strong state* since "the central issue of the Non-Capitalist Road is the issue of power."[19] Political power, concentrated in the hands of the variegated elements of the NLM, is the absolute precondition for the success of the NCR, because:

> The special quality of the Non-Capitalist Road is that as it proceeds it solves not only the general democratic tasks but also several tasks of the socialist revolution. Not only does it eliminate the remnants of feudal

relations, it also confines and even wipes out the capitalist economy by means of nationalizing foreign capital and contains the activities of private national capital.[20]

The NCR's mission, therefore, is a dual one: the elimination and/or containment of two modes of production. The strong state, created by what amounts to a revolution "from above," must be prepared for resistance from traditional interests and strata, and from both foreign and domestic capital. It thus must be invested with a certain degree of relative autonomy, standing in some measure above the society in which it functions. As a union of "all the healthy forces in the nation,"[21] it must conform to the imperatives of development and concentrate especially on (import-substituting) industry to establish the basis for a growing, balanced industrialization. If the state and cooperative sectors can expand rapidly and efficiently, not only will the primary goal, development, be realized within a comparatively short time—perhaps even within a few decades[22]—but further social preconditions for the eventual transition to socialism will be created. A growing proletariat will furnish both the mass basis and driving force of socialism and at the same time prevent the national bourgeoisie from particularizing non-capitalist development. The peasantry, by being involved in the burgeoning state sector and by increases in its material and educational enablements, will be drawn into an alliance with the proletariat. The increasingly revolutionized masses will then act as a spur and inspiration to the other "national" classes, who will polarize into genuinely progressive and reactionary factions. The progressive elements among the "national" leadership, taking their cue from the masses and from their growing nationalist consciousness, will gradually form as a vanguard party and perceive a need for socialist ideology. Therefore:

> Like iron to a magnet, left wing revolutionary democrats are drawn to scientific socialist theory and real existing socialism. The historic mission of revolutionary democracy in the "Third World" is to undertake the kind of socioeconomic transformations that will open the door to eventual socialist development. This is very feasible where the unity of all anti-imperialist forces is maintained, and where revolutionary democracy seeks the support of the socialist world system.[23]

Here, the importance of *mass mobilization* to the success of the NCR is evident. There exists in the NLM a sometimes more, sometimes lesser divergence of interests and outlooks between a composite élite that exercises hegemony and a mass on behalf of whom power is held. The resulting incongruence produces a need for constant mutual adaptation or "dialectic." The more rapidly mobilization and social consciousness are effected, therefore, the more likely is the NLM to proceed from the "stage of the revolution for the people" to the "stage of the revolution realized by the people." Conversely, the more the process is delayed or held back—e.g. by imperialist machinations or intra-élite rivalry—the more bleak are the prospects for a successful completion of a NCR strategy. "This fact," writes Ibrahim and Metze-Mangold, "demonstrates that the class character of the State of National Democracy cannot be determined solely according to *who* leads it, but to an equal degree according to the social *substance* that its concrete measures display."[24]

Of particular analytical relevance here is the fact that a pronounced element of subjectivism—perhaps "voluntarism" inheres in the theory. There is nothing inevitable about either the class composition of the revolutionary-democratic state nor about the pace and effectiveness of mass mobilization in a progressive direction. Embourgeoisement is possible even as proletarianization proceeds. Reaction may temporarily defeat the movement toward socialism (Ghana, Indonesia). Thus in Nasser's Egypt the dynamics of the NCR were said to have produced an alliance among the leading potentially revolutionary cadres as against the masses, while in the People's Republic of Yemen there ensued a progressive proximation of base (mass following) and superstructure (political élite). However, as the State of National Democracy proceeds toward the fulfillment of its historical tasks—rapid development, creation of a proletariat, forging of links to world socialism, establishment of economic preconditions for socialism, etc.—the contradictions begin to resolve themselves as the progressive forces in the hegemonic alliance coalesce and carry the masses along with them. The now more self-confident, more autochthonous state, having expanded its domestic market on the strength of state-promoted accumulation and raised its level of domestic savings and investment, having as well rationalized agriculture and begun industrialization, would be in a position to "exploit" foreign capital in reverse, as it were. Since the imperialist countries for the time being represent the major source of capital accumulation on a world scale, and since the socialist countries would be faced by an impossible number of requests for aid and investment from the many new non-capitalist roaders—which is another way of accounting for a chronic shortage of deployable capital among the state-socialist countries—it would be possible, under the changed conditions, to utilize capital inflows and technology transfers from the advanced capitalist states for one's own purposes. The resultant more rapid development of the new socialist countries would in a sense make imperialism into a factor strengthening the very forces that will ultimately negate it.[25]

This exploitation of the profit motive by developing countries is of course based on a crucial—and basically non-demonstrable—assumption that the capitalist countries will continue to invest in, and grant aid to developing countries that nationalize foreign holdings, curtail profits, and ally with the advanced communist countries. It also entails a constant political danger alongside its immense potential economic advantages, namely that the developing country adopting such a strategy may be subjected to regressive pressures. Here again, therefore, the major precondition for adopting this strategy is the strengthened state. Careful government regulation of both grants and credits from the West, it is assumed, will lead to further expansion of the state sector and a determining role for it in the national economy. Nevertheless, such capital and technology inflows must be scrupulously weighted beforehand and only accepted under certain well-defined conditions, for instance: (1) absence of any sovereignty-undermining provisions; (2) use of such funds to correct the deformed sectors of the economy; (3) efficiency of operations being financed must be greater than capital costs (interest, services, etc.); (4) markets, both domestic and foreign, must be assured for goods produced with the aid of foreign inputs; (5) bilateral government-to-government credits to be given preference over direct foreign investment in order to monitor the imported capital and ensure its utilization in the interests of national development; (6) joint ventures to be controlled by the recipient state; (7) tax breaks, if granted, to be linked to firm time limits; and (8) all investments involve an obligation to train local personnel in the relevant technical and managerial skills.[26] In this way, industrial development and with it class formation of the proletariat and mass mobilization of the population will be accelerated, thus more rapidly eliminating the need for foreign investment/aid/technology, which can then be phased out.

These then represent in simplified form the main components of the NCR theory. To sum up this section, it is worth recalling that, far from a fixed, definable stage of socio-historical development, the NCR is a fluid, dynamic process—"not socialist development proper but a specific period of *creating* the material, social, and cultural *conditions* for the transition to socialist development."[27]

Exigencies and Adaptations

Precisely this processual, transitional quality of the NCR model helps to explain its further differentiation and diffusion over time. The admission of foreign capital and technology, just described, is an initial example of the capacity of the theory to adapt to exigency, in this case to the limited availability of capital and know-how—and for that matter, lack of a broad, multi-sectored, scientific-technological fund—in the actually existing socialist countries.

From the late sixties onward, external and internal factors have tended to transform and qualify the conditions under which the NCR was originally formulated. From about the fall of Khrushchev until the mid-seventies, rigid bipolarity succumbed to peaceful coexistence, and the People's Democracies, faced with economic slowdown and internal structural problems, concentrated more on domestic savings and internal restructuring. At the XXIIIrd Congress of the CPSU, Brezhnev emphasized building communism at home as a precondition for getting on with "international tasks." "Moderation," "gradualism," "pragmatism," and, above all, "economic rationality" became the watchwords of communist development, while relations with the South were characterized more and more in terms of the "international division of labor" and "mutual advantage." The notion of *mnogoukladnost* (multi-structured or multi-layered) was increasingly used to account for the diversity of the Third World and the complexity of state socialism's relations with it.[28] Among other things, these premises rationalized closer links between aid and trade, and the CMEA countries began to register a series of positive trade balances with the South. Indeed, such trade in the 1970s became an instrument to resolve certain problems and dysfunctions of Eastern European economies by means of such techniques as dumping, sale of obsolete technology, purchasing raw materials cheaply at fixed prices, and then selling them dearly on the world market, etc.[29]

Where Khrushchev had held out the prospect of development within a generation, his successors have emphasized its gradual, protracted nature. The new leaders expanded the scope of Soviet foreign policy beyond active support for comparatively few regimes to include the capitalist roaders as well. In the mid-sixties, credits were allocated to Morocco, Nigeria, Iran, Malaysia, Singapore, the Philippines and several conservative Latin American countries. This pragmatic approach actually increased Eastern European prospects for cooperation with the South, since countries hitherto apprehensive about entering into relations with socialist states could now do so with less concern about ideological penetration.[30] Thus, from this perspective, the communist countries acquired a growing interest in the maintenance of the global status quo.

However, it would be rather simplistic to infer from all this that the state-socialist countries' policies toward the Third World somehow began to converge with those of the capitalist West. For one, the means were different. Where capitalism strives toward ownership of whole sectors of the economy and branches of production, state socialism[31] attempts to establish a greater basis of equality between partners and does not seek a systematized extraction of surplus from the less developed countries. Second, although the NCR thus became an apologetic concept to justify, e.g., cooperation with repressive military regimes, an enhanced role in global arms trade, and dealings with reactionary, corrupt, and even anti-communist governments in the Third World, massive support was at the same time forthcoming for revolutionary liberation movements. It is important to establish the existence of this two- or three-track model of communist relations with the South, since state-socialist policies cannot be neatly fit into any single category. Indeed, ambiguity and flexibility are the defining characteristics of the model as well as the policies emanating from it.

By the mid-seventies, Soviet economic growth, like economic development throughout the North, was hampered by the global economic crises that characterized this era. At the same time, the newly liberated NCR states in Africa (Angola, Mozambique, Ethiopia) as well as Afghanistan threatened to place impossible financial and military demands on Eastern Europe, even while some relatively advanced NCR states had regressed toward capitalism (Egypt) or fallen stagnant in their evolution toward socialism (Burma). In this context, several revisions to the theory (and hence to praxis as well) were called for:

(1) The two-camps/two-economies theory of the global economy yielded to the more realistic notion of interdependence within a growing international division of labor. Just as the Third World itself was differentiating into OPEC states, NICs, regressively underdeveloping areas, etc., so the mutual interdependence of all states advanced to the forefront of the theory. The 1974 *Great Soviet Encyclopedia* confirmed this line of thinking:

> In its initial form the world market was based on the capitalist mode of production and was the world capitalist market. At present the world market takes in the full international division of labor as practiced between the world's two socio-economic systems. The world market has expanded in scale as social production has become increasingly internationalized.[32]

(2) State capitalism emerged as a guiding concept. While state capitalism had been coined to apply to certain measures to be taken by the State of National Democracy, and related to state control of the key sectors of the economy, the notion was now coupled with an emphasis on economic incentives, market rationality, and comparative advantage (where once state expansion, political rationality, and import substitution respectively had made up the essence of the theory). Profitability, in this connection, became a norm and central prescription.

(3) Parallel to these, the role of actually existing socialism as mentor and protector was downplayed in favor of greater "collective self-sufficiency" (e.g., via the Group of 77) and "local self-reliance."[33]

(4) Finally, a "dialectical" dimension entered into several of the organizing concepts of the NCR theory. Nationalism, as a motive force, was no longer presumed to be simply and invariably progressive; it might also and equally operate to reinforce regressive petit-bourgeois class domination. Leadership in the national democratic coalition might therefore be personalistic and arbitrary rather than progressive and consolidating, particularly where neocolonial relations remained effective. Indeed, within each newly independent state, tendencies were at work both to combat imperialism and simultaneously to come to terms with it, and a given country might therefore be anti-imperialist *and* anti-Soviet.[34]

It is this shift in Soviet thinking—if not total revision, then certainly a re-ordering of ideological priorities—in line with changing conditions that leads Richard Löwenthal to speak of a paradigmatic transformation from "anti-imperialism" to "counter-imperialism," where the latter signifies a stable, growing, peaceful, and rather complacent anti-imperialist bloc.[35] This counter-imperialist tendency has been reflected in Soviet approaches to the NIEO during the past decade: "The growing integration of the Soviet economy with an acknowledged single world market made Moscow lose zest for a radical restructuring of international economic relations for the benefit of the developing countries."[36] Whereas the communist countries began by supporting the South's demands for a NIEO, that support has been mitigated as the non-NCR South has increasingly styled the industrialized socialist countries as part of the same North against whose interest the NIEO must realized. The Soviets and East Europeans have countered with several objections to the Brandtian NIEO, *viz.*: (1) that it is indifferent to domestic reforms and thus maintains élite rule; (2) that it departs from universalist principles and works to the exclusive interest of the South; and (3) that it is non-Marxist in as much as it has no anti-capitalist goals, leaves the world capitalist economy intact and assists selected underdeveloped countries to develop into "subimperialist" powers.[37]

The state-socialist countries have, however, consistently supported the non-aligned movement on the grounds that here the anti-imperialist interests of East and South intersect; but they have failed to put forward an alternative radical plan for restructuring global economic relations beyond the continuing advocacy of a leading Soviet role in the Socialist Community of States. In no small part, this failure is seen in the South as rooted in the new concern for gradual change, comparative advantage, and world-market stability.

The renewal of the Cold War in the 1980s, coupled with Soviet reverses in agriculture and a shrinking economic base, merely exacerbated these conservative tendencies and set off a substantial theoretical debate among scholars and politicians. More and more, the "pragmatists" are prevailing with their call for moderation, for a proper mix of state control and private enterprise—reminiscent of Lenin's NEP measures—and their advocacy of "national" capitalism as opposed to "dependent" capitalism.[38]

Analysis and Critique

It is not at all surprising, therefore, that the Eastern European politicians and ideologists find their NCR-based theories increasingly overtaken by world communist movements rooted in Southern conditions; not only by rivals such as Maoists or Guevarists, but by those who see themselves as proceeding along the Non-Capitalist Road as enunciated in the theories of actually existing socialism. For instance, Abdul R.M. Babu, the Tanzanian Marxist-Leninist, advocates an instant revolutionary transformation for Africa based on a presumed militant proletarian class consciousness.[39] The former (and late) Secretary-General of the Yemeni Socialist Party has also argued for rapid and complete withdrawal of his country from the world capitalist system on the strength of aid and cooperation from the socialist countries.[40] The Mozambique delegate to UNITAR has made a strong and implicitly critical plea for more Soviet assistance in the immediate construction of socialism.[41]

Precisely these kinds of statements, emanating from regimes subjectively following the NCR, tend to undermine the central theoretical proposition and ideological strength of the NCR, namely the anti-imperialism-grounded identity of interests between developed socialism and the Third World. While this premise basically still applies, the socialist division of labor deduced from it and the increasingly divergent views about the timing and intensity of the NCR are nevertheless potential sources of conflict.

Moreover, the Soviet Union also operates as a great power and the Eastern European People's Democracies as components of a power bloc. As such their interests structurally depart in important ways from those of the South. Allusion has already been made to communist support for despotic, corrupt, or anti-communist regimes in the Third World. Certainly the model, already broadly conceived, is subject to pressures of diplomatic, power-political and economic exigency. Thus, if one sets aside the temporal dimension, the NCR appears to contain a whole series of contradictions, as summarized by Clarkson:

. . . there can be no development under capitalism vs. there must be more capitalist development; the proletariat is weak and lacks class consciousness vs. the proletariat must lead an alliance with the peasantry; imperialism resists third world industrialization vs. imperialist aid facilitates important industrial development; independence can only be achieved by breaking ex-colonial ties with imperialism vs. independence is only relative and will grow while maintaining trading relations the West; the rural bourgeoisie is the enemy of agrarian development vs. the rural bourgeoisie is leading capitalist development in the countryside.[42]

Conversely, this apparent eclecticism finds its counterpart in the tendency in the South to take from the model what is required for local needs. For Nehru it helped resolve the nationality question and promote industrialization through economic planning; for Nkrumah its attraction was the disciplined one-party system; and for Sekou Toure it provided a strategy of state control of foreign aid.[43]

Another way of examining the NCR paradigm is to recall that it has been formulated in the state-socialist countries, more or less as official ideology, on the basis of their observations of structures and processes prevailing in the South. As such, the NCR is a Northeastern prescription for world order. All its main components—strong state, "modernizing" élite, mass mobilization, socialist orientation—relate isomorphically to the Soviet experience of development and, whichever actual road may be taken due to local conditions, ultimately converge with the interests of the developed communist states whose social, economic, and political system it will sooner or later proximate. In fact the theory expressly precludes: (1) a "Third Way" or "convergence" of communism and capitalism in Third World societies;[44] (2) development strategies founded on the "basic needs" of the majority of the population, since these are considered to be "utopian";[45] and (3) any notion of an absolute North-South or "rich-poor" dichotomy in the world system, which masks the real coincidence of interests between East and South and makes actually existing socialism part of the problem rather than the solution.[46]

The theory also precludes a fourth developmental approach: any reliance on traditional values, beliefs, institutions, or ways of life as a basis for indigenous or autocentric development. Apart from isolated references to communal ownership, all "pre-capitalist relations"—which are usually styled as feudal despite the allusions to communal property—are clearly and unambiguously a hinderance to development. Parasitism, corruption, inertia, unproductivity, and immobilism are the defining characteristics of this stage, which the NCR means to overcome with a total transformation of "backward" society into an integrated, mobilized, developing society.[47]

The NCR is further hampered by a very imprecise class analysis. The dynamics of the National Liberation Movement are presumed to produce a progressive tendency within its leadership. Yet in practice most Third World liberation regimes have developed into a single party (or military establishment) serving few interests but their own. Far from mobilizing the masses for socialist development, these élite agencies consciously aim at depoliticization, self-aggrandizement, and braking any trends toward popular participation in economy and society. Similarly, state capitalism in the South has, by and large, made the state into a collective capitalist functioning for the benefit of a growing state élite (as in India, Mexico, Nigeria, Argentina, Brazil and the Shah's Iran, to mention a few prominent examples from the literature on the NCR). Rather than acting as an instrument in the transition to socialism, therefore, the state in most cases has become a mere facilitator and legitimator of capitalist development.

Even the NCR's reliance on the "national" elements of the underdeveloped state is highly problematic, since it assumes a link between nationalism and progressiveness. However, those groups which are made up of representatives of all ethnic groups, religions, and sectors of society—almost by definition an élite in any case—within the arbitrary, colonially drawn boundaries, may be anything but dynamic and progressive, as the state élites of Nigeria or Indonesia (military or civilian) clearly demonstrate. While such groups often are the "modern" harbingers of "national sovereignty" as against neocolonial domination,[48] they are just as often induced to act as compradors, local agents of foreign capital, or counter-revolutionary enforcers. The NCR's adherence to such categorical concepts too often leads it to ally with repressive, reactionary, or particularistic élites at the expense of supporting subnational groups—the Eritreans, Kurds, or Pushtus for example—who may represent more progressive revolutionary forces. A more literal interpretation of the logical consequences of this notion would suggest the local military to be the ideal agent of the NCR. Indeed, Bassam Tibi argues that most National Democratic States said to be on the Non-Capitalist Road are in fact military regimes, few of which actually qualify as agents of an NCR-type regime.[49]

Recently, a few authors have begun to abstract the essential features from the NCR—the strong state, an educated and conscious vanguard, state capitalism as motor of accumulation, mobilization from above for a "cultural revolution," rejection of traditional values and forms, a developed Northeast as a model—and to argue that it in fact amounts to an Eastern European variant of "modernization theory."[50] There is actually much in this thesis. Both modernization theory, whether in its stages-of-growth (Rostow), nation-building (Almond, Pye, Verba) or political order (Huntington) formulations, and the NCR in its several varieties, start from the primacy of the political. This suggests élite control of the state apparatus in order to ensure state-directed accumulation. In the one case, the élite is presumed to be educated and capitalist oriented, in the other to contain a revolutionary potential. Either way, the development process is imposed and guided from above and aims at emulation of development processes already accomplished elsewhere. Indigenous starting points, aspirations, and potentials are regarded as obstacles to be overcome. Science and technology as well as rationality and efficiency are prescribed as organizing principles of social change. Thus, popular participation, in both models, is reduced even as mass mobilization is advocated, whether the process is described by Huntington as the creation of political order[51] or by Ponomarev as leadership of a "revolutionary avant-garde."[52] By the same token, both models seek to "create" a sustaining mass basis of legitimacy for the realization of their goals, the one a proletariat, the other a bourgeoisie.

Tibi's relentless critique of the NCR may be further examined in light of Elsenhans' and Löwenthal's observations. For him, the theory of the National Democratic State, the NLM and the NCR are nothing more than "an unhistorical superimposition of the Soviet model of development onto the peripheral countries . . . even though it contains a few modifications." Thus, the National Democratic State is in essence a replica of the Soviet state in so far as "both display a bureaucratic independence of the state apparatus vis-à-vis the classes of society." Moreover, a determining criterion of NCR states is whether or not they share Soviet foreign policy goals; in this way the Shah's Iran or the élites of reactionary oil-producing states can be passed off as "anticapitalist" and "national democratic."[53] Following Marcuse and Negt, Tibi also addresses the problematic of the strong state. In his view the NCR confuses state ownership with a Marxian socialization of the means of production, and in this way degrades the liberating function of communal ownership into a means of state-bureaucratic control. The Marxist theory of emancipation is converted into a theory of production, the negative dialectic transformed into a positive one serving merely to legitimate Soviet domination of Third World societies.[54]

A Progressive Core?

A central problem of analytical constructs that posit the NCR as an instrument of domination or as equivalent to modernization theory is that they absolutize and essentialize certain characteristics and goals that may actually be temporally limited, exiguous, or transient phenomena, even while they ignore respective starting points and goals. Like the

Cold War "theory" of totalitarianism,[55] these approaches—if used for more than simple heuristic purposes—may in fact be deployed more for purposes of demonization of an ideological opponent or vindication of a capitalist-oriented status quo than for insight and understanding.

For instance, the basic premise of modernization theory, namely the prescription of capitalist relations of production for the Third World, stands in stark opposition to the anti-capitalist, anti-imperialist premises of the NCR. If the NCR is to be seen as modernization theory, then it is modernization theory with a class content and progressive core. The inflated state of the NCR must be strong in order to withstand the presumed counter-offensive of imperialism from without and reaction from within. Its élites are assumed to be able to become independent and self-sufficient, while the masses are imputed with a democratic potential. The purpose of the National Democratic State is to create the material preconditions for socialism. All this contrasts with the assumptions and intents of Western modernization theory. By way of conclusion, this "progressive core" of the NCR may be discerned in terms of at least two fundamental questions: (1) How does the NCR operate in praxis to help "liberate" and "guide" countries in the South; and (2) How relevant is the People's Democracy model itself to the goals and aspirations of these countries?

In relation to the first question, the anti-imperialist premise of the NCR, just alluded to, has to be further elucidated. The position of the People's Democracies and their elementary interests within the still essentially bipolar world political-economic system compel them to oppose the global manifestations of transnational capital. At the very least, actually existing socialism is at present the sole alternative socioeconomic formation to world capitalism. Without its presence, much different outcomes of the anti-imperialist struggles in, for instance, Viet Nam, Mozambique, Cuba and, presently, Nicaragua may be envisioned— even while not losing sight of converse tendencies such as Afghanistan and Czechoslovakia. From this perspective, it is impossible to reject out of hand Castro's "natural alliance" thesis, advanced at the Sixth Summit of Non-Aligned Countries in Havana in 1979: that an objective or structural identity exists between the interests of the developing countries and those of the industrialized communist states.[56]

Following Salua Nour,[57] one might push the progressive core concept to its analytical limits. Even though the Soviet Union must often behave as a great power, he argues, and despite its increasing search for cheap raw materials and outlets for its manufactured goods, it does not produce permanent structural imbalances and systematic dependency in the same way that international capitalism does. This is mainly because the Soviets do need allies in the anti-capitalist struggle and their loyalties can only be assured by a consistent anti-imperialist course. The Soviets and their industrialized allies do make errors (friendship treaties with repressive governments, tied development aid, half-hearted support for local revolutionary movements, etc.), but these are insignificant, the argument goes, compared to the means of control utilized by the advanced capitalist countries: corruption, backing coups, reinforcing the repressive apparatus, creation of structural dependency, etc. True, the People's Democracies have increased their global military presence and become a major proliferator of armaments. Again, however, communist arms aid concentrates on building up the local military with a view to eventual self-sufficiency as opposed to Western attempts to use it as a means of further deepening dependency relations. To be sure, Northeastern and Southern interests do not always converge in this sphere; they often do, as in the case of military harbor construction in Algeria, South Yemen, and Somalia or the build-up of the Syrian and Egyptian forces before 1967; but differences arise as well, as when Egypt's interests in offensive weapons to combat Israel clashed with Soviet interests in maintaining the status quo in the Middle East.

However that may be, Soviet interests are served by any and all developments that tend to undermine world capitalist hegemony. Thus, apart from various conservative policies and alliances, the industrialized communist states do continue to concentrate their support behind revolutionary regimes and movements, and other countries and groups of countries attempting to dislodge themselves from the world capitalist order, the same order that Western proposals such as the Brandt Report attempt to vindicate.[58]

The second and final aspect of the NCR relates to the validity of the People's Democracy model for Southern conditions. After all, the end point of both "Socialist Orientation" and the NCR itself is, as has been shown, state-socialism. Indeed, as Löwenthal has demonstrated, the concept of People's Democracy, as implemented in Eastern Europe in the late forties, very closely corresponds to the model of National Democracy.[59] Although it is quite impossible within the confines of the present topic to discuss actually existing socialism as a development model,[60] it is worth recalling that the elements of communist development outlined above—forced industrialization, vanguard leadership, etc.—do seem to exert an attraction to Third World countries (or at least their élites) in proportion to the degree of their underdevelopment. However, as these countries evolve into NICs, OPEC states, export-led developers and the like, the model seems to decline in relevance. This tendency correlates with the increasingly apparent dysfunctions and limitations of the Soviet-type model itself.

On the pathologies of actually existing socialism, a growing body of
literature, based on "immanent critique," has already evolved, as linked
with names such as Marcuse, Šik, Bahro, Djilas, Medvedev, Deutscher,
et alia. Setting aside some important differences of emphasis and nuances,
these critiques all conclude: (1) that state-socialism has nowhere fulfilled
the human emancipatory purpose of Marxism; and (2) that real economic
growth and development have not proceeded beyond a certain stage.
Concerning the former, Rudolf Bahro posits "a new antagonistic order
the other side of capitalism" and argues that the elimination of private
ownership of the means of production is separated "by an entire epoch"
from universal human emancipation.[61] For him, the "Gordian Knot of
bureaucratization and uneven development" ultimately thwarts any chance
of realizing socialism in the Marxian sense of human liberation. Thus:

> . . . there is no way, Marx implies, that a pre-capitalist country can
> industrialize without either wage-labor or extra-economic compulsion. One
> of the two is needed. The abolition of capitalist private property here
> means a decision in favor of terror—for an unending torment of devel-
> opment, if no stable dictatorship comes into being—and the specific problem
> then consists in the productive function of this terror.[62]

In this model of industrialization without emancipation, it is precisely
this terroristic-bureaucratic structure needed to trigger development in
pre-capitalist or underdeveloped society that prevents that development
from becoming self-sustaining.

For Senghaas, the deficiencies of actually existing socialism become
apparent with the transition of the economy from its extensive to intensive
phases, when the excessive controls exerted by the political superstructure
produce economic problems such as declining capital productivity, industrial supply bottlenecks and continuing deferral of consumer needs.[63]
Or, to cite Bahro once more:

> Criticism of the present condition of the Soviet state system can be summed
> up in the simple fact that it has still not advanced one single step beyond
> the structures that were created in the very specific conditions of the 1920s
> for [the dictatorship of the proletariat]. In this rigid continuity, the Soviet
> Union finds it difficult to complete even the foundations of socialism,
> precisely because this is not simply a technical task. Soviet society needs
> a renovate communist party, under whose leadership it can use the
> productive forces that were developed in the decades of industrializing
> despotism to break out to new shores, towards genuine socialism.[64]

These concluding considerations by no means negate the NCR, particularly its "progressive core." But they do suggest anew the dynamic

quality of "development," its variability over time and space, and the real problems of adapting this, or any, development model formulated under conditions far removed from those where the model is supposed to be applied.

Notes

1. A few remarks about this chapter are in order. I have to thank Professor Toivo Miljan who first prodded me to develop a more or less coherent analysis of the NCR by inviting me, in the fall of 1984, to present a seminar to his international development class at Wilfrid Laurier University. He then proposed a more careful and comprehensive formulation for inclusion as a chapter in his reader entitled *A Political Economy of North-South Relations* (Peterborough, Oct. 1987). The present chapter is a somewhat revised version of that chapter. Ms. Sandra Couch, a graduate student at the University of Guelph, produced an outstanding study, *Communism in the Third World: Prescriptions for Development* (Mimeo., April 1985) from which I have learned much. My thinking on the topic has also been influenced by a series of discussions with Brigitte Schulz of Seattle University, whose outstanding study of GDR aid to Africa is a comprehensive and concrete examination of the NCR in practice.

In addition to Soviet and other East European sources, I have chosen to rely especially on the East German literature on the NCR, (1) because many key Soviet sources—to which I had no direct access—have only been translated into German, and (2) because GDR development theory is in many areas (mass basis of the anti-imperialist revolution, individual country studies, etc.) more comprehensive—and indeed more "orthodox"—than that produced elsewhere in Eastern Europe. For analogous reasons, a number of the—surprisingly few, in the West—most informed critiques of the NCR are found in the West German literature.

2. For instance reasoning of the kind presented by S.T. Hosmer and T.W. Wolfe (*Soviet Policy and Practice Toward Third World Conflicts*, Lexington 1983) who write (p. 1) that: "The USSR appears to possess an untiring urge to expand its influence and to reduce that of its rivals in the Third World. In addition, the changing and troubled international environment has become increasingly vulnerable to Soviet opportunism at a time when the USSR's capabilities to project power into the Third World have increased." Indeed, the purpose of their study is to justify and rationalize the buildup of American "countervailing power" to Soviet "aggression."

3. Elizabeth Kridl Valkenier, *The Soviet Union and the Third World* (New York 1984), p. 11.

4. R. A. Ulyanovsky, *Socialism and the Newly Independent Countries* (Moscow 1972), p. 9.

5. Stephen Clarkson, *The Soviet Theory of Development. India and the Third World in Marxist-Leninist Scholarship*, (Toronto & Buffalo 1978), p. 4.

6. Authors' Collective, *Klassen und Klassenkampf in den Entwicklungsländern* (E. Berlin 1969), Vol. 1, p. 13.

50   William D. Graf

7. *Ibid.*, p. 13; further see the official statement by Erich Honecker which defines the socialist community of states as "the main revolutionary force of our epoch and a reliable bastion against imperialist policies of war and aggression," *Neues Deutschland*, June 16, 1971.

8. Gerhard Hahn, "Das sozialistische Weltsystem und die Entwicklung des anti-imperialistischen Kampfes der Völker Asiens, Afrikas und Lateinamerikas," *Nichtkapitalistischer Entwicklungsweg*, Report of a Conference held in Leipzig 1973 (E. Berlin 1973), pp. 78–79.

9. On this, see Albert Szymanski, *The Logic of Imperialism* (New York 1981), pp. 57–60.

10. *Klassen und Klassenkampf* . . . p. 16 *et seq.*

11. P. Polshikov, *Capital Accumulation and Economic Growth in Developing Africa* (Moscow 1981), pp. 120–124.

12. See Lothar Rathmann & Hartmut Schilling, "Probleme des nichtkapitalistischen Entwicklungsweges der Völker Asiens und Afrikas in der gegenwärtigen Etappe der nationalen Befreiungsbewegung," *Nichtkapitalistischer Entwicklungsweg* . . .

13. I.L. Andreyev, *The Noncapitalist Way. Soviet Experience and the Liberated Countries* (Moscow 1977), p. 11.

14. See the article by J. Josweg, H. Kroske and H. Schilling in *Grundfragen des anti-imperialistischen Kampfes der Völker Asiens, Afrikas und Lateinamerikas in der Gegenwart* (E. Berlin 1974), pp. 279–281.

15. But see N.A. Simonia, *On the Specifics of National Liberation Revolutions* (Moscow 1968); V.L. Tyagunenko, *Problems of Present-Day National Liberation Revolutions* (Moscow 1969); V.L. Tyagunenko, "World Socialism and National Liberation Movements," *Kommunist*, No. 8, 1973; E. Tarabin, "The National Liberation Movement: Problems and Prospects," *International Affairs*, No. 2 (February 1978), pp. 59–68.

16. See Hahn, "Das sozialistische Weltsystem . . . ," p. 82.

17. *Klassen und Klassenkampf* . . . , Vol. 1, p. 11.

18. This analysis evokes that of Guinean revolutionary leader and theorist Amilcar Cabral, which was formulated a few years earlier (1964); see his "Brief Analysis of the Social Structure of Guinea-Bissau," reproduced in P.C.W. Gutkind and P. Waterman (eds.), *African Social Studies: A Radical Reader* (New York, 1977), pp. 226–233.

19. *Nichtkapitalistischer Entwicklungsweg* . . . , p. 21.

20. *Klassen und Klassenkampf* . . . , Vol. 3, p. 295.

21. *Ibid.*, p. 308.

22. Martin Breetzmann, *Die Industrialisierung der Entwicklungsländer: Stand, Probleme, Perspektiven* (Frankfurt 1970), p. 8.

23. Clarence J. Munford, "The National Liberation Movement in Theory and Practice—Nine Theses," paper presented to Socialist Studies Society Conference, Guelph, Ont., June 1984, Mimeo., p. 67.

24. Salim Ibrahim & Vera Metze-Mangold, *Nichtkapitalistischer Entwicklungsweg: Ideengeschichte und Theoriekonzept* (Cologne 1976), p. 86 (emphasis in original).

25. Gert Kück, "Zu einigen Zusammenhängen zwischen politischen und ökonomischen Faktoren bei der Gestaltung der Aussenwirtschaftsbeziehungen der Länder auf nichtkapitalistischem Weg," *Nichtkapitalistischer Entwicklungsweg* . . . , p. 279.

26. This catalogue is inferred from a variety of sources. The conditions are summed up by Heinz Josweg, "Probleme der Finanzierung von Entwicklungsprogrammen durch Inanspruchnahme ausländischer Finanzquellen in Ländern auf nichtkapitalistischem Entwicklungswege," *Nichtkapitalistischer Entwicklungsweg* . . . , pp. 314–315. Further, see Robert S. Jaster, "Foreign Aid and Economic Development: The Shifting Soviet View," *International Affairs*, Vol. 45 (1969), esp. p. 462.

27. R. Ulyanovsky, "Foreword," to Andreyev, *The Non-Capitalist Way* . . . , p. 26.

28. C.R. Saivetz & S. Woodby, *Soviet–Third World Relations* (Boulder and London 1985), p. 12.

29. Salua Nour, "Die Beziehung der Sowjetunion zur Dritten Welt: Beitrag zur Emanzipation der Entwicklungsländer oder Weg in eine neue Abhängigkeit?" in: Jose Linhard & Klaus Voll (eds.), *Weltmarkt und Entwicklungsländer* (Rheinstetten, Neu 1976), p. 209.

30. *Ibid.*, p. 206.

31. "State socialism" here refers to the political-economic ruling structures of the industrial Eastern European states; it should be distinguished from "state capitalism" or the strategy of economic development pursued by state socialism for the underdeveloped areas.

32. Cited in Valkenier, *The Soviet Union* . . . , p. 46.

33. "Gap Between the West and Newly-Free Countries," Department of Centralized Materials (Moscow, April 1982), Mimeo., pp. 11–13.

34. Y. Alimov, "The Newly Free Countries in World Politics," *International Affairs*, September 1981, pp. 22–24.

35. Richard Löwenthal, *Model or Ally: The Communist Powers and the Developing Countries* (New York 1977).

36. Valkenier, *The Soviet Union* . . . , p. 110.

37. *Ibid.*, pp. 118–120.

38. Thomas J. Zamostny, "Moscow and the Third World: Recent Trends in Soviet Thinking," *Soviet Studies*, XXXVI, No. 2 (April 1984), pp. 227–230.

39. A.R.M. Babu, *African Socialism or Socialist Africa?* (London 1981); for a critique of this work, see my review in *Canadian Journal of African Studies*, Vol. 18, No. 2, 1984.

40. Abdel Fattah Ismail, "A New Vanguard Party," *World Marxist Review*, 22 (January 1979), p. 24.

41. *Working-Class and National Liberation Movements: Joint Struggle Against Imperialism, For Social Progress* (Moscow 1981), p. 43.

42. Clarkson, *The Soviet Theory* . . . , pp. 251–252.

43. Couch, *Communism in the Third World* . . . , p. 5.

44. The authoritative *Klassen und Klassenkampf* . . . invokes Goethe to reject this possibility: "It is said that truth lies between two extreme views. By no means. What lies between them is the problem." (Vol. 3, p. 331).

45. Valkenier, *The Soviet Union* . . . , p. 90.

46. Horst Grienig, "Bürgerliche Theorien des Dualismus," *Nichtkapitalistischer Entwicklungsweg* . . . , p. 349.

47. On this, see Babu, *African Socialism* . . . , *passim*; also Rathmann & Schilling, "Probleme . . . ," pp. 46–47.

48. S.I. Tyulpanov, *Essays on Political Economy. The Developing Countries* (Moscow 1969), pp. 88–92.

49. Bassam Tibi, "Zur Kritik der sowjetmarxistischen Entwicklungstheorie," *Handbuch der Dritten Welt 1975* (Stuttgart 1975), pp. 78–79.

50. In particular, Hartmut Elsenhans, *Abhängiger Kapitalismus oder bürokratische Entwicklungsgesellschaft? Versuch über den Staat in der Dritten Welt* (Frankfurt & New York 1981), ch. IV (1).

51. Samuel Huntington, *Political Order in Changing Society*, New Haven 1976.

52. Boris N. Ponomarev, "Urgent Theoretical Problems of the World Revolutionary Process," *Kommunist*, No. 15, 1971.

53. Tibi, "Zur Kritik . . . ," p. 83.

54. See *Ibid.*, p. 80.

55. For a critique of "totalitarianism" see my "Anticommunism in the Federal Republic of Germany," *Socialist Register 1984* (London 1984), pp. 175–177, and the literature cited there.

56. See Para. 2f of the Economic Declaration of the "Final Declaration of the Conference of Heads of State or Government of the Nonaligned Countries," 3–7 September 1979, Havana, n.d. (Mimeo.).

57. Nour, "Die Beziehung . . . ," pp. 202–205.

58. On this, see my "Anti-Brandt: A Critique of Northwestern Prescriptions for World Order," *Socialist Register 1981* (London 1981), pp. 22–24.

59. Löwenthal, *Model or Ally* . . .

60. But for a synopsis and discussion of the relevant literature, see O.P. Dwivedi, W.D. Graf, J. Nef, "Marxist Contributions to the Theory of the Administrative State," *Indian Journal of Political Science*, XLVI (January–March 1985) No. 1, pp. 1–17.

61. Rudolf Bahro, *The Alternative in Eastern Europe* (London 1977), pp. 20–21.

62. *Ibid.*, p. 27.

63. Dieter Senghaas, "Sozialismus: Eine entwicklungsgeschichtliche und entwicklungstheoretische Betrachtung," *Leviathan*, No. 1, 1980, p. 33.

64. Bahro, *The Alternative* . . . , pp. 118–119.

4

Socialist Transformation and Soviet Foreign Policy in the Gorbachev Era

Peter W. Schulze

The Primacy of Domestic Reforms and Flexibility in Foreign Policies

After the long reign of Leonid Brezhnev, the Soviet Union showed signs of political immobility, economic stagnation, and social decay. Economic inefficiency, as well as the waste of scarce human and material resources, were structurally caused by inflexible planning and arbitrary interventions into economic mechanisms. The behavioral patterns and attitudes of plant management, administrative and planning cadres, production workers, and service employees were formed accordingly. In general these were intolerable and irreconcilable with the operative requirements of modern industrial production and social progress. Challenges emanating from the impact of information technologies, flexible manufacturing, and CAD/CAM/CIM systems on the labor force and the relations of production within industrial branches and between industry, the ministries, and the educational field were not addressed. In retrospect, ironically, the very assets of the Brezhnev era (the consolidation of the political domain, the stabilization and creation of some homegeneity among factions of the ruling elite, and the re-establishment of social codes and judicial norms for the political process by removing fears for personal safety) brought with them the high price of bureaucratic ossification. Status quo attitudes of the old guard and their pursuit of particular group interests rendered the system structurally incapable of dealing with the very transformations it successfully helped to generate; namely, complex economic interdependencies, social differentiation, and the enhancement of Soviet power in the international system.[1] The success of Gorbachev's reform policies, defined in terms of revitalizing the Soviet social system and bridging the gap with advanced capitalist countries in production standards, will depend upon the mobilization of the Soviet masses. Even more important is the question of selecting the proper cadres and regaining in general the active support of decisive layers of the Soviet elite. This will determine the outcome of the reform process.[2]

Traditional mass campaign formulae (the "revolution from above" concept) aimed at forging maximum utilization and mobilization of human and material resources over a limited period of time either by hidden or openly repressive means. Such concepts corresponded to the economic and organizational level of development at that stage of Soviet accumulation. The limits of centrally directed mass campaigns, principally a substitute for social planning and participation of the masses in economic and socio-political decision-making processes, became obvious in the mid-seventies. Capital, material, and human resources were either exhausted or resource allocations and ever more costly capital investments failed to yield the desired returns. Rates of economic growth, of labor and industrial productivity, stagnated. In other words, economic inter-dependence (domestic and international) and social differentiation had reached a stage of complexity in which repressive methods of integration and economic growth had become ineffective, counterproductive, and historically outdated.[3]

Stagnation and even decline of the international Soviet position culminated in the latter part of the Brezhnev era. In contrast, the world economy experienced dramatic shifts and saw the emergence of new economic centers (the Pacific Basin) and the growing relevance of countries which a decade ago were still considered underdeveloped. Such countries responded to the new wave of information and communications tech-nologies with their revolutionary consequences for traditional production methods. They were able to defuse new technologies over traditional industrial sectors, upgrading and modernizing them. On such a basis were they able to entertain export-led growth strategies and compete effectively in nearly all sectors (textiles, steel, autos, chemicals, semi-conductors, consumer electronics) with such advanced industrial areas as the European Community, the United States, and Japan.[4] Effective sectoral restructuring and organizational changes became synonomous with economic success.

This process did not go unnoticed in the USSR. During the Central Committee meeting of January 27, 1987, a meeting postponed three times, the legitimacy of revolutionary reforms was theoretically articulated by Mikhail Gorbachev. He emphasized the systemic nature of the Soviet crisis and linked it to the obsolete theoretical concepts of socialism which had remained from the thirties and forties; periods in which Soviet society had to face totally different problems. Alexander Galkin has stated:

> The main objective of our policy is a democratization of all echelons of Soviet society. That is to say, restructuring and creation of competence and behavioral patterns of the Soviets as well as democratization of the Party, including secret ballots at all levels. This includes the democratization of economic life, such as the election of management, of university chancellors, and rectors. Some universities are already in compliance with the reform. However, a plurality of political parties is not a practical proposal of our political system.[5]

Objectives and Scope of the Socio-Economic Reform

Allow us to introduce a somewhat provocative thesis. Any doubt as to the seriousness of the present leadership with regards to transforming Soviet society and economy, and adapting the USSR to changed international conditions, would seem to us to be outdated. Of course, we can argue about the results and the depth of reforms, about their chances for success, and with regard to the time factor needed to obtain palatable results.

There is a very perplexing contradiction which seems to render Soviet policies somewhat ambivalent. While there is little doubt as to the seriousness of the present Soviet leadership to modernize the country economically and to open social processes which could breathe new life into ossified bureaucratic structures, the Soviet leadership seems to have no clear concept of the future role of the country in the international system. Uncertainties with regard to its long-term international strategy are reproduced in regional questions, despite the leadership's remarkable flexibility, which was successfully demonstrated in the ongoing arms limitations talks with the US. Soviet foreign and security policies are dominated by the debate on domestic reforms. However, the "primacy of domestic policies" implies an external dimension. To regain international respect and a new momentum for Soviet foreign policy after the long period of immobility necessitates successful completion of the domestic reform of Soviet society and the adaptation of its production system to world standards. Gorbachev and other members of the Politburo have stated over and over that the reform objectives of *perestroika, glasnost,* and *samoupravlenie* may eventually be attained only in a long, painful process, full of contradictions and setbacks and opposed by many groups, that will be extended well into the twenty-first century. Such a process will traverse several stages. During the CC meeting of June 8–9, 1987, the beginning of the second stage was seen to correspond with the end of the current Five Year Plan in 1991. As was repeatedly stressed, the next three years will be decisive. It is our opinion that they will be less influenced and certainly not determined by events in Washington, Bonn, or Tokyo. The opportunities for success will be decided by the compliance and support of local and regional layers of the Soviet economic, administrative, and political elite.

As recently as two years ago, no one in the West or in Eastern Europe would have given it a second thought that the Soviet daily *Pravda* would be passed from hand to hand in East Berlin or Prague, or even sold on the black market in Romania. To imagine slogans, like "We want Gorbachev" on East Berlin's or Prague's walls, or to imagine that the highest party representative of a traditionally oppressive power and members of Western and Eastern peace and environmentalist movements would spend hours together in debate, as happened recently in Prague and Moscow, would have caused concern among friends. Rudolf Bahro, a former GDR economist and author of *The Alternative*, a devastating Marxist analysis of the political and economic modes of "real socialism," a book for which he was imprisoned and later exiled, stops short of euphoria in interpreting Gorbachev's ascendance to power. Bahro, now active in the West German peace movement, sees Gorbachev as a representative of a new political generation in the USSR which was mobilized by Khrushchev's call for change and his renunciation of the Stalinist political system at the 20th Party Congress. However, his generation was not strong enough then to stop another layer of the political, economic, and cultural elite, educated and formed under Stalin, from attaining power. The Brezhnev era, despite its conservatism, reliance on bureaucratic institutions, and its lack of political energy, was not "criminal."[6] Consequently, the system did not dehumanize the young reformist generation which began its own version of the *long march through Soviet institutions* in the sixties. According to Bahro, Gorbachev is both modernizer and exponent of disciplinary renewal. He is both "quasi-czar" and probably a "Soviet Dubcek." However, it must not be forgotten that Dubcek always remained a "party soldier" and this is also true regarding Gorbachev.[7]

His programmatic concepts of *glasnost* (openness), *perestroika* (reorganization of systemic structures), and *samoupravlenie* (active and responsible participation for citizens, workers, and management) are politically limited by the constellation of forces (interest groups, institutionalized and factional elites) which constitute the *governing coalition* in the Politburo, Party Secretariat, and the Central Committee. These political factions formulate the ruling consensus and platform for policy actions by integrating conflicting interests in a compromise formula. Expectations, therefore, of radical and rapid structural changes in the Soviet economic, political, and social order would be wishful thinking. Furthermore, it is of extreme importance, both methodologically and theoretically, to clarify first what is understood by change; in which direction and of what quality. What can we expect then? Simes, who refers to the same historical experience as Bahro, doubts that even the introduction of "Stalinism with a human face" is a formula for creating a working modern society.[8]

Why not? If there is one common point on which all the diverse ideological currents of anti-Stalinist opposition movements in the USSR since 1919 can agree, it is regarding a critique of the oppressive power centers controlled by political-administrative Party cadres far removed from the Soviet people and not subject to any social control from below.

The history of Soviet socio-economic reforms, from the "revolution from above" concept under Stalin to the introduction of economic stimuli for raising productivity rates under Khrushchev and Brezhnev, is full of failures. These have been due to contraditions among the ruling factional interest group of the *nomenklatura* and petty resistance from subalternate bureaucrats, managers, peasants, and workers. However, the failures have a structural explanation which is directly linked to the nature of the Soviet political system. Most economic reforms so far have been isolated and fragmented from their socio-political environment. They did not combine an overall program to change simultaneously with economic conditions as well as such factors which acted as social and political counterproductive barriers. They intended to solve underlying problems in their various structures by the application of immanent means. For example, economic reforms oscillated around either of the two poles of centralization or decentralization of decision-making power; to give more authority to the plant managers, or to reduce it, or to decentralize and strengthen the central planning authority at the same time. Most of these programs were coupled with material and financial incentives for better work performance on the part of Soviet laborers and for technical and administrative plant management cadres. As long as the incentives paid off, or the increased local authority of plant managers produced results, there was no need for further innovations and improvements down the line. When the reform impetus weakened and material deliveries stopped, bureaucratic inertia and the fear of incurring failure took over.

In Soviet theory on social development, the stages of "building up and improving the material-technical base of socialism" were clearly separated from the "development of socialist democracy." As long as Soviet industrial production practices, as distinguished from their the-

oretical tenets, exploit and regard human labor solely in its capacity as
a means for raising productivity and for filling the goals of the various
plans, collective labor will not be integrated with the process of production
as a social organization and as the genuine source of innovation and
production.

To overcome this structural antagonism, Soviet society has had to be
freed from its Stalinist entanglement; i.e., an end to the *political interdiction
of Soviet citizens*. Rudimentary principles of socialist democracy were to
be restored in order to revitalize social dynamism. In other words, the
diachronical, step-by-step logic of building socialism, introduced during
NEP and Stalin's call for "socialism in one country" have had to be
revised. Instead of building first a new material-technical base and then
upon that the political superstructure of socialist democracy which of
course never happened, the concepts of *glasnost, perestroika*, and *samoupravlenie* emphasize social and political dimensions as a prerequisite
for reform. The socio-economic process started with small steps such
as publishing the agenda of the Politburo, campaigns to discuss issues
of Soviet life in the newspapers, and of bringing the remote political
institutions back into contact with everyday Soviet reality. The limits
within which sensitive issues of Soviet life could be voiced widened
substantially in the course of the last few years. Mass communications
channels are involved in the process of information exchange from below
and above.[9] However, the discourse of openness does not limit itself to
changes in cultural and everyday Soviet life. The democratization campaign, now in full cry in the media, seems to focus on three main
objectives:

a) to limit the obstructive inertia of the middle layers of Soviet
   bureaucracy. This fight is as old as the system itself and has
   consumed earlier generations of reform minded Bolsheviki;

b) to win the active support of the Soviet intelligentsia by alleviating
   systemic oppression and opening avenues to express dissent in
   established forms as the newspaper projects of various dissident
   groups suggest;[10] and

c) to convince a skeptical and reluctant public which will not show
   any interest in social and political participation unless it is convinced
   that its social and material well-being is at stake.

There was a shift from limited institutional reform to a campaign for
democratic openness in Gorbachev's initial approach. It proceeded from
cultural topics into the core field of societal integration, questioning
elements of the Stalinist model of state to society relations. By doing
so, the implicit question arises as to what will be the role of the Party

in the period of transition and thereafter. In his address to the 27th Party Congress Gorbachev chastized the Party for having become partly a bureaucratic institution, devoid of efficiency and dedication. He reminded the Congress that there is no "such thing as the Communists' vanguard role in general; it is expressed in practical deeds" and that the Party can only resolve societal problems successfully if it is itself in "uninterrupted development, free of the 'infallibility' complex."[11]

The Leninist principles of criticism and self-criticism have to be restored in order to achieve a better education of Party cadres to raise their consciousness and to enrich the interchange of ideas in Party life and to strengthen collective work and eliminate attitudes that have closed the Party organizations to criticism. As a means for achieving such objectives Gorbachev proposed in January, 1987 reforming the electoral system on the local and district levels for Soviets and Party secretaryships. Voting would be by secret ballot and voters could choose from between more than one candidate. If carried through, this could be of significant importance for the overall process of restructuring Soviet society. This process is continuing as the results of the Central Committee meeting in June, 1987, suggest. For the first time in nearly fifty years the CPSU called openly for a Party conference to be held on a confirmed date (June 1988) in order to review the progress of *perestroika, samoupravlenie,* and *glasnost.* Candidates for the conference should be elected by secret ballot at Central Committee meetings in eleven of the fifteen Soviet Republics. In the Ukraine, Byleorussia, Uzbekistan, and Kazakhstan candidates should be chosen at regional Party committees. It is not yet clear if these are also to be by secret ballot.

Gorbachev's comet-like ascension and the swiftness with which he strengthened his political power base, a process far from complete, as the confirmation of several former close associates of Brezhnev during the 27th Party Congress would suggest, seems even more remarkable if we accept the widely held notion that he did not command significant institutional backing in the beginning. To build his own political base he has had to:

1. rely on "personal associations" for the "alliance building process" to establish a "governing coalition" of interest groups in the Politburo and the Secretariat of the CPSU;[12]
2. introduce a new political style into Soviet politics; and
3. dominate the programmatic discussion regarding the most important topics of social and economic change.

However, aided both by international developments unfavorable to Soviet interests as well as a stagnating economic performance, including a decline in productivity rates since the mid-seventies, Gorbachev succeeded in linking these two crucial questions regarding future Soviet development with his own political ambitions and his concept of socio-economic reform.

Before him, during the short interregnum of Yuri Andropov, criticism emerged within the Soviet intelligentsia as to the faltering economic and political performance of the Brezhnev era. It touched upon the question as to which economic, political, and cultural cadres should guide the Soviet Union out of the morass and deal with the challenges forced upon the country by the effects of the third industrial (informational) revolution. As earlier historical cases, the "question of cadres" (their selection, qualification, and new functions) had two aspects. First, is the objective need to improve economic efficiency, technological innovation, and to overhaul the politico-economic administration. Discussions regarding moral, political, and professional criteria for the selection of the new cadres who would master these tasks were widespread in the period preceding the 27th Party Congress in 1986.[13]

Secondly, in using this debate for his own purposes, Gorbachev obviously has managed to broaden his base of intra-party support by purging the Old Guard in the name of efficiency, anti-corruption, modernization, and the streamlining of local, regional, and national administrative apparatuses. Since March, 1985, for example, in addition to extraordinary changes in the Politburo and Secretariat, which resulted in a supportive majority, Gorbachev succeeded in having outsted about 25 percent of all 157 First Secretaries of territorial and regional Committees (including seventy-nine members of the Central committee of the CPSU). Five of the fourteen voting members of the Politburo gained their position under Gorbachev in 1985 and an additional three were appointed at the Central Committee meeting of June 26, 1987. In that same month Defense Minister Sergei Kokolov was forced to retire after a teenage West German pilot landed his plane on Red Square. Earlier, in February, 1987, the Khazakhstan Party Secretary, Dinmuhammad Kunaev, was dropped from the Politburo and subsequently expelled from the Central Committee because of accusations of corruption and inefficiency with regard to Party affairs. In the case of non-voting members of either the Secretariat or the Politburo the ratio is even more favorable to Gorbachev. Of six non-voting members of the Politburo four have been elected since 1985.[14] In the Secretariat his supporting ratio seems to be even higher. This does not mean that Gorbachev's position is as strong as he would like it to be, but opposition will not come from the Brezhnev Old Guard, which is in retreat. Contrary to Western opinions, which often tend to link his fate as General Secretary to successful performances in foreign policy, Gorbachev's position seems to be much more conditioned by domestic developments. Despite the lack of tangible results in economic performance so far, there are neither visible alternatives to his policies, nor are there any indications that a new core of oppositional forces is ascendant.[15]

A New Model of Societal Synthesis or Integration?

Let us point in this context to some changes in the political process which could be observed recently. These changes are neither dramatic nor substantial, but they reflect an underlying gradual shift in the relationship between the economic and socio-political structure of Soviet society. Such changes were not introduced by Gorbachev. They could rather be defined as a historic achievement of the Brezhnev era and the Khrushchev years, in which some of the worst heritages of the Stalinist epoch were overcome. The elimination of massive, widely applied state terror as a means of direct economic, political, and administrative actions of the Soviet state led to the revitalization of socialist justice and minimal guarantees of civic and constitutional rights. It would seem not simply a matter of difference in form if political leaders, declared ideological deviators, are no longer shot or killed with an axe, but merely jailed or exiled. The purge of the representatives of the *ancien regime* no longer menaces the personal safety of the Old Guard which survived the Brezhnev era stigmatized with political and social immobility, nepotism, corruption, and institutionalized bureaucratic inertia.

Obviously, *the methods of political control and social guidance have changed over time.* Today material and social incentives take the place of more direct means of political rule. Any program of reform intended to mobilize Soviet workers and peasants in order to increase labor productivity and industrial production and to ensure a constant and reliable output of high quality commodities, must take into account those systemic factors. Considering these shifts, we can postulate a *fundamental change in the Soviet model of social integration.* Furthermore, during the two decades of Brezhnev's rule, the reconstitution of the CPSU as the dominant political body in Soviet society, responsible for formulating developmental perspectives contributed to a *consolidation and harmonization of the nomenklatura as the ruling societal class. Brezhnev's "corporatist" and conservative style of exerting political leadership facilitated the creation of an institutionalized process of interest representation in the leading policy bodies of Soviet power.*

To accede to his present position Gorbachev has had to accept and respect the principles of consensual, integrating norms and rules; i.e., the manner in which the *nomenklatura* regulates its internal factional conflicts. The political implications of such a consensus are ambivalent.

On the one hand, they restrict the scope of political and social innovations introduced by the new leadership. The traditional concept of a Stalinist type "revolution from above" seems to have lost considerable leverage as a means of social mobilization. If this thesis can be supported by sufficient evidence, it would enable us to modify current perceptions of the USSR, and to ask questions which are somewhat obstructed by questionable theoretical assumptions as to how we may define a true reform of Soviet society. Important questions are: which substitute instruments/actions for societal integration are provided by the political system? Are elements of a new societal form of integration already manifest? Is there evidence of a weakened power of the change-from-above concept? If yes, are the causative factors social differentiation and industrial/technological/informational diversification? If the tendency continues on an even larger scale to utilize high technology in production and services, producing transformational effects in the industrial structure and changes in the requirements for highly qualified, skilled personnel, will such a trend, in the long run, lead to a withdrawal of étatist omnipresence? Can we assume, regardless of the economic model, that with the increase in technological-industrial complexity, semi-automatization and greater flexibility of the production line, reduced demand for serial labor, as well as growing sectoral economic interdependence, the methods and instruments for social and economic management will change irreversibly to reduced levels of political control (and government interference in social and economic life) and greater degrees of socioeconomic guidance, even allowing elements of limited participation?[16]

On the other hand, one may be tempted to consider that the possible success of reform opponents would indicate either a tendency towards wider political fragmentation in Soviet decision-making bodies, or a harbinger of other than collective forms of political leadership. In the course of such developments, the reintroduction of "reforms from above" concepts would either obstruct or instrumentalize fragile efforts to expand autonomous participation of economic and social groups in the political process. Here we can point to astonishing phenomena aside from the changes in style and presentation during the recent Party Congress. In order to obtain an endorsement and to legitimize his reform projects, Gorbachev needed a favorable constellation of political forces either supporting, or at least not blocking him. Since March 1985 it seems that he has been able to create such a platform for his project. However, interesting enough, discussions and reconfirmation patterns at the 27th Party Congress suggest that we finally can observe a Soviet style "checks and balances" system in operation between the executive arms of the Party, the Politburo, and the Secretariat on one side, and the legitimizing Central Committee on the other side.[17]

The above should suffice for the moment to indicate the importance of questioning several of the perceptions which predominate in Western academic and political circles. Some correctly describe the USSR as an immobile, bureaucratic society, based on an inefficient, unproductive, and wasteful economic system which is ruled by a repressive, ossified political order insensitive to innovative socio-economic, structural change. We have no objections to such a description which lists the most obvious deformations of the Soviet system. However, to describe the social and political form correctly is not necessarily equivalent to an analysis either of the relationship between its systemic elements (the political, economic, and the ideological structures) or of the forces of societal synthesis.

At this point a few methodological remarks should be made. At the risk of stating the obvious, it appears necessary to recapitulate that any society which follows:

1. an *étatist* type of economic accumulation, based on central planning and the non-existence of private ownership of the means of production, will
2. coin its political institutions and processes according to the underlying economic basis, and
3. will create value systems and sets of ideological norms different from societies and economic orders which emanate from the Western model of civilization.

This poses immediate analytical problems. Descriptions of phenomena in those societies, regardless of the richness of empirical data they process, have little analytical value if they operate with categories and methods derived from theories not applicable to the subject under investigation. Most descriptions of Soviet society derive their analytical instruments, their methods, and categories from theories of Western societies. This leads, for example, to an unjustified transfer and application of categories central to qualifying Western societies, but of relative irrelevance in determining and explaining the transformational potential of Soviet type social and political formations; concepts such as market, parliamentary democracy, and political pluralism. By applying external parameters to measure change or structural transformation in these societies, one imposes from the beginning normative verdicts by the very categories used. *Reform and real change to a more efficient economic system is exclusively identified with market economies* (mixed economies or the resurrection of capitalism). Parliamentary democracy based on a multiparty system is regarded as the *conditio sine qua non* for the free expression of political opinions. *Planning and democracy are regarded as antagonistic.*[18] Therefore, any policy which fails to aim at these tenets is barely noted or accepted as reform. Even worse, attempts to turn out more efficient and rational planning often are interpreted as steps into a failed Stalinist past, and identified with the exercise of more direct or authoritarian forms of social and political control. Such policies, it is assumed, correspond to the intensification of ideological struggles between Western and Socialist societies in international and regional relations. Rather than following such an approach with their predictable results, but little insight into the constellation of social, economic, and political forces and their conflicting, contradicting interests in supporting or restricting systemic changes, we propose to concentrate on internal Soviet debates regarding the future developmental path of the system.

More than two years into the Gorbachev era, it is still too early to evaluate the reform. To concentrate exclusively on tangible structural changes, measurable in quantitative units over a predictable period of time, would yield little insight into the dynamics of the ongoing process. Undoubtedly we have both to alter some of our predictions and try to integrate the emerging themes of the reform process into a longer historical perspective. Very often observers expect quick and drastic solutions to the towering domestic problems and to the dangerous foreign policy heritage of Soviet global overcommitment during the Brezhnev era. They were correct in their assumptions and prejudices. Gorbachev's impact on Soviet domestic and foreign policy during the first two years was neither impressive nor was daring reform introduced.[19] Only since the latter part of 1986 and 1987 did he seem to seize the initiative in domestic and foreign affairs. Ever since a barrage of Soviet foreign policy proposals, like the limitation of strategic weapons, elimination of INF and shorter range missiles in Europe (double-zero option), non-first-use, discussion of a defensive military doctrine for both Warsaw Pact and NATO countries, and proposals for establishing nuclear free and chemical and biological-free zones in Europe have kept the Atlantic Community out of breath. In domestic policies the reform pace was slower. However, there are certain elements which seem to confirm the assertion that the Soviet Union has arrived at a decisive point in her evolutionary process in which systemic change not only seems to be unavoidable, but is launched by the existing leadership. Evidence for such a finding is limited and scattered, and has to be pieced together like a mosaic.

However, we have noticed over the last three decades a substantial and fundamental shift in policies of societal integration. The present leadership and, even more so, any future political leadership, will be confronted by, and has to deal with, a new, well-educated, urbanized, and socially differentiated generation reaching maturity. This new generation is barely connected to the Soviet past, indifferent to ideological tenets, and open to "post-modernity" influences centered around such issues as "quality of life" which plague Western policy makers and have in some instances upset the traditonal power base of party politics. This is by no means an argument for "convergence" but on the surface many issues and problems of the West do exist in slightly different forms in "real socialist" societies as well, especially those linked to both youth cultures. As the social base of the USSR is undergoing changes, induced by shifts in the ensemble of the forces of production, and contradictions derived from inertia and the resistance to change on the part of ossified, political institutions, these processes leave their impact on both the dominant value system as well as on the methods of political rule.

These changes happened gradually, no declared reform from above was necessary. Debates and theoretical discourses within the Soviet intelligentsia initiated or accompanied such processes. We cannot sufficiently comment on these discussions which have been in progress since the mid-seventies and deal with theoretical problems of Soviet development, such as:

1. What is the stage of socialist development the USSR and other socialist societies are traversing?
2. What is the nature of conflicts and contradictions between social groups and classes in the present stage of socialist development?
3. What are the perspectives of the international socialist movement with regard to the relationship between *developed socialist* and advanced capitalist countries?
4. What are the perspectives of Third World countries for entering a non-capitalist path of development?

The remainder of this chapter will focus on two interconnected fields in which changes are already underway and more are to be expected: domestic socio-economic reforms and a redefinition of Soviet objectives with regard to external relations, particularly in the Third World.

Towards a Reassessment of Soviet Policies in International Affairs: Linkages between the "New Thinking" in Domestic and Foreign Policy

Despite legitimate reservations with overemphasizing linkages between external and internal imperatives of Soviet policies, there seems to emerge some correspondence between a "new thinking" with regard to matters of social and economic reform, and a "new vision" as to the Soviet Union's role in the international system. A more pragmatic, flexible foreign policy, seeking to reduce tensions between both superpowers and to achieve arms reductions, is an important element in the restructuring of Soviet society. To some degree such a policy could secure the reform process against undesirable external developments and facilitate shifts in material and human resources from unproductive military facilities to civilian production.

Such a trend is neither unique to the Gorbachev administration nor without historical precedent. It would be very wrong to generalize that domestic reform periods correspond with détente elements in foreign policies, or vice versa. Numerous stages in Soviet history suggest the opposite. We have experienced stages of extreme domestic oppression that corresponded with intensified trade and political contacts with the capitalist countries. We could see domestic terror accompanied by a policy of pragmatic adjustments in Soviet policies after 1935. The initiation of NEP at the Tenth Party Congress went hand in hand with the prohibition of factions. However, during the course of NEP we saw the most vivid debates on industrial and transformational strategies taking place between Preobrazhensky and Bukharin. Again during the Khrushchev era, aspects of de-Stalinization were combined with a new approach in foreign policy, leading to détente and the formulation of the theory of peaceful coexistence.

It would be wrong to attribute solely the reorientation of Soviet foreign policy objectives, especially with regard to Western Europe and on some Third World issues, to Gorbachev. On the contrary, this process had already started near the end of the Brezhnev era.[20] However, the political immobility of Breshnev's Old Guard was too deeply entrenched to free Soviet foreign politics from its self-inflicted INF dilemma and the resulting consequence of international semi-isolation. The following interlude of Andropov's reform initiatives were too shortlived to achieve substantial momentum toward change. While some elements and the direction of a reform movement in the domestic domain became clear, Soviet foreign policies again suffered from incoherence and lack of analysis of Western Europe. Finally, Chernenko's leadership of the Party can be mainly interpreted as a calculated interregnum, as buying time without complicating the difficult process of regrouping and realigning social and political forces within the *nomenklatura*. The period functioned as a shield while a new governing coalition, based on new formulae of power compromise and interest distribution, was generated within the ruling elite.

Such a thesis does not aim at minimizing the initating role of the present Soviet leadership in the restructuring and revitalizing of Soviet foreign political objectives. Gorbachev's ascendency and the remarkable rapidity with which he succeeded in strenghening and consolidating his position within the political system were a prerequisite for implementing on a pragmatic basis new Soviet foreign policy objectives.

Let us recapitulate a few of the ideas in the ongoing Soviet debate with regard to foreign policy objectives and point to three structural elements which emerge and seem to be indicative of the "new thinking":

a) the impact of shifts between global economic growth centers, internationalization of production, R&D, and control over national policies;
b) redefining and revitalizing the role of collective security concepts and international organizations for conflict resolution; and
c) a critical reassessment of Soviet overcommitments in regional affairs.

Neither the draft of the Party Program nor the discussions during the 27th Party Congress put extreme emphasis on foreign political issues. The underlying assumption of Soviet leaders is apparently that a strong economy will provide the necessary basis as well as the instruments for a robust foreign policy which can deliver advantages in the ideological struggle between the superpowers.[21]

To preserve the hitherto gained position, the following are the guiding principles of Soviet international policy:

1. to be militarily-strategically respected as an equal by the other superpower;
2. to play an active part in solving international disputes, primarily in crisis areas of the Third World and the Middle East;
3. to strengthen and to maintain the coherence of the socialist commonwealth of nations;
4. to render "necessary" support for internationalist movements and struggles without jeopardizing the Soviet Union's security; and
5. to end the war in Afghanistan without sacrificing the physical survivability of the Afghan Communist Party.

Gorbachev's consolidation of political leadership in the Party accelerated a realistic reassessment of Soviet foreign policy objectives. Paradoxically, despite the political immobility regarding domestic issues in the late Brezhnev era, such a process of adapting foreign policy to altered conditions was well underway. It surfaced then from time to time in intellectual debates. This extraordinary phenomenon was partly caused by a "scientific revolution" in Soviet foreign policy. Since the latter part of the Brezhnev era we could observe that academic institutions, which functioned as advisory agencies for the political process, attained growing importance. The impact of long-term and differentiated analysis of foreign policy is undeniable. It contributed to a perception of a sophisticated Soviet leadership regarding international developments and regional issues. The dynamization of Soviet foreign policy under Gorbachev in order to overcome international isolation as a result of Afghanistan, the downing of the Korean airliner, and the failure of Soviet policy to stop the deployment of INF missiles in Western Europe, reflects the influence of such advisory institutions. As indicative of a few of the modifications in perceptions of the external world, the Soviet leadership:

a) is ready to accept the existence of the European Community and has developed substantial interests in participating in EUREKA and other high technology programs, such as the EC's space project;
b) can differentiate between various currents of conservatism in Western societies;
c) sees the limits of exploiting differences between West European and American security positions, but is more sensitive to the specificities of West European security interests;
d) presumably has understood that self-proclaimed socialist governments in Third World countries develop more often into liabilities than reliable allies;
e) follows with increasing interest the emerging patterns of economic conflicts between leading capitalist countries; and
f) finally recognizes that Soviet influence, especially in the Third World, *cannot be maintained over a long period of time by non-economic means.*

Despite the fact that nearly all these themes could well be integrated into a coherent and general foreign policy strategy, there are still perplexing contradictions between some elements. Apart from fundamental statements by Gorbachev as to the avoidance of war and the necessity of peaceful solutions, the Soviet leadership seems not to have derived a clearer concept regarding the future role of the USSR within a rapidly shifting international economic and political order. It is not at all clear as to which elements will dominate Soviet foreign policy thinking; a more status quo oriented approach on the basis of economic and political détente with core countries of the West, a policy of selective globalism, or a policy of isolationism. Even speculations regarding the reopening of the German question circulated not long ago, causing serious concern not only in leading West German conservative circles, but especially among the Federal Republic's West European allies and her Eastern neighbors. In an unusual article that appeared in *Pravda* and *Izvestia* on September 17, 1987, Gorbachev seemed to revitalize a traditional concept of former Soviet foreign policy. He addressed the need to enhance the capacity of international organizations, such as the United Nations, the Security Council, and the International Court of Justice, to take on more responsibilities for preserving global and regional stability and to develop a role in the monitoring of compliance with arms control agreements.[22] Without doubt such proposals were partly prompted by actual tensions in the Persian Gulf, the Iran-Iraq War, and the deployment of NATO naval units. More than that, however, they indicate a more fundamental shift in Soviet thinking; i.e., that peace-keeping efforts and international stability have become matters of "global" dimension and are no longer simply bi-polar responsibilities. Such ideas culminate in Gorbachev's thesis of ruling out any attempts, direct or indirect, to influence the development of countries which are "not one of our own."[23] The destabilization of existing governments from the outside is impermissible.

Global Overcommitments and Shifts in Soviet Third World Policies

Since 1977 internal Soviet debates have focused on the relationship between the socialist states and the Third World. This resulted in the renunciation of the ambitious project of creating a "socialist world market" competing with the capitalist one. This concept proved to be as unrealistic as the one intended to involve newly industriazed countries (NICs) in tripartite economic schemes in which the USSR would become an active partner. By the end of the seventies both concepts had proved to be failures. International solidarity and preferential economic treatment characterized the first stage of Soviet Third World policies; the second stage saw attempts to build a "socialist economic world order" upon East-South relations; the third stage stressed interdependence of global economic development and sought to integrate Third World countries into tripartite arrangements.

Elements of the last concept are still valid, but present internal Soviet debates indicate a rather radical break with previously held theoretical positions, taking into account a sober reassessment of the results of socialist development performance. Core elements of an emerging consensus stress that:

a) underdevelopment can only be overcome by integrating the South into the existing division of labor on a global scale;

b) as long as the world market remains dominated by superior Western economic standards of technology and production, even *socialist countries in a developed stage* (to use the term introduced by Gorbachev), will be unable to free themselves from, or act against, such externally imposed standards.

Both arguments carry an implicit and bitter message for Third World socialist liberation movements and countries:

1) There are no shortcuts for building a socialist society and political transformations are not enough to guarantee structural changes;
2) Less developed countries have to accept for the foreseeable future the dominance of the capitalist world market and use it as a resource for their own development;
3) Soviet economic, political, and military assistance to these new states who wish to enter the socialist stage will be rather limited and given selectively. Such countries cannot expect relations like those between the USSR and Cuba, Vietnam, or with East European countries.[24]
4) They must obtain support for their economic development from other industrialized regions or countries like the EC or Japan. This implies the necessity of diversifying trade, attracting foreign investments, and of speeding up social change with economic growth.

Disillusion with the prospects for social transformation on the part of those movements and declared socialist states, on the one hand, and continuing increased economic and military demands for assistance, on the other, seemed to prepare the ground for a critical and sober evaluation of the USSR's relationship to liberation movements in the Third World. Thus, and measured against the abyssmal Soviet economic performance and indications of systemic crisis, the leadership was confronted with carrying an intolerable burden of "global overcommitments" and simultaneously threatened by a worsening of East-West tensions which originated partly from those very overcommitments. In regard to East-West relations, Gorbachev has been most outspoken in denouncing the concepts of "winnable or limited nuclear wars."[25] Likewise, he has stressed over and over again the need for normal relations with the West and China. Gorbachev's predecessors had already indicated some reluctance to concede CMEA membership to self-defined socialist countries in the Third World and to take on financial and material support along the magnitude of her obligations to Cuba. Even countries like Mozambique and Angola were denied membership in the organization and, together with Nicaragua, were advised to diversify trade and financial relations in order to obtain support from capitalist countries.

    Its most articulate expression of caution and lack of confidence that socialist transformation could be achieved in Third World NICs, even in the medium term, was underlined in an interview given by Victor Goncharov, Deputy Director of the Institute of African Studies of the USSR's Academy of Sciences on Soviet policy in Southern Africa.[26]

Refuting South African assertions, often reiterated in Western circles, that Soviet objectives aim at cutting the sea lanes around the Cape of Good Hope, Goncharov stressed that neither the USA nor the USSR have any vital interests in the region. In Goncharov's view the region ranked alongside the Middle East as a strategic issue after the prevention of nuclear war, the socialist countries of Europe, the USA, China, and Western Europe.[27] Goncharov called the military-strategic importance of the sea lanes a "myth" and stressed that any disruption of economic trade and financial linkages would hurt the socialist world as well as the West. He underlined that, in the framework of the "so-called new political thinking we should take into account the global problems and the global consequences of our behavior in every part of the world."

Assessing the prospects of solving the problems of national liberation with a campaign for socialist transformation, Goncharov was very pessimistic. Alluding to Lenin, he characterized such currents in the African National Congress as "an infantile disorder" which could threaten to separate the ANC from the black population. He foresaw a long and escalating national liberation struggle of about ten years and expressed no hopes for a "quick victory." Transforming a victorious black South Africa into a socialist society may not be achieved "in 25 years, but in a century . . . I am an optimist."[28]

Gorbachev stated the rationale and the main objective of the Soviet Union's international position during the Peace Forum in Moscow in February 1987: "I will state with full responsibility that our international policy is more than ever determined by domestic policy, by our interst in concentrating on constructive endeavours to improve our country. This is why we need lasting peace, predictability, and constructiveness in international relations."[29]

This *primacy of domestic policy* carries the hidden message that the Soviet Union must be relieved of intolerable economic burdens and cease being the primary source for stabilizing socialist regimes elsewhere, including its East European glacis. The chronic Polish and Romanian crises, persistant economic and military aid obligations to Vietnam, Cuba, Ethiopia, etc., and the war in Afghanistan have either drained the Soviet economy or put constraints on her in perspective. Furthermore, the sluggish performance of the Soviet economy itself, and the ongoing arms race which threatens to spill over into the militarization of space, are additional factors which limit the importance of Third World developments in present-day Soviet thinking. The failure of the economic tripartite integration model, due to shifts in world trade and capital flows, which were never able to be influenced by Soviet behavior, indicated two trends. First was the growing importance of NICs as international economic actors and their increasing independence from the political and military influence of both superpowers (Brazil, Argentina). Second was the inattractiveness of Soviet industrial commodities for NICs. They simply bypassed the USSR.

The present Soviet leadership finally seems to have realized that the determining factor for Soviet external (especially Third World) relations rests on the capability of the domestic economy to deliver assistance for socio-economic transformation. In this regard successful economic reconversion, modernization, and social reform become the bases for new concepts of Soviet international policies. Moreover, the ambitious goals of Soviet Third World policies seem to have reached their limits by the end of the seventies. To borrow from Lenin, the time is ripe to call for a cautious and "orderly political retreat" without losing too much credibility among militant, socialist oriented, Third World élites. Considering the foreign policy priorities in Gorbachev's project, which cannot be separated from the overriding objective of strengthening, revitalizing, and, most of all, modernizing Soviet economy and society, there is very little doubt as to where the focus of Soviet national interests will be. His efforts to regain the political initiative for conflict reduction and confidence building measures in East-West relations relegate Third World problems to a position of less importance on the Soviet foreign political agenda.

The time has come for a "strategic retreat" from Third World conflicts. The retreat will be gradual and orderly, in the sense that the USSR will seek international agreements to defuse conflicts, but will also allow minimal guarantees for their own interests as well as to safeguard their clients or allies.

Notes

1. Alex Nove, "What's Happening in Moscow," *The National Interest*, Nr. 8, Summer 1987, p. 14f.

2. Seweryn Bialer, "Reform und Beharrung im Sowjetsystem: Ausgangslage, Schwierigkeiten, und Aussichten der Politik Gorbatschows," in: *Europa-Archiv*, Nr. 2, 1987, p. 47.

3. *Ibid.*, p. 47; Peter Knirsch, "Perspektiven der sowjetischen Wirtschafts-politik," *Europa-Archiv*, Nr. 23, 1985, p. 715.

4. See the remarkable speech by Gorbachev in Vladivostok, July 28, 1986 in *Europa-Archiv*, Nr. 16, 1986, p. D457ff. He stresses the necessity to contain military-industrial influences on political decisions in both superpowers and to throw overboard now obsolete security doctrines based on class theory or cold war ideologies in either camp. They were causing a "primitive automatism" in the international dialogue. Instead Gorbachev points to growing international economic and political interdependencies, acknowledges the profound shifts in the world economy, and asserts that the emergence of the Pacific region as an

Socialist Transformation and Soviet Foreign Policy

73

important factor in the international system demands a reassessment of national policies under global determinants.

5. Interview with Professor Alexander Galkin, Vice-Chancellor of the Institute of Social Sciences at the Central Committee of the CPSU in *Die Tageszeitung*, 10 September 1987, p. 7.

6. Rudolf Bahro, "Keine Routine," in *Die Tageszeitung*, 1 March 1986, p. 22. Under the impact of the military intervention of Warsaw Pact troops in the CSSR in 1968, Bahro has asked the rhetorically important question, "Who can send troops against a Soviet Dubcek?" For the differences in political style, climate, and the generational attitudes of the Khrushchev period and the circumstances facing Gorbachev, see Dimitri K. Simes, "A Tough Speech, but will Gorbachev Deliver?" in *The New York Times*, 11 March 1986. Simes argues that a call for stability and preservation is not high on the leadership's political agenda, as it was after the tumultuous and erratic reform movements of the Khrushchev period ended. Equally significant seems to be that the Soviet system lived through three rapid successions in leadership. Indicating a definite termination of the Brezhnev era, these successions were not accompanied by, nor did they cause, any social and political unrest in the USSR or in Eastern Europe, despite internal and external circumstances unfavorable to the Soviet political system. Under Brezhnev stability was achieved but the price was stagnation and decay in the social and political order. We fully agree with Simes' argument that Gorbachev's political mandate is to "modify the system in order to change it."

7. Interview with Zdenek Mlynar, *Die Tageszeitung*, 7 March 1986. As both a former comrade-in-arms of Dubcek and fellow student with Gorbachev in Moscow, Mlynar is convinced that Gorbachev will struggle relentlessly to initiate more than mere technocratic reforms from above. In his opinion Gorbachev is a reformer comparable to Dubcek who will try hard to launch economic reform and combine it with aspects of democratization and limited self-government on the local level. According to Mlynar, such reforms will not be confined to the party level but will touch upon social issues. The reliance on the possible arrival of a new enlightened czar, a la Peter the Great, as some Western observers and Soviet dissidents are inclined to do, renders too much weight to the subjective factor in history and seems to be at least questionable, if not an invalid and even dangerous remedy. Contrary to the hope and silent confidence that a "ruthless visionary" may arrive, there is evidence to assume that socio-economic changes over the long run seem to depend to a lesser degree on strong political leadership or charismatic personalities than on the continuous pull and push effects of modern, complex, and interdependent industrial processes along with the massive defusion of information technologies.

8. Simes, "A Tough Speech . . . " p. 3.

9. The change and effects of *glasnost* are most explicit in films and art. See, for example, "Gorbachev Trying to Line Up Artists' Support in Fight Against Decaying Bureaucracy," *Los Angeles Times*, January 8, 1987. The Secretary for Ideological Affairs, Alexandr Yakovlev, proposed Elem Klimov, a former blacklisted moviemaker, as president of Goskino, the state film organization, in May, 1986.

The annual congress of Soviet writers in June, 1986, was less dramatic, but the results were of a similar calibre when Sergei Salygin was elected president. If the liberalization process of Soviet arts and films continues to proceed at the same speed it would be more profound than similar developments during NEP. Such intrepid liberalizations would attack both the institution of Soviet censorship *(Glavlit)* and, what may be of even more importance in the long run, the system of intermeshed, semi-feudal favoritism which blossoms on greed, servility, and corruption.

10. In freeing Andrei Sakharov, Gorbachev took a bold step in indicating the seriousness of *glasnost*. Above all tactical considerations, which focussed predominantly on individual factors, this move is to be seen in the context of the Soviet state's very complex, fragile, and conflictive relationship with its own intelligentsia. In a way, Gorbachev's move is comparable to the policy of the early Bolsheviki of integrating the former czarist economic and technical intelligentsia for NEP and the enforced industrialization at the end of the 1920s. More than anyone before, the new Soviet leadership seems to realize that the modernization and structural reorganization of the country cannot be done without the active participation of the Soviet cultural, technical, and economic intelligentsia. For further discussion, see Peter W. Schulze, *Herrschaft und Klassen in der Sowjetgesellschaft. Die historischen Bedingungen des Stalinismus*, Frankfurt: Campus Verlag, 1977.

11. Gorbachev's address to the 27th CPSU Congress, in *The Challenges of Our Time. Disarmament and Social Progress*, Highlights, 27th Congress, CPSU, New York 1986, p. 90f.

12. Seweryn Bialer/Joan Afferica, "The Genesis of Gorbachev's World," *Foreign Affairs*, Vol. 64, No. 3, p. 623. Contrary to the Brezhnev era, in which Brezhnev enjoyed institutionalized support from the beginning, Gorbachev's power base within the governing coalition reflects personal ties rather than institutional support. This very fact, however, does not necessarily preclude a successful reform process. On the contrary, the gradual and strategic placement of Gorbachev supporters in state, economic, and cultural institutions could assure *that the new cadres have to initiate changes first before they can start building their own fiefdoms.* They eventually will develop particular instead of societal interests and thereby will become bureaucratic office holders who are more interested in preserving the status quo of material and social distribution. Consequently, their interests will be confined to that which benefits their petty empires. Such developments seem to be a structural element of the political system, caused by the political interdiction of society.

13. *Pravda*, 27 March 1985; *Sovjetskaja Rossija*, 1 May 1985; *Pravda*, 20 June 1985. The selection of Nikolai Talyzin as head of GOSPLAN may be a first step into the direction of seriously attacking the problem of modernizing the economy. Talyzin was Minister of Telecommunications from 1975. We may even deduce a second indication from the selection of such an important cadre, who as head of GOSPLAN will be responsible for formulating and implementing both the new Five Year and the Perspective 15 Year Plan. Talyzin was Deputy Chairman of the Council of Mutual Economic Assistance (CMEA). He would

be the best informed with regard to the experiences of economic reform in Eastern Europe. His appointment may indicate a move towards greater cooperation among the CMEA countries.

14. *Los Angeles Times*, 27 June 1987.

15. See Gorbachev's speech to Communist Party leaders in June, 1987, in which he acknowledged opposition from subordinate bureaucrats, managers, and party officials to his reform policies. His strength is founded in the belief that there is no alternative to the ongoing reform, as incomplete and defective as some of it may be. *Los Angeles Times*, 13 June 1987, p. 10.

16. In other words, if we accept a correlation between increasing structural-industrial-technological complexity in the Soviet economy, on the one hand, and altered methods of social control and exertion of power, on the other, this correlation must eventually affect the political process and later the constellation of social forces. Changes in the economic structure have produced corresponding transformations *in and between social groups* (social differentiation). They will eventually spill over into the political sphere, because no political system can exist for a long period of time without adapting to structural demands, unless it is ready to use *excessive force against its own citizens to secure their compliance*. Such a policy, of course, is quite likely to have counterproductive effects and could in turn endanger the stability of the system. The chronic, continuing crises in Poland and the CSSR are example enough of the catastrophic consequences of repressed reform movements.

17. 183 members (or 59.6 percent) of a total 319 members of the Central Committee *were re-elected*. Among the reconfirmed members of the Central Committee were prominent exponents of the Brezhnev Old Guard like Ponomarev and Kuznetzov. While commanding a solid majority in the Politburo, despite the survival of veterans like Kunaev and Viktor Shcherbitsky, a restricting and controlling majority of former Brezhnev appointees rules the Central Committee. The delicate path Gorbachev has to walk was clearly stated during Party Congress speeches. His initial critique and call for support for the retirement of certain cadres was somehow dampened by remarks of Yegor K. Ligachev. *Los Angeles Times*, 7 March 1986; *Washington Post National Weekly*, 24 March 1986, p. 16.

18. Among others, I. Adirim, in an article on perspectives and the actual state of economic reform in the USSR questioned the correctness of putting too much emphasis on Soviet planning as the core element and culprit for faltering economic performance. The Western notion that such a conservative, inflexible, regulative, and centralized mechanism determines every aspect of Soviet economic life is formally correct, but rather abstract. In any case, according to Adirim, it is an extremely simplistic notion to believe that the planning mechanism determines the economy and there are no feed-backs; for example, a dependence on planning information coming from the economic system as such. He quotes a member of the Soviet Academy of Social Sciences, A. Abalkin, who precisely questions whether operative decisions (plans) can regulate the diversification of products and guide scientific-industrial innovations. Even a long-term perspective for economic sectors is problematic in achieving. Furthermore, a presumably genuine task of planning to facilitate balanced and even growth is unthinkable

without taking into consideration the totality of all economic mechanisms. Adirim's provocative thesis is that planning is *not the guiding but the guided links of the chain in the Soviet system of administration;* i.e., the Soviet economy, while being principally directed through plans, in reality more often responds to other mechanisms. *Osteuropa,* Nr. 12, 1985, p. 898.

19. The argument "nothing new in the East," hitherto a repetition of the traditonal "muddling through" policy of earlier Soviet administrations, was frequently heard in Western circles. The left-leaning Parisian daily newspaper *Liberation* ridiculed Gorbachev's performance during the Congress of the CPSU as "Gorbat-show."

20. The pressure for change grew during the last years of the Brezhnev era. All sensed that something went wrong; that there was a pressing need for change in the factories, among the technical intelligentsia, in the Party apparatus; and on all levels. During this entire time period a potential accumulated which aimed at social change. This was the objective part, but there were subjective factors as well which supported change. If it would not have been for Gorbachev, than someone else would have come along. Interview with Prof. Alexander Galkin, Vice Chancellor of the Institute of Social Sciences at the Central Committee of the CPSU during a conference in Frankfurt, West Germany on the "USSR in a Process of Restructuring," in *TAZ,* 10 September 1987, p. 7.

21. In this regard, Gorbachev's foreign policy resembles that of Reagan since 1981. The focus on domestic, especially economic, issues should lead to a stronger and primarily defensive foreign policy. This definitely does not mean that the USSR will change one iota of her international obligations or commitments. The preservation of the hitherto achieved position in the multi-layered struggle with the USA will be predicated upon solving the domestic economic crisis.

22. *New York Times,* 8 October 1987, pp. 1, 4.

23. *Ibid.,* p. 4.

24. Two examples illuminate this changing Soviet position and support the argument that especially economic aid for countries of "socialist orientation" has become a serious Soviet concern. One is the refusal to accept Mozambique and Angola as members of the CMEA, and the second is the insistent pressure on Nicaragua to diversify its sources of economic and financial support to countries *outside* the CMEA.

25. See, *inter alia,* Adam Ulam, "What's Happening in Moscow," *The National Interest,* Nr. 8, Summer 1987, p. 12.

26. "Soviet Policy in Southern Africa," interview with Dr. Victor Goncharov, by Howard Barrell, *Work in Progress,* July/August 1987.

27. *Ibid.,* p. 4.

28. *Ibid.,* p. 7.

29. Mikhail Gorbachev's *Address to Participants in the International Forum for Nuclear-Free World,* Moscow, February 16, 1987, p. 5.

5

The Socialist Countries' Conception of the New International Economic Order

Helmut Faulwetter

With socialism new forms of economic relations have emerged over the past decades. These forms are based on the principle of equality and mutual advantage, most-favored nation treatment, and a planned and long-term inclusion of the domestic economic needs of the partner countries. Their creation and expansion has limited the field of action for the laws and mechanisms of capitalism. However, the economic relations between the socialist and imperialist countries to date have scarcely acquired any of these features. Imperialism continues to discriminate against the socialist countries. A new situation was created through the emergence of national liberation revolutions. The developing countries have made demands with regard to overcoming their economic backwardness and thus for a considerable change in the division of labor of the capitalist world economy. The dependence of the developing countries on the core imperialist states and their transnational monopolies to date has kept the former poor through their enormous exploitation and has simultaneously steadily reproduced this condition on the part of the developing countries which was created by colonialism. A democratic transformation of these relations can bring the developing countries economic growth capable of overcoming the hunger and poverty of their populations. Broad segments in international economic relations thus demand changes which are particularly important for the vast majority of the developing countries.

Support for Progressive Transformations at the Political Level

It is well known that the capitalist world economic system functions on the basis of its inherent laws, even if with steadily growing frictions

and with enormously heightened disproportions and contradictions. They
are often referred to as the "laws of the market." It is to these conditions
that the countries of Asia, Africa, and Latin America have been subjected
since colonial times. The mechanisms utilized by monopoly capitalism
in the "countries with developed market economies" and the institutions
created by them exploit even more effectively and "noiselessly" than
the colonial system was ever able to do.

This must inevitably lead to a situation in which the developing
countries began to rebel against these conditions. Only such a process
of organized resistance has offered and will continue to offer the
opportunities necessary for voicing and executing their interests which
function in accordance with democratic rules. This process is what has
brought into existence a common position on the part of the developing
world and the socialist countries.

UNCTAD's official history thus says with regard to the fifties and
sixties:

> The shortcomings of the GATT system were becoming increasingly manifest.
> Its lack of a solid institutional basis (the proposal to provide it with one
> by creating the Organization for Trade Co-operation (OTC) in 1955 failed
> to materialize for lack of United States support), its omission of major
> areas of interest to developing countries (viz. non-recognition of the special
> importance of trade to economic development and exclusion of the Havana
> Charter provisions for commodity arrangements), its assumption of equality
> and reciprocity among unequal trading partners, its excessive preoccupation
> with the reduction of trade barriers among the industrialized market-
> economy countries, its relative neglect of developing countries and its
> virtual lack of consideration of the place of the socialist countries of Eastern
> Europe in the GATT system—these deserve mention.[1]

As a result of a common decision in Cairo in 1962 of thirty-six states
in Asia, Africa, and Latin America, the creation of a "Conference on
the Problems of Developing Countries" was demanded. "The Cairo
Declaration called for an international conference on all vital questions
relating to international trade, primary commodity trade and economic
relations between developing and developed countries within the framework of the United Nations."[2] The authors of this volume found it
necessary to describe in more detail this process to which the then UN
General Secretary U Thant referred to as "one of the most important
events since the establishment of the United Nations."[3]

> The socialist countries of Eastern Europe, which from the mid-1950s had
> been pressing for such a conference, readily supported the call in the
> Cairo Declaration. It was, however, not without a great deal of reluctance

and resistance that the United States and other major trading nations finally agreed to the ECOSOC decision adopted in August 1962 to convene such a conference.[4]

With Resolution 1785 (XVII) the General Assembly decided in December 1962 to convene the conference. Here it is also important to note that:

> The decision to set up UNCTAD did not come about easily or smoothly. Western powers which had rejected the ITO proposal, and had the strongest objections to the creation of any new United Nations machinery in the field of trade and development, gave in only in the last.[5]

The position of the socialist countries with regard to these questions was, and continues to be, determined not by opportunism or even simply tactical considerations. It reflects a characteristic feature of socialism. The relationship between real socialism and national liberation was clearly defined from the beginning. V.I. Lenin already characterized it on the eve of the socialist revolution in Russia:

> We will make all efforts to get closer to the Mongols, Persians, Indians, Egyptians and to affect a fusion with them. We are of the opinion that it is our duty and that it is also in our own interest to do so since socialism in Europe otherwise will not be secured. We will make every effort to grant to these people who are even more backward and more oppressed than we, "unselfish cultural aid"; i.e., to help them in the transition machine use that will make work easier in democracy and socialism.[6]

Since the concept of a democratic transformation in global economic relations began to crystallize as a program and task for the international community of states, the socialist countries have supported this process as well as the content of those demands found anchored in documents of the United Nations and its organizations. This was so when this process was initiated, particularly the declaration and program of action of the Sixth Special Session of the UN General Assembly in April, 1974, as well as the "Charter of Economic Rights and Duties of States," which, in fact, represents the "constitution" of this new anticipated order.

Let us take the German Democratic Republic, for example. It declared through its Foreign Minister at the Sixth Special Session of the UN General Assembly:

> The government of the GDR views the development of economic cooperation which is as equal as it is stable, and of mutual advantage as the best

possibility for effectively helping the developing countries to overcome their economic difficulties.[7]

These sought-after new forms of economic cooperation should have equality as their core and rest on such important principles as

> sovereign equality of states, . . . rights to the free choice of one's own path to social and economic development, . . . to the control over their natural resources . . . unencumbered decisions concerning the type of foreign economic relations . . . elimination of discrimination in economic relations . . . the regulation and control of foreign investments, including the control of the activities of multinational corporations, most favored nation status in international trade, non-discrimination through regional economic groupings.[8]

It is only thanks to the determined actions of all anti-imperialist forces that these basic principles became the main features of the "Charter" passed by the General Assembly six months later. The same applies to important subsequent documents of UN organizations.

The responsibilities of the socialist countries in contributing to the determination of the direction and the main points anticipating changes in these documents cannot be overlooked. From the beginning the GDR also defined the conditions which needed to be overcome as well as the factors responsible for these conditions:

> The origin of these problems lies in decades and centuries old colonial exploitation. Even today they are maintained and in fact deepened by the imperialist countries through neocolonial forms of exploitation of the natural wealth and labor power of developing countries. Thus these states also bear a political as well as moral obligation to help overcome the consequences of colonial and neocolonial exploitation. Likewise, it is the undeniable right of developing countries to receive compensation for the material damage incurred through colonialism and the still ongoing neo-colonialism.[9]

The GDR consistently supported the maintenance of this line of argument in the confrontations concerning the reorientation of international economic relations. Its Foreign Minister declared in 1975 before the XXXth UN General Assembly that:

> the young sovereign states face the necessity of overcoming the colonial structure of their national economies and their international economic relations. We support their just demands, raised at both the Sixth and the

Seventh Special Sessions of the United Nations, for a new international economic order.[10]

The core imperialist countries do not grant the developing countries this right, just as they generally have in the past and even now continue to fight against democratic transformations in international economic relations. For example, they did not vote in favor of the "Charter of Economic Rights and Duties of States" in the UN General Assembly, unlike the governments of roughly 150 states on this planet. A leading member of the US Delegation at the Seventh Special Session declared: "The United States can and will not accept interpretations that the world currently is heading toward something which calls itself a new international economic order."[11] The head of the delegation from the Federal Republic of Germany at UNCTAD IV in Nairobi in 1976 interpreted and answered the demand for a new international economic order ("speaking for the Federal Government"): "The idlers in the developing countries should first get used to working themselves before they ask for monies gained through hard work in other countries."[12]

Imperialism (especially the United States) has increasingly resisted right up to the present the application of basic democratic principles to international economic relations; not only in the creation of practical economic relations but also in confrontations in international political fora. This is why the process of transformation has currently slowed down considerably and, in some areas, has even come to a complete halt.

The GDR belongs to those countries which early on pointed to the ensuing dangers for the development of international relations in general and for the developing countries in particular:

The German Democratic Republic advocates the opinion that it is an important and urgent task of UNCTAD V to give new impetus to the further restructuring of international economic relations on a just and democratic basis and to promote such relations through concrete measures . . . the situation of the developing countries continues to be characterized by inequality and discrimination within the system of international capitalist division of labour. Full national sovereignty of developing countries over their natural and other resources is still not guaranteed. The negative impact of the activities of transnational monopolies on developing countries has not been overcome, but continues to increase. Protectionism and discrimination in trade on the part of the main capitalist countries and their monopolies are aggravating. Transfer of technology in reverse, the brain drain, is becoming an additional source of profit for capitalist monopolies and an obstacle to the national progress of developing countries. Serious problems encumbering international economic relations, such as

inflation, unemployment, growth difficulties, imbalances and currency
instabilities, continue to exist in capitalist world economy [sic]. The implementation of fundamental social and economic changes in developing
countries is being openly or covertly sabotaged and in some cases thwarted
by reactionary forces.

Accordingly,

the German Democratic Republic supports without reservation the implementation of the justified demands of developing countries. . . . For her
this stance is not determined by tactical considerations, but results from
the essence of her socialist order of society.[13]

The leading political force in the GDR, the Socialist Unity Party (SED),
marks as an important element of its international policies:

Our support goes to all peoples who fight for their national liberation,
for their equal position in international relations, for economic development
and social progress. . . . We find it necessary to overcome the international
division of labor which was created by imperialism and serves neocolonial
exploitation, and to create international economic relations based on
equality.[14]

This is in agreement with the Program of the Party, since it promotes
"actively the deepening of the alliance between the German Democratic
Republic and the peoples of Asia, Africa, and Latin America who fight
against imperialism and neocolonialism."[15]

The Practice of Economic Relations of a New Type

This position as outlined above also finds its reflection in real economic
relations. Thus let us look again at the GDR's foreign economic relations.

During the past three decades its foreign trade volume with developing
countries has grown more than twenty times. It is a reliable supplier
and customer. Its products are competitive both in terms of prices and
quality. In order to give developing countries which have problems with
their own exports the opportunity to make purchases, the GDR accepts
payments in the form of goods; if desired exports and imports are
balanced against each other. While this helps to increase the export
power of the respective developing countries, it also prevents massive
indebtedness as a part of their foreign economic relations.

Anchored in many treaties are equality, most-favored nation status,
as well as the principle of mutual advantage. These determine the nature
of actual relations. There are neither the transfer of dividends, monopolistic

price fixing, the pirating of labor, enticements for smuggling and capital flight, nor speculations with the resources of the partner. The GDR has no customs or other discriminatory barriers vis-à-vis the exports of developing countries.

Along with other socialist countries the GDR offers developing countries very favorable conditions in its offers of long-term arrangements in raw materials trade, in scientific-technical cooperation, in the training of cadres, etc. Long-term trade or even more extensive economic treaties, should the third world partner so desire, are adjusted in terms of the structure of exchanges in goods and services to fit the interests of both sides in a planned fashion. In case both sides are interested, bilateral committees work out and supervise the agreed-upon obligations. This enables specific interests to be introduced and considered. In such cases the market no longer regulates such features and processes as the structure of trade, the determination of prices, and the general conditions of exchange. This takes place instead through the respective official representatives of the partner countries. At present the GDR maintains governmental treaties concerning trade, cultural, as well as scientific-technical relations with over sixty developing countries. They regulate a type of cooperation which, at the economic level to date, has principally focussed on the creation and expansion of raw materials and turnkey industries (particularly in machine building and in metallurgy), the development of the energy sector, an increase in agricultural production, on certain areas of infrastructure and the training of experts.

For example, in a large number of countries the GDR participates in both the preparatory work and in the construction of installations that produce raw materials, the building of factories (e.g., in the cement industry, in the power station sector, in light industry) in supplying equipment for machine building, for the processing of agricultural products, and in polygraphy. Support goes primarily to the state sector in developing countries, since this is the most important instrument for overcoming economic dependence. As a matter of principle, all of the projects built with the help of the GDR are the property of the developing countries and a part of the public economic sector. This sector was aided tremendously by the GDR in such countries as Algeria, India, Iraq, PR Yemen, Syria, and in sub-Saharan African countries such as Guinea and Sudan. As far as its capabilities permit, the GDR grants developing countries advantageous long-term credits. They are free of any type of political demands or conditions.

The main goal of this support is to enable the developing countries to reach their economic independence as quickly as possible and to create an economy with a structure increasingly showing its own capacity to reproduce as well as to enable rapid growth. Since the core of these efforts in most developing countries will be in industry, roughly two-thirds of the means made available by the GDR have been for the construction of industrial plants and in energy producing installations. This share is three to six times higher than that with non-socialist economic partners of the developing countries.

The GDR has, and continues to offer, economic and technical aid to developing countries with hundreds of economically important goals. The GDR, just as the other socialist countries, is famous for its enormous accomplishments in the area of training and other qualification projects in developing countries. During the last years hundreds of thousands of persons have been trained in scientific, technical, and production techniques, either in the developing countries themselves or at institutions in socialist countries.

To have beneficial partners in the socialist countries has had the additional fundamental advantage for developing countries in the past decades of breaking open, or at least softening, a series of oppressive monopoly conditions (e.g., in the export of installations, in technology transfer, in the granting of credits, in transport, the construction of infrastructural installations, the supply of military equipment, etc.). Transnational corporations of the imperialist countries have increasingly been forced into making concessions, often merely because of the presence of foreign trade enterprises of socialist countries in these markets.

The further deepening of socialist economic integration within the CMEA expands the opportunities for expanding relations with the developing countries. The signing of treaties concerning economic and scientific-technical cooperation between the CMEA and individual developing countries marks new conditions for doing so. Based on these treaties multilateral projects can be realized in various sectors of the economy and in science and technology.

The volume and quality of this cooperation and the support of developing countries naturally depend to a large extent on whether it will be possible to strengthen the GDR itself in all respects. These relations depend not only on the growing economic power of the GDR, but must, at the same time, contribute toward satisfying the foreign economic objectives of the GDR. It is in this that, in the final analysis, the dialectical relationship between economics and politics is reflected. The more successfully and effectively the economy of the GDR develops, the larger will be its leeway in foreign economic activities. This can only be created, however, if foreign economic relations themselves make a growing contribution to the growth process of the economy. This is of extreme importance for the economy of the GDR because it is involved particularly intensively in foreign trade. As a matter of fact, at present almost 40 percent of the gross national product is materially redistributed via foreign trade. This means that all territorial movements of foreign trade must be viewed from criteria of effectiveness and that thus, for example, the consideration of mutual advantage becomes an objective requirement. This applies as well to relations with the developing countries.

It was particularly during the beginning years (the fifties and sixties) that these relations presented considerable difficulties for the GDR. There were no "traditional" contacts on which the foreign trade of the country could have based itself. Its enterprises were confronted with conditions and effects which are typical for the capitalist world market but incompatible with the socialist economic system; spontaneity, the impact of crises on production, the currency system, etc. The effects of the "cold war" created an unfavorable climate for the establishment and expansion of economic relations between the GDR and developing countries. The rapid expansion of these relations was, nevertheless, possible because the GDR was, and continues to be, an attractive trading partner for many developing countries.

The relations between the socialist and developing countries continue to take place in an environment in which the market laws of capitalism prevail and in which the international monopolies are active. They are touched by disturbances in the capitalist world economy as well as by deliberate activities of the MNCs.

Due to the economic warfare of aggressive imperialist circles, particularly beginning in the fifties, as well as the deep economic crisis of the eighties, the conditions worsened for the socialist countries in trading with the countries of the capitalist world market. The long-lasting economic slide in most capitalist countries and the concomitant disturbances in currency relations, sometimes high rates of inflation, record interest rates, sagging prices, foreign trade restrictions including an embargo; all of these factors have had far-reaching effects on international trade and thus also on the foreign trade of the socialist countries with the developing countries. The US policy of high interest rates does not only have consequences for credit policy, but also influences deeply the level of prices, inflation, and has a negative impact on the economic crisis in the capitalist countries with all their contradictions. This also burdens the socialist countries in their trade with developing countries. For example, the credit embargo closes off to the GDR finance opportunities which are necessary to the normal handling of business with countries of the capitalist world market. At the same time the high interest policy enormously increases the costs of credits. The competitive struggle, hard fought in the capitalist markets, in addition to the trade barriers directed against the GDR and other socialist countries, makes sales more difficult.

In order to gain an impression about the economic relations between socialist and developing countries economic aid must also be mentioned. The Soviet Union, for example, until 1981 annually granted "official development assistance" (ODA) at a level exceeding 1 percent of GNP.[16] In 1982 and 1983 the GDR provided 0.79 percent, and in 1984 0.82 percent of its national income for ODA.[17]

The volume and quality of the economic relations of socialist countries with those developing countries which are interested in equal and mutually advantageous relations led Fidel Castro to the following assessment:

> We have developed our economic relations with the socialist countries. In our relations with them we have created a new type of international economic order and are neither victims of the laws of unequal exchange nor of protectionism, nor of a too high rate of interest, nor of an overvaluation of the ruble, nor of protectionist measures, nor of dumping on the part of socialist countries. Thus we have reached a solid basis for a secure economic and social development. . . . We have fair and stable prices as well as their adjustment to our export prices which stand in relation to the price increases of goods imported by us.[18]

Nations Must Live Together in New Ways

The nuclear age does not allow human beings today to allow disagreements to develop into conflicts which would have to be solved by military means. Peoples and their governments instead should avoid everything which could create dangerous tensions. The environment also no longer can bear its growing abuse. There is not one country which alone can maintain or save the environment for people on the entire planet. All countries are called upon to act upon a common and coordinated policy.

In the same fashion, hunger, unemployment, immiseration, and hopelessness in the lives of hundreds of millions of human beings are no longer tolerable in a world which possesses the material means with which to eliminate and overcome them all. The economic effects of this situation alone are reason enough to demand of all governments in all countries that they petition for change and contribute toward it.

Economic backwardness is also a chain for socio-economic changes. It is a decisive obstacle to the creation of relations of production under which human beings can harvest for themselves that which they have sown.

The enormous economic problems of the developing countries in addition burden the global political climate. As Mikhail Gorbachev has noted:

The misery of the developing countries is an enormously important global problem. It is precisely this and nothing else that causes the many conflicts in Asia, Africa, and Latin America. This is the truth, no matter how much the ruling circles of the imperialist powers would like to say about the "hand of Moscow" in order to justify their neocolonial policies and global claims.[19]

Nobody can argue against the necessity of eliminating this emergency situation. The mechanisms responsible for this misery and hunger continue to function, however. The raw materials markets of international capitalism, dominated by MNCs, bring for the developing countries steadily declining export prices and, thus, a growing uncompensated drain of the income produced in those developing countries to the capitalist industrialized countries. The enormous pressure of borrowed capital from huge banks and the simultaneous deterioration of the economic framework of the developing countries leads to their enormous indebtedness. This in turn increases their dependence and exploitation.

The governments must do something concerning these questions. Practice shows that administrative interventions in the market economies is possible and effective. Western states use protectionism to an enormous extent; public support cements old production structures by creating an international division of labor in flagrant contrast to the comparative advantage of other countries (e.g., in the case of sugar and meat). Individual MNCs dominate vast production and market areas without concern for what are often called the "requirements of the market." So-called managed trade has assumed large proportions. The imperialist states take enormous funds out of the economic cycles and use them for the arms industry and preparation for war, for example. The former Assistant Secretary General of UNCTAD, Jan Pronk, thus says of these governments:

The present situation whereby governments opt for completely unilaterally managed trade, shifting their problems of economic disequilibrium at home onto the shoulder of weaker countries, is perverse.

He reaches the logical conclusion that:

We need a new consensus, some degree of managed international trade on the basis of multilaterally agreed principles. These should not only apply to international trade proper but also to investment and production policies underlying international trade.[20]

The identical principles underlying these demands and the already historically established position of the socialist countries is surely immediately obvious. Interventions by Western governments or the monopolies of these countries into the market processes, into the "rules of the game of the markets," are possible. Why, however, this should be possible only at the expense of billions of human beings on this planet and not for their benefit is undoubtedly impossible to justify.

The emergency situation in developing countries, which has become an important global problem in the interdependent living of mankind, thus demands of the Western governments that they rethink their economic policies. For the socialist countries it has always been an important concern, as outlined at the beginning of this chapter, to promote this process. If it needs to be stated that in the current epoch, the danger exists that not all human beings on the planet have a future, it is stated simultaneously that a new international economic order is an imperative, no matter what the chosen steps might look like, or what the names and concepts utilized for it will be. It is thus also aspects of a global policy which today determines the position of the socialist countries with regard to questions concerning a new international economic order.

Notes

1. *The History of UNCTAD 1964–1984*, New York: UNCTAD, 1985, pp. 9–10.
2. *Ibid.*, p. 10.
3. *Ibid.*
4. *Ibid.*
5. *Ibid.*
6. V.I. Lenin, *Werke*, Vol. 25, Berlin 1960, p. 61.
7. Speech by the Minister of Foreign Affairs of the GDR, Oskar Fischer, at the Sixth Special Session of the General Assembly of the United Nations, New York, April 1974.
8. *Ibid.*
9. *Ibid.*
10. Speech given by the Foreign Minister of the GDR, Oskar Fischer, at the XXXth Meeting of the UN General Assembly in New York, September 1975.
11. *Europa-Archiv*, 1975, Vol. 21, p. 596.
12. *Frankfurter Rundschau*, 1 June 1976.
13. Statement by the Minister of Foreign Trade of the German Democratic Republic, Horst Soelle, to the Fifth United Nations Conference on Trade and Development, Manila, 14 May 1979, p. 2 ff.
14. Report of the Central Committee of the Socialist Unity Party at the IXth Party Congress, Rapporteur Erich Honecker, Berlin 1976.
15. Program of the SED, Berlin 1976.
16. UNCTAD, TD/302.

17. UNCTAD, TD/304; *Horizont*, 12/1984; *Horizont*, 8/1985.

18. Fidel Castro, "Es gibt keine Alternative" (There is No Alternative), conversation with US Congressman Mervin Dymally and Professor Jeffrey Elliot concerning economic problems, *La Habanna*, 29 March 1985, pp. 27–28, 124.

19. Politischer Bericht des Zentralkomitees der KPdSU an den XXVII. Parteitag der Kommunistischen Partei der Sowjetunion, Berlin 1986, p. 24.

20. Jan Pronk, "The Case for a World Public Sector," in *ifda Dossier 54*, July/August 1986, p. 65.

6

A Critique of the Socialist Countries' Theory and Practice of the New International Economic Order

Kunibert Raffer

Introduction

By demanding a New International Economic Order (NIEO) the periphery has expressed its strong discontent with the present world economy, and with its own disadvantaged position within the global economic and political framework. These demands for changes, therefore, cover a wide range of topics; practically all aspects of North-South relations. Nevertheless some especially important issues, such as the Common Fund, can be singled out.

Due to the asymmetry in West-South and East-South relations NIEO-demands were mainly addressed to the OECD member countries. Socialist Countries (SCs) were understandably eager to present capitalist countries as those responsible for all the negative effects of North-South relations, thus intensifying the impression that the NIEO, or changing the present order as such, was exclusively a matter concerning West-South relations. In international fora SCs adopted a policy of supporting the South in resolutions and declarations and of praising their own economic relations with the periphery as flawless and mutually advantageous. SC sources sometimes use the latter two adjectives as a logical characterization of East-South trade. Data that could prove this claim are not as readily provided.

SCs have always rejected the division of the world into rich and poor nations, dividing it instead into capitalist and socialist states and sub-dividing the former into developed and developing nations. According to the official view only the West has the duty of redressing evils suffered by the periphery during colonialism and through exploitative trade.

When the loss of foreign exchange earnings arising from fluctuations in primary commodities exports of Least Developed Countries was discussed at UNCTAD VI, for example, the spokesman for Group D (the socialist countries) stated that the malfunctioning of the market economy system had created the deplorable situation of the periphery and that compensatory financing schemes "were *therefore* not applicable to the relations of Group D countries with the developing countries."[1] As early as 1964 at Geneva the socialist countries had backed demands by the periphery against capitalist countries while refusing to implement any acts of solidarity that were more substantial and binding. This attitude explains also the reactions of SCs toward attempts to implement demands contained in the NIEO list. As early as 1980 C.W. Lawson noted that "support was modified, becoming increasingly tentative as the debate moved from the stage of rhetorical posturing to that of actual concessions."[2] Since the beginning of serious negotiations on NIEO demands at UNCTAD IV, where SC support for the periphery had become more equivocal, Lawson thought it feasible to analyze SC positions as a single bloc. This view is also held by Barbara Despiney, who characterizes the Soviet position vis-à-vis the periphery as "generally marked by the profound conviction that the mere existence of the socialist system is already beneficial to international relations, and consequently for developing countries. The official declarations of CMEA member states are noticeably similar to those of the Soviet Union."[3]

No developed CMEA country has signed the Common Fund Agreement so far and Group D is the only group at UNCTAD that has taken no steps to do so, despite the fact that they neither voted against the establishment of the fund in the first place, nor against unanimous resolutions at Belgrade stressing the importance of the fund and demanding its entry into force by January 1, 1984. On the other hand, the Soviet Union, like the United States, was quick to protest against the allocation of votes among the groups that had been fixed by the 1979 resolution on the fundamental elements of a Common Fund. Evidently Lawson is right in remarking that the socialist states have also been as "quick to appreciate the dangers inherent in creating institutions dominated by LDCs"[4] as have Group B members.

Western researchers analyzing the behavior of European CMEA countries in international fora often describe these countries' actions as determined by their self-interest,[5] or conclude that long run interests of SCs are closer to those of the West than to those of the South.[6] The struggle to implement NIEO demands shows this especially clearly. In several international negotiations at UNCTAD, UNIDO, or the Law of the Sea Conference the industrialized CMEA countries have, in effect, opposed the position of the Third World, while being more supportive in matters in which they might equally benefit.

Ideologically the SCs might feel ambivalent about the NIEO. As Brigitte Schulz has shown in an analysis of the GDR, solutions that do not entail a "socialist orientation" are strongly rejected. Solutions offered by the *dependencia* school, such as de-linking, are even attacked as "petty bourgeois." Development toward socialism also means "close alliance with the countries of real socialism, as they alone hold the key to a 'scientific' understanding of the development process."[7] Clearly, this claim to leadership is at odds with the basic ideas of the NIEO, while, on the other hand, "anti-imperialist solidarity" demands support against exploitative international relations.

The main arguments as to why the SCs have no obligation to redress the plight of the periphery have to do with the colonial past and the contention that the world capitalist system is the source of all the periphery's problems. Romania, having declared itself a developing country and being a member of the Group of 77, presents itself obviously as a member of the group of would-be receivers rather than would-be donors. Nevertheless, for the purposes of this chapter the socialist countries are comprised of the six European CMEA countries (CMEA-6) and the Soviet Union.

Neither this historical argument nor the effects of the capitalist world system shall be discussed here. Although tsarist Russia had more colonial commitments[8] than Austria-Hungary or Switzerland, it was not among the leading global colonial powers and certainly did not shape the history of Africa and Latin America. Given the shares of East-South trade relations both in SC-exports and in periphery-exports it is only fair to acknowledge that SCs are definitely not the driving force of the global economy.

The call for an NIEO, however, was caused by present economic structures and the desire to change them seeks to give the periphery a fairer share in global progress. Obviously, the conditions of trade, relative prices of periphery exports, accessibility to markets for Southern products, and changes in international economic institutions are important. Therefore the essential question is neither the colonial past as such, nor who is primarily responsible for the Old Economic Order, but whether East-South relations are qualitatively different from the West-South pattern. If the pattern is basically the same, the socialist countries, though not actively shaping the global economy, are also profiting from these structures. Anyone buying at "non-remunerative" prices puts the seller at a disadvantage, irrespective of who created the trading system. Trade can only qualify as mutually advantageous if it differs from exploitative trade by objective criteria; prices, conditions, etc. To see whether NIEO demands apply equally to East-South relations, structures, prices, and conditions of trade, as well as SC, aid must be analyzed.

The Structure of East-South Trade

While consistently denying any historical obligation to redress the problems of the periphery, contrary to the capitalist countries, some socialist countries (the USSR, Czechoslovakia, Hungary, and Poland) agreed as early as 1964 to raise the level of their trade with the South in general, and to increase in particular their imports of primary products.[9] This policy has to be explained in view of the above mentioned attitude of the SCs: trade with them is definitely seen as something positive as such, conducive to development, and as a new and positive element in the construction of the New International Economic Order. This explains a phenomenon unique to East-South relations: the increase of trade between the East and the Third World is always cited as something seemingly laudable although detailed statistical information on the conditions of trade is less readily provided. Thus all representatives of European CMEA-countries at the UNCTAD VI session emphasized growth rates of trade with or imports from the South. However, the UNCTAD policy paper on trade relations among countries having different economic and social systems (item 13d, TD/280) shows figures like "foreign trade-turnover," import and export time series in current prices, and the growth rate resulting therefrom, while disaggregated country data on a higher SITC-digit-level are as unobtainable as meaningful unit prices of imports and exports. Rough calculations as to how much a global (or regional) STABEX-like system covering the core or Nairobi commodities would cost the Soviet Union or the Six European CMEA-members thus cannot be done.

Information readily available covers topics like the number of projects (bilateral, tripartite, or multilateral) that have been completed or were planned ("more than 6,400" by 1982), examples of single projects, the number of long-term agreements ("now more than 450") or the number of developing countries ("over 100") that have signed such agreements.[10]

Official UNCTAD publications judge trade with CMEA to be "beneficial to all participants involved, especially to the developing countries."[11] UNCTAD Resolution 95 (IV) of 31 May 1976 in fact calls for an intensification of East-South trade, an appeal SCs have obviously welcomed much more than calls for active participation in changing the existing economic framework.

According to UNCTAD over 90 percent of East-South trade is conducted under bilateral intergovernmental agreements.[12] The traditional form of exchange prevailing in the past was the clearing arrangement. This type of transaction is possibly best characterized by the term "comparative disadvantages" used by Nayyar and Schoeller.[13] Mutual advantages, according to this view, stem from the possibility of exchanging goods that could not be otherwise sold on the world market. Schoeller mentions the example of Mozambican tea, a third class quality tea by international standards, that was exchanged for manufactures from the GDR, also not highly competitive in international markets. Understandably no partner is especially keen to barter "hard" export goods under such agreements. There is, on the other hand, a mutual advantage in such a deal if both countries get what they otherwise could not buy, be it for lack of foreign exchange or for other reasons.

These clearing arrangements were gradually replaced by payments in freely convertible currencies and nowadays the latter system prevails. According to UNCTAD, clearing was only still being used in a few instances by early 1982. "Even where clearing agreements are still operational they have usually been concluded at the request of the developing countries concerned. Experience shows that this does not preclude the settlement in convertible currencies of the surplus arising from the imbalance of trade turnover."[14]

This tendency, often classified as an "improvement" of payment relations,[15] can also be seen in a slightly different perspective: socialist countries have been able to accumulate significant balance of trade surpluses with developing countries. To effect a *de facto* exchange of soft to hard currencies via the settlement of these surpluses is a very tempting possibility in view of the CMEA hard currency deficit *vis-à-vis* the West. Although this is "a tricky and underresearched subject and no firm conclusion can be drawn concerning the precise magnitudes," partly because of limited data, István Dobozi seems to be right when he observes: "The balance of trade surplus registered by the socialist countries is to a significant extent in hard currency which can be used to finance partially the trade deficit *vis-à-vis* the West. In 1982 the surplus of the CMEA 6 *vis-à-vis* the South amounted to 72 percent of these countries' deficit *vis-à-vis* the West, which provided a possibility for the socialist countries to finance a part . . . of their hard currency deficit *vis-à-vis* the West." As Dobozi further notes, in 1981 the surplus of these countries with the South was even larger than the deficit with the West: "This then suggests that if their surplus *vis-à-vis* the South had been in hard currency, the socialist countries would have gained a net hard currency benefit from their trade with the non-socialist world."[16]

Or, put in different words: during the past a certain, though relatively modest, part of the accumulating debts of the South has been used to provide hard currency to SCs. The exact amount cannot be assessed. "Guestimates" of the hard currency percentage of East-South trade range from roughly 60 percent to "a significant extent," while the East enjoyed a cumulative surplus of $30 billion with the South between 1971–81.[17] However, this tendency is quite similar to Western policies of exporting to countries that have to borrow from the Euromarket to honor their obligations.

Furthermore Grosser and Tuitz believe that hard currency and debt problems of CMEA countries led to a more restrictive import policy in the mid-seventies: "In this context the transition in East-South trade to payments in hard currencies may have turned into a limiting factor for the developing countries' manufactured exports. Since the East apparently prefers Western manufactures to those of the South, imports of manufactures from the South are prone to be hit hard by the restrictive import policies of the East."[18] The question of (non-tariff) trade barriers is, by the way, a topic socialist countries simply refuse to discuss. During the discussion of NTBs to agricultural exports of the South at the 10th session of the Committee on Commodities, the spokesman for Group D even threatened to leave: "On the basis of such approaches, countries of Group D would not be in a position to participate in further deliberations on that subject."[19] Although it is correct to stress differences—as the resented document does—between economic systems which imply different instruments of economic policy, it seems somewhat exaggerated to try to prevent any discussion by invoking the principle of non-discrimination against socio-economic systems, as was done on this occasion. It could, for instance, be discussed as to why tropical fruits and beverages are subject to such high excise duties in SCs since high "taxes" or "excise duties" on imported goods are a well known instrument for hindering trade that is sometimes also applied by market economies. Levcik and Stankovsky see this policy as a major constraint on greater consumption of these products in SCs and advocate the reduction of these duties and the increase of imports within Five Year Plans as steps to raise imports from the South—a demand that had already been formulated by the Group of 77 in the Manila-Platform.[20]

As on many other occasions the spokesman stressed the increase in his group's foreign trade since the 1970s. Such statements clearly disregard the composition of East-South trade, best described by the catchword "Machines for Raw Materials." Its pattern is very similar to the traditional North-South trade composition criticized by Raúl Prebisch. Judging future perspectives regarding East-South trade there is some reason to assume that this pattern is going to hold in the near future.

According to Nayyar: "Available evidence suggests that at least 85%, if not more, of the exports of developing countries to European CMEA countries—USSR as well as Eastern Europe—were constituted by primary products and raw materials throughout the period of the mid-1950s to the late 1970s." Considering that almost ⅔ of total world exports to European CMEA consists of manufactured goods he concludes: "Clearly, the composition of East-South trade, at least as far as the developing market economies are concerned, is not significantly different from that of North-South trade."[21] For the centrally planned economies of Asia statistical data show a better picture.

Obviously the attitude prevails in the East that the developing countries should primarily supply urgently needed raw materials, or at best semi-finished products of a low degree of processing in exchange for exports of manufactures, particularly capital goods.[22] During the recent past this attitude seems to have become stronger since the share of manufactured imports from the South declined considerably. Between 1972 and 1980 it halved from 18 percent to 9 percent. The share of developing countries in total mineral and fuel imports of SCs increased from 9.9 percent to 21.1 percent during the last decade. Obviously the famous increases in oil prices distort the picture to a certain extent. However, if we look at imports of manufactures from the periphery as percentages of total imports of manufactures, SCs display a slight decline between 1965 and 1980 (2.2 percent in 1965, 1.8 percent in 1980). At the same time Developed Market Economies show a strong increase, more than doubling the percentage of imports from the periphery in their total imports of manufactures during that period (1965: 3.4 percent, 1980: 8.7 percent) as one can see from Figure 1. Furthermore the pattern of East-South trade in manufactured goods is characterized by an increasing trend until 1971, when 5 percent was reached, and a steady decrease after that period. Clearly, market shares of the periphery were lost to the West during this period. Increases in total trade are thus not a convincing argument in the discussion of trade barriers.

The present dependence of the six European CMEA countries on Soviet deliveries of raw materials and the problems of increasing Soviet exports to these countries substantially—as is clearly documented by cuts in Soviet deliveries of oil or the increased "hardening" of natural resources in intra-CMEA trade—make a diversification of sources necessary. A rise in imports of several major fuels and minerals, mostly from developing countries, seems inevitable. Even if successful conservation policies are assumed imports from the South will become "staggering in terms of finance . . . the combined imports of six commodities (oil, natural gas, copper, bauxite, iron ore, phosphate rock)—at current market prices—will amount to about 40 billion dollars in 1990."[23] These pressing needs will very likely not allow any increases in imports of manufactures from the South, especially since a preference for Western manufactures may be assumed. It might, therefore, be said that SCs presently hold exactly the point of view which the West held during

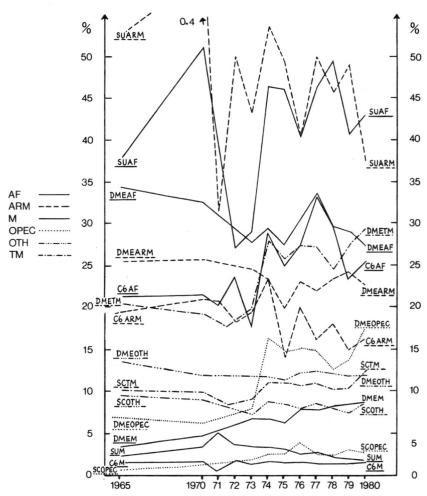

Figure 1. Shares of the South, OPEC, and non-OPEC Countries
in Selected and Total Imports of Developed Market Economies,
Socialist Countries, the Soviet Union, and the Six Small CMEA
Members in 1965 and the 1970s

Figure 1 (Cont.)

The curves in Figure 1 show the evolution of the shares of imports from the
South by
   DME   Developed Market Economies
   SC   Socialist Countries
   SU   Soviet Union
   C6   Six Small CMEA Countries
in percentages of total (worldwide) imports of product groups
   AF   All Food Items (=SITC 0+1+22+4)
   ARM   Agricultural Raw Materials (=SITC 2-22-27-28)
   M   Manufactures
Thus SCM, e.g., means the share of imports of manufactures from the South by
SCs in total SC-imports of manufactures. Furthermore
   TM   Southern share in total imports of a country group
   OPEC Imports from OPEC as percentages of total imports of a country group
   OTH   Total imports of OTHer (=non-OPEC) South as percentages of total
         imports of a country group
Thus: DMEOPEC, e.g., means the share of DME-imports from OPEC in total DME-
imports (worldwide).

Note: As the UNCTAD-Handbook does not give data for 1971 and 1972 (except
         for total imports of DME and SC, where averages for 1971/1972 are
         shown which are reproduced between the two resp. years in the figure)
         1971 and 1972 percentages are mostly missing.

Sources: UNCTAD, **Handbook of International Trade and Development Statistics**,
         (various issues) "Agricultural trade ...," TD/B/C.1/239, op. cit.,
         p. 24.

---

the fifties and which still determines its position *vis-à-vis* the South,
though to a lesser degree.[24] East-South economic cooperation centers,
therefore, on extractive industries and resource development: the biggest
and most often quoted compensation deals (e.g. the Soviet-Moroccan
phosphate "deal of the decade" or the Guinean bauxite deal) try to
secure raw material supplies. In the *Press Bulletin* of January 18, 1984
(No. 959) the Moscow Narodny Bank states that "most agreements on
compensation co-operation involve mining industries."

The advantages of exports to SCs are a certain diversification of
markets, as long as Eastern countries compete for commodities and do
not cooperate with other Northern importers. It also offers the opportunity
of selling more than would otherwise be possible.

The argument of stable import markets for periphery exports also
deserves a comment. As can be seen from Figure 1 total import shares
of the South to SCs were rather stable between 1965 and 1980, while
shares in total imports of the periphery to the West increased. Within
the South's share that of OPEC increased, while that of other developing
countries decreased by one percentage-point between 1965 and 1980
for imports to the SCs. The increase in Western imports from the
periphery was simply the result of OPEC. The share of other peripheral
countries remained remarkably stable.

The greater degree of fluctuations in agricultural imports from the South compared to total CMEA-imports (to which the UNCTAD-document quoted above under footnote 16 draws attention) might also have been one reason for the strong reaction of Group D. The document argues that this greater instability in agricultural imports is caused by an essentially residual role of East-South trade as a source of supply used to make up shortfalls in domestic production of certain commodities.[25] Other factors, like the relatively small aggregate, the overall hard currency situation of SCs at given points in time, or the possibility of using periphery imports as balance of payments adjustment devices must, however, also be taken into account. Some of these motives are strikingly similar to economic policies of Developed Market Economies which are often criticized by the SCs.

In 1981 and 1982 the six European CMEA countries cut their imports from the periphery by more than 10 percent each year. This was considerably more than the decline in imports from other sources. In 1982 the Soviet Union also cut its imports from developing countries. In some individual cases this drop was extremely pronounced. After switching from clearing to hard cash, Soviet imports of agricultural goods from Turkey virtually stopped in 1983. In 1981 and 1982 Soviet imports had already declined by over 35 percent each year.

Information available on East-South trade and its commodity composition, it may be concluded, does not indicate positive differences between East-South and West-South trade. Therefore we turn next to prices and terms of trade of this exchange to see to what extent mutual advantages and positive effects for the periphery can be found.

Prices and Terms of Trade in East-South Trade

Another topic, and possibly the most important with regard to foreign trade, is prices. It has to be asked whether there is a significant difference between prices paid by the West and those by the SCs. Since prices alone may be misleading, information on terms of trade would be more conclusive. Given the well known difficulty with data, the analysis must often rely on case studies or whatever detailed information is available.

Trade agreements between Eastern and Southern governments are usually guided by world market prices. They are not invariably fixed, but are subject to periodic adjustments in accordance with fluctuations in the world market. Thus the Soviet-Moroccan phosphate deal determines that prices should be renegotiated annually, and the GDR and Syria have agreed to tie the prices of exchanged goods to ruling world market prices. This was also a stipulation between the GDR and Cyprus.[26]

The question of prices actually paid in trade between SCs and the periphery is difficult, if not impossible, to answer. Information on prices must be treated cautiously because of the possible effects of barter, or such trade which cannot be assessed from prices alone. Price comparisons of manufactured exports from the SCs, as Jean Diambou writes, are practically impossible because these prices are never published.[27] According to the sources available to Diambou the Soviet Union "frequently" buys at prices below the world market price. In some cases the difference is quite substantial. Prices above the world market level have also been paid. CMEA-members, most notably Cuba, have especially benefitted from highly favorable pricing.

Even at ruling international prices an actually less favorable outcome is possible. An agreement between the GDR and Mozambique covering tantalite gives the former a monopsony at the ruling international price. However, this prevents Mozambique, an important exporter, from actively influencing this price. Furthermore the imported technology allows only an exploitation of 65 percent of the deposits, compared with 95 percent using Western technologies.[28]

However, as has been already pointed out, prices of Southern exports alone, especially with regard to the scarcity of available information, do not allow an evaluation of the effects of the trade. To do this it is necessary to have a look at CMEA export prices as well. If one assumes like Schoeller that CMEA exports, especially machinery, are of inferior quality compared to the corresponding Western products, even selling at world market prices would mean overpricing unless similar quality differences exist with regard to the respective imports from the periphery.[29] Even if such differences exist (i.e., if the terms of trade are exactly the same as in West-South trade) exchange at world market prices still means that terms of trade trends, like the recent sharp decline of raw material prices, are a common feature of North-South trade, irrespective of which group of countries in the North is trading with the periphery. Very short run fluctuations, of course, are mitigated by agreements containing periodical (e.g. annual) price adjustments.

For the Soviet Union, Raimund Dietz, in a study of Soviet–East European trade, derives terms of trade for Soviet–Third World exchanges from Soviet sources.[30] His time series shows a deterioration of Soviet net barter terms of trade *vis-à-vis* the periphery (excluding CMEA members) which closely resemble Western terms of trade as given by the UNCTAD Handbook.[31] According to Dietz, Soviet terms of trade for all goods fell from 100 in 1970 (or 105.4 in 1973) to 81.9 in 1981. According to the handbook the net barter terms of trade of Developed Market Economies *vis-à-vis* other regions fell from 111 in 1970 to 89 in 1981, amounting to a 20 percent reduction. For the region "America" which is, of course, strongly influenced by the US, the figures are 112 (1970) and 87 (1981) respectively, which is a decrease of 22.3 percent. Although these figures, especially for the USSR, must be treated with caution and the terms of trade are not specifically those of West-South trade, it may be said that the capitalist world market behaved like Soviet-South trade in the 1970s, at least as far as terms of trade are concerned.

Studies devoted to the terms of trade in East-South relations generally do not present significant conclusions, as Dimitri and Lavigne point out.[32] Due to the difficult data situation they often cover relatively short periods, a (very) limited number of products, and are quite frequently case studies covering only one peripheral country. Among SCs the Soviet Union is naturally by far the most frequently studied country. While the studies reviewed by Dimitri seem to suggest—the author formulates very cautiously—that SC terms of trade might be better, Lavigne refers to sources supporting the contrary thesis. Both authors stress the precariousness of the data situation. This poses the question as to why SCs are so reluctant to provide better statistical coverage, at least to the standard usual in the West, if their trade relations are indeed so much better than the exploitative trade of capitalist countries.

In evaluating East-South terms of trade, and it must be assumed that the same is valid for Soviet trade, it must also be mentioned that SCs quite often prefer buying from Western intermediaries rather than paying agreed higher "minimum" prices to the exporter.[33] Direct East-South trade may therefore give a false and biased picture of real (that is, direct and indirect) East-South trade. Agreed prices are in such cases more or less declarations of intent.

To make prices really comparable, it would finally be necessary to examine loan conditions granted to the South. This involves the tricky question of how to compare soft currency loans given at 3 to 5 percent to normal Eurocurrency conditions, and the question as to whether and to what extent these "soft" loans are finally indirectly "hardened."

For my argument the conclusion supported by available information is reasonable; i.e., that the possibility of East-South exchanges in general occurring at terms of trade better than those of the world market can be excluded. However, in cases when these world market prices contain elements of hidden transfers of profits from the periphery to the West, such gains accrue to all who buy at these prices. In this respect no mutual advantage other than the Ricardo-Torrens perception of comparative advantage can be perceived. Any trade at these terms is unequal exchange according to critical development research.

In the case of tripartite cooperation, especially favored by the East, it is logically impossible to differentiate between Northern partners. As multinationals will not offer their goods cheaper if an Eastern partner participates, only the existence of such a partner would ultimately constitute a mutual advantage. As can be shown with the example of an integrated pulp and paper mill in Cameroon, constructed with Austrian and GDR participation and quoted as an example of success by UNCTAD,[34] such cooperation may turn out to have shortcomings familiar to critics of Western exports. Apart from the fact that this mill ceased operation in 1983 for technical reasons—immediately on being quoted, so to say— it had led to public criticism in Austria. It threatened to destroy the livelihood of local fishermen through its effects on the environment and had been built for export only because a big international bank involved had declined to give credit for a small mill supplying the domestic market which had been initially desired by Cameroon.

Looking at the history of economic thought in SCs an interesting phenomenon can finally be discerned. Unequal exchange was theoretically debated there before it attracted much attention in the West, and was regarded as the main instrument of international capitalist exploitation in the fifties. Santalov even calculated Southern losses of US$15–16 billion per year for the period 1948–1952.[35] At the beginning of the sixties Gunther Kohlmey of the GDR argued that SCs cannot ignore ruling world market prices as long as capitalists dominate this market, but since prices are only one aspect of international relations, other special arrangements should compensate for this shortcoming.[36] In his remarks on East-South, however, he only expressly mentions the traditional mechanisms of trade like long term agreements and (contrary to intra-CMEA trade which also suffers from inequality of exchange) not transfers like international aid. Finally, during the seventies, the topic of "unequal exchange" was dropped and refuted by Soviet economists as "inappropriate theoretically and practically of little importance."[37] Incidentally this theoretical conclusion developed at the same time as East-South trade started to become relatively more important.

In the meantime the argument has been brought forward that East-South trade would be qualitatively different from West-South trade; i.e., being trade among equal partners and free of exploitation. As Jürgen Klose argues, the quantitative growth of East-South trade has made new theories necessary. Academically Klose echoes official declarations by simply stating that while capitalism exploits, exploitation by SCs is unthinkable. However, he fails to provide any convincing argument for this conclusion.[38] Unequal exchange theory, by contrast, has elaborated an objective measure of non-equivalence: whenever homogeneous factors of production are rewarded differently—or more technically: if the double factoral terms of trade differ from one—exchange is unequal.[39] Obviously it does not matter between what types of countries trade takes place.

Aid by SCs

Very much as in the case of trade relations, the estimation of aid figures is a difficult and cumbersome business. Official information made available shows high percentages, such as the Soviet statement in the ECOSOC of July 1982 claiming an average of 1.0 percent of GNP as aid given during 1976–1980, rising from 0.9 percent in 1976 to 1.3 percent in 1980. However, they do not necessarily produce a better impression. Apart from verification problems they allow, according to the UNCTAD secretariat, no "meaningful comparison" with other donors, nor can it be ascertained whether they "are consistent with internationally agreed upon norms established by the General Assembly in the International Development Strategy."[40]

However, if one takes the estimates of the Development Assistance Committee (DAC) of the OECD and adds price subsidies, the CMEA-6 gave about as much as Italy did while the Soviet Union was around (and sometimes above) DAC-averages during the recent years. Actually there is little economic reason why these payments should not be added. If "normal" world market prices were taken into consideration and the differences with the actually paid (subsidized) prices were granted in cash, these subsidies would constitute aid by DAC-norms. In other words, a different accounting technique would change the picture. The reason why DAC does not recognize these payments as aid seems to be political; if they did they would accept that the USSR contributes substantially more than the US, a country which, like the socialist group, has never accepted the 0.7 percent target. The only DAC member interested in recognizing such payments as aid, France, is obviously less influential than the US and other countries which do not want such payments included. Whatever the reasons are, they are not economic.

For the sake of fairness it should also be added that the method of converting from the System of Material Product Balances to the (Western) System of National Accounts adopted by the DAC was the method of the IBRD (World Bank), which renders the lowest percentages of CMEA-aid. If the DAC adopted the conversion method of the Joint Economic Committee of the US Congress, aid percentages would increase up to 1.6 times the figures officially presented by DAC.[41] It must also be remembered that this comprises as aid only those flows of SCs which are recognized by the DAC of OECD as Official Development Assistance. Without trying to decide which method is better it can be remarked that it is obviously impossible to get both low GNP-values per capita and low aid percentages by the same method. The choice of the DAC and the existence of the conversion method of the Joint Economic

Committee seem to be an attempt to both keep one's cake and eat it at the same time, but in different places.

In a thorough and very detailed analysis of estimates of Soviet Official Development Assistance (ODA) published by the Development Assistance Committee (DAC) of the OECD, Walter Kaiser proves that these figures cannot be correct. As Soviet sources only provide data sporadically and in insufficient detail (and never in a verifiable way) Kaiser relies on Western sources, such as those from the US (including the CIA) and the DAC itself. As his findings are not yet available in English, a short presentation of his main conclusions is called for.[42]

Generally, the DAC presents extremely high GSP-estimates, up to 72 percent higher than the CIA, and higher than the IBRD estimates that were published until 1980. While the 1980 report explained that the World Bank method had been used, additional information provided by the World Bank had led to another estimate done by the DAC itself. The 1984 report claims that the DAC "had used the GSP-data published by the World Bank until 1980."[43] After the IBRD stopped publishing GSP-data, so-called "extrapolations" of the IBRD time series were used according to the DAC. As Kaiser points out these "extrapolations" show apparently no continuity with the IBRD series and render unbelievably high rates of growth for the USSR; nearly 15 percent both in 1981 and 1982! During this period the Net Material Product (NMT) grew by 3.4 and 4.2 percent in 1981 and 1982 respectively. The CIA-GSP grew by 2.7 percent in both years. GSP figures for the same year were changed quite substantially in later reports without any explanation (e.g. for 1981 by more that a quarter of the estimated CIA-GSP). Generally, inconsistencies, incompatibilities, and incorrect results have abounded during the last decade.

Regarding subsidies to Cuba, Kaiser proved that these had been recognized explicitly as ODA by the DAC until 1974! In the case of Vietnam such subsidies were recognized until the beginning of this decade. Since 1974 price subsidies to Cuba were excluded without mentioning the change of the method of estimation. The 1980 report of the DAC excluded them explicitly for the first time. Naturally this most remarkable way of calculation changed Soviet percentage shares drastically. Incidentally, this change occurred after the USSR had surpassed the US percentage. It transformed the USSR from an around-average-donor to a tightfisted miser. It should also be added that price subsidies qualify as ODA according to the definition used by the DAC itself.

Kaiser concludes that the data were manipulated to provide a basis for attacks on the Soviet Union (and SCs in general) in international fora. He backs this conclusion with meticulously researched material. The upward revisions of the early 1980s were, according to Kaiser, triggered by the fear of finally losing credibility. Apparently growth rates of the dimension mentioned above for 1981 and 1982 cannot be extrapolated forever.

Kaiser also scrutinizes the figures presented by the Soviets in 1982. Due to restrictions on information the author feels unable to make a final conclusion. However, he is able to show that the USSR also manipulated the figures by using GSP instead of NMP or by using rubles instead of dollars. The latter mistake (confusing the currencies) renders 40 percent higher values on average. Kaiser is also surprised that the DAC, in contrast to the heavy critique based on its own incorrect data, has not drawn attention to this fact. Although the USSR is, as far as one can judge from available information, not a tightfisted donor, Kaiser thinks that "propagandist and wrong presentation" has had a "boomerang effect."[44] This statement need not be restricted to aid.

Conclusion

East-South economic relations are neither better nor worse that West-South relations; both are basically guided by self-interest. Differences in detail exist, of course, but the broad line is the same. Licensing agreements, the growth of countertrade in the West, long term contracts in mining, or the coming into existence of "socialist transnationals" further diminishes the differences. If trade with the West is exploitative, trade at the same prices and conditions with SCs must also be so, unless one is prepared to accept the fact that clearly different systems are in themselves a sufficient condition for beneficial effects. The demands of the NIEO thus address the whole North. Insofar as these demands aim at changing present structures, the history of colonialism—although it formed the present economic relations—can be no excuse for profiting from these existing structures which put the South at a disadvantage.

Notes

1. UNCTAD, Sixth Session, Summary Record of the 200th Meeting (TD/ SR.200, 12 August 1983), paragraph 19 (emphasis added, K.R.).

2. C.W. Lawson, "Socialist Relations with the Third World: A Case Study of the New International Economic Order," *Economics of Planning*, No. 3, 1980, p. 150.

3. Cf. Barbara Despiney, "Les pays socialistes dans le débat sur le nouvel ordre économique international," *Bulletin de Liaison du Colloque "Vers quel nouvel ordre mondial?"*, Septembre 1983 (1), éd. par le département d'Économie Politique, Université de Paris VIII, p. 4.

4. C. W. Lawson, "Socialist Relations . . . ," *op. cit.*, p. 152.

5. Cf. *Ibid.*, pp. 148, 160.

6. Despiney, "Les pays socialistes . . . ," *op. cit.*, p. 12; or: Marie Lavigne, "East-South Trade in Primary Products: A Model Borrowed from the North-South Pattern?," *Journal für Entwicklungspolitik*, vol. 2, n. 2, 1986, pp. 18ff, who speaks of an "objective collusion" with developed market economies (p. 28); cf. also Kunibert Raffer, "Ost-Süd: Vorbild oder Abklatsch der West-Süd-Wirtschaftsbeziehungen?," *Journal für Entwicklungspolitik*, vol. 2, n. 2, 1986, esp. p. 16.

7. Brigitte Schulz, "The Road to Socialism in the Periphery: East German Solidarity in Theory and Practice," *Journal für Entwicklungspolitik*, vol. 2, n. 2, 1986, p. 67.

8. Cf. V. I. Lenin, "Der Imperialismus als höchstes Stadium des Kapitalismus," in V. I. Lenin, *Ausgewählte Werke, Bd. I*, Moskau, 1946, p. 745.

9. Cf. R. M. Cutler, "East-South relations at UNCTAD: Global Political Economy and the CMEA," *International Organization*, Winter 1983, vol. 37, n. 1, p. 124; U.N. Economic and Social Council, "Possible Future Development of Trade between the Socialist Countries and the Developing Countries," E/CONF. 46/L. 17, 12 June, 1964.

10. UNCTAD VI, "Trade relations among countries having different economic and social systems and all trade flows resulting therefrom," Item 13d-policy paper, TD/280 (14 February 1983), p. 15.

11. *Ibid.*, p. 17 (paragraph 50).

12. *Ibid.*, p. 17 (paragraph 51).

13. Deepak Nayyar, "Some Reflections on East-South Trade and the Division of Labour," ID/WG 357, 31 March 1982, (document reproduced without formal editing), p. 3; Wolfgang Schoeller, " 'Komparativer Nachteil' und 'wechselseitiger Nutzen,' Zur Kooperation zwischen COMECON und Entwicklungsländern am Beispiel Mozambiks," *Deutschland Archiv*, Nr. 12, Dezember 1983, pp. 103ff.

14. UNCTAD VI, "Trade relations . . . ," *op. cit.*, p. 19 (paragraph 58).

15. Cf. *Ibid.*; Eva Palócz-Németh, "Der Handel in Industriewaren zwischen Ost, West und Süd und seine Auswirkungen," *WIIW-Forschungsberichte*, Nr. 67, Jänner 1981, Wien, pp. 51f. who calls it a "substantial progress."

16. István Dobozi, "The Prospects of East-South Economic Interaction in the Changing International Environment," *Vienna Institute for Development, Occasional Paper*, 83/4, pp. 3ff.

17. ECE, "Economic Survey of Europe in 1983," United Nations (Pre-Publication Text: Part II), Table 4.3.7.

18. Ilse Grosser and Gabriele Tuitz, "Structural Changes in Manufacturing Industries in the European CMEA Area and Problems of Trade in Manufactures between CMEA Countries and Developing Countries," ID/WG.357/5, 25 January 1982, p. 111.

19. Report of the Committee on Commodities on its tenth session (26 January–8 February, 1983) TD/B/944/TD/B/C. 1/247, Trade and Development Board, Official Records, 26th Session, Supplement No. 4, p. 28; the document to which the spokesman specifically referred was TD/B/C.1/239 (12 January, 1983) titled "Liberalization of Barriers to Trade in Primary and Processed Commodities,

Agricultural trade expansion and protectionism with special reference to products of interest to developing countries," esp. paragraphs 25–33.

20. F. Levcik and J. Stankovsky, *Industrielle Kooperation zwischen Ost und West* (Studien über Wirtschafts- und Systemvergleiche, Vol. 8), Vienna/New York, 1977, p. 143.

21. D. Nayyar, "Some Reflections . . . ," *op. cit.*, p. 7.

22. Cf. Grosser and Tuitz, "Structural Changes . . . ," *op. cit.*, p. 133.

23. I. Dobozi, "The Prospects of East-South Economic Interaction . . . ," *op. cit.*, p. 1; Cf. also István Dobozi, *Projected Trends of World Raw Material and Energy Markets until 2000* (Studies on Developing Countries, No. 110), Budapest, 1982.

24. Kunibert Raffer, "Raw Material Supply of Western and Eastern Countries: The Case of African Minerals," in I. Dobozi and P. Mándi (Eds.), "Emerging Development Patterns: European Contributions," *Selected Papers of the 3rd General Conference of EADI*, Budapest, 1983, esp. pp. 494–495.

25. "Liberalization . . . ," TD/B/C.1/239, *op. cit.*, p. 25.

26. Cf. Grosser and Tuitz, "Structural . . . ," *op. cit.*, p. 114; Hansjörg F. Buck, "Abbau von Rohstoffengpässen durch Handel mit Entwicklungsländern, DDR-Wirtschaftsbeziehungen mit Entwicklungsländern am Beispiel Syriens, Zyperns und Kuweits," *Deutschland Archiv* 1, Jänner 1983, p. 57; Jean Diambou, "Faiblesses et qualités des relations Est-Sud," dans: Marie Lavigne (éd), *Strategies des pays socialistes dans l'échange international*, (Série: Sciences économiques, études internationales), Paris, 1980, p. 125; UNCTAD VI, "Trade . . . ," *op. cit.*, p. 17 (paragraph 54); Schoeller, "Komparativer . . . ," *op. cit.*, p. 1309.

27. Diambou, *ibid.*

28. Schoeller, "Komparativer . . . ," *op. cit.*, p. 1309.

29. *Ibid.*; Jiri Elias, *Die Aussenwirtschaftsbeziehungen des COMECON mit den Entwicklungsländern unter besonderer Berücksichtigung Südasiens*, (Europäische Hochschulschriften, Vol. 159, Series V), Bern/Frankfurt-am-Main/Las Vegas, 1977, p. 164, generally speaks of overpriced exports.

30. Raimund Dietz, "Advantages and Disadvantages in Soviet Trade with Eastern Europe—The Dimension of Prices," in: *Joint Economic Committee of the Congress of the US (JEC)*, East European Volume 1984 (forthcoming).

31. UNCTAD, *Handbook of International Trade and Development Statistics 1983*, New York 1983, Tab. 2.5.

32. Cf. Alexandre Dimitri, "Le systeme des Prix," in: M. Lavigne (éd), *Les relations Est-Sud dans la économie mondiale*, Paris 1985 (mimeo), vol. I; this study was published in English (*East-South Relations in the World Economy*) at Westview Press; Lavigne, "East-South Trade in Primary . . . ," *op. cit.*, esp. pp. 26ff.

33. I. Angelis, "Some Issues Concerning Economic Relations between the ČSSR and the Developing Countries," in I. Dobozi (Ed), *Economic Cooperation between Socialist and Developing Countries*, Budapest, 1978, pp. 173ff.; Cf. also I. Dobozi, "Arrangements for Mineral Development Cooperation between Socialist Countries and Developing Countries," paper presented at the Hungarian-Italian Roundtable, November 23–24, 1982, Budapest (mimeo), p. 42.

34. UNCTAD VI, "Trade . . . ," *op. cit.*, p. 25 (paragraph 87).

35. Cf. Jan Otto Andersson, *Studies in the Theory of Unequal Exchange between Nations*, Abo Research Institute, 1976, Annex 1, pp. 167 ff.

36. Gunther Kohlmey, *Karl Marx' Theorie von den Internationalen Werten mit einigen Schlussfolgerungen für die Preisbildung im Aussenhandel zwischen Sozialistischen Staaten*, (Probleme der Politischen Ökonomie, Vol. 5), Berlin/DDR, 1962, p. 96 and p. 79; cf. also G. Kohlmey, "Karl Marx' Aussenhandelstheorie und Probleme der Aussenwirtschaftlichen Beziehungen zwischen Sozialistischen Staaten," *Wirtschaftswissenschaft*, August 1967, p. 1235.

37. Andersson, "Studies . . . ," *op. cit.*, p. 168.

38. Jürgen Klose, "Some questions relating to the mode of operation of the law of value in the economic relations between socialist and developing countries," *Economic Quarterly* (Institute for the Economy of Developing Countries, Hochschule für Ökonomie, Bruno Leuschner, Berlin/GDR) 2/1982, pp. 3ff. His view is criticized by Raffer, "Ost-Süd . . . ," *op. cit.*, pp. 14ff.

39. For a survey on theories of unequal exchange cf. Kunibert Raffer, *Unequal Exchange and the Evolution of the World System, Reconsidering the Impact of Trade on North-South Relations* (forthcoming from Macmillan, London & St. Martin's Press, New York).

40. Cf. UNCTAD VI, "International financial and monetary issues," Item 11—Policy paper, TD/275 (26 January 1983), p. 67 (paragraph 271).

41. *USSR: Measures of Economic Growth and Development, 1950–1980*, Studies prepared for the use of the Joint Economic Committee, Congress of the United States, December 8, 1982 (97th Congress, 2nd Session), Washington, DC; according to the JEC Chairman the "volume was prepared by the CIA at the request of the Joint Economic Committee." (*Ibid.*, preface).

42. Walter Kaiser, "Die Entwicklungshilfeleistungen der Sowjetunion in den OECD-Publikationen," *Journal für Entwicklungspolitik*, vol. 2, n. 2, 1986, pp. 32ff. This article is based on Kaiser's master's thesis of the same title, approved at the University of Vienna in 1986.

43. *Ibid.*, p. 34.

44. *Ibid.*, p. 48.

7

Patterns, Determinants, and Prospects of East-South Economic Relations

Istvan Dobozi

Introduction

Relationships between the European socialist countries belonging to the Council for Mutual Economic Assistance (CMEA)[1] and the Third World have an ideological, political, strategic and economic dimension. While a great deal of scholarly attention has been directed to the political and strategic forces underlying East-South relations, until recently the economic dimension has not been thoroughly and comprehensively investigated. Though the current decade has seen an impressive growth in the amount of scholarly literature related to East-South economic relations, state-of-the-art economic analysis continues to be rather imperfect and non-systematic.[2] It is quite symptomatic that a rigorous econometric analysis of determinants of East-South economic exchange hardly exists.[3]

As Table 1 shows, East-South trade does not constitute a major flow of world trade. In 1984 the value of the European CMEA countries' exports to the developing countries was US$29 billion, corresponding to a mere 1.5 percent of world exports. It is slightly up from 1.4 percent in 1975. This implies that in the period 1975–1984 East-South trade expanded only marginally more dynamically than world trade as a whole. However, East-South trade looks more significant in relation to the total trade of the two groups of countries. In 1984, 16.6 percent of CMEA exports went to the developing countries, up from 15.8 percent in 1975, but down from 21.4 percent in 1980.

In sharp contrast, in 1984 only 3.6 percent of total developing country exports was directed to the European CMEA countries; down from 4.7

Table 1. East-South Trade in the Context of World Trade Flows

1975, 1980, 1984 (billion dollars)

Exports from		World	Developed market economies	Developing countries	European CMEA countries	CMEA6	USSR
World	1975	872.7	573.2	209.2	82.6	47.3	35.3
	1980	200.2	135.1	466.0	144.1	81.9	52.2
	1984	190.7	126.8	438.7	148.3	79.8	68.5
Developed market economies	1975	577.2	402.0	143.9	22.9	14.4	13.5
	1980	126.8	902.6	295.1	46.3	22.2	24.1
	1984	123.6	901.3	266.0	38.6	14.0	24.6
Developing countries	1975	218.1	151.0	53.2	10.3	4.1	6.3
	1980	558.6	391.6	138.9	16.5	6.5	10.0
	1984	469.0	305.7	132.9	17.0	6.9	10.1
European CMEA countries	1975	77.4	20.2	12.2	44.4	28.8	15.6
	1980	155.1	58.2	33.2	78.6	51.7	26.9
	1984	175.0	50.7	29.0	89.8	57.9	31.9
CMEA6	1975	44.1	10.6	4.9	27.9	12.3	15.6
	1980	78.7	20.7	9.1	46.4	19.5	26.9
	1984	83.4	20.6	10.9	49.9	18.0	31.9
USSR	1975	33.3	9.6	7.3	16.4	16.4	
	1980	76.4	27.6	14.1	32.2	32.2	
	1984	91.6	30.1	18.1	39.9	39.9	

Exports to

Source: United Nations, **Monthly Bulletin of Statistics**, June 1983 and May 1986.

percent in 1975 and up from 2.9 percent in 1980. These figure imply asymmetrical importance of mutual trade flows: the CMEA countries depend relatively more on East-South economic exchange than do developing countries. This circumstance may be one important reason why most studies focus on the Soviet and East European motives behind East-South trade and find those of the South to be of much less significant concern and, thus, less clearly identified.

The main aim of this essay is to discern some fundamental forces underlying East-South economic interactions. More specifically, I wish to find out what kind of implicit international division of labor has evolved between East and South. Is there any trade model capable of explaining the pattern and determinants of East-South trade? Section I addresses these issues.

Although the scope of direct East-South interaction is found to be rather limited from the point of view of both groups of countries, a rapidly increasing competition has evolved between the East and South on third markets, particularly those of the OECD for manufactured goods. In this context, several issues need to be addressed: the scope and intensity of a mutual competitive threat, the evolution of relative competitiveness over time, and the identification of forces underlying the changes in the competitive positions. Section II is devoted to a discussion of these issues.

Experience shows that more developed and economically stronger nations' adjustment to external imbalances often occurs at the expense of less developed or economically weaker nations. In this context the following question comes up: given CMEA's middle position between West and South and the East's serious financial imbalances with the West in the recent period, has the East used its trade with the South as a vehicle of external adjustment? In Section III an attempt is made to provide an answer to this question.

Aid ties between East and South constitute a most controversial dimension of overall relations, especially since several CMEA countries have recently gone public about their assistance in quantitative terms. Section IV addresses the question as to whether the East is an under-performer in the provision of economic assistance.

An important suggestion of the chapter is that over the past decades a relatively limited direct economic interdependence has evolved between the two groups of countries and, generally speaking, they are of residual importance for one another. The domestic and international environment however will undergo considerable changes in the following period with possible impact on the conditions and expansion of East-South exchanges. In Section V an attempt is made to discern the most important "push" and "pull" factors which are expected to condition the prospects for East-South economic relations.

I. The Pattern of East-South Trade: A Replica of East-West Trade?

Statistical studies abound regarding the commodity composition of East-South trade. There is considerable agreement that, contrary to some past Eastern claims about a "new type" of international division of labor, the commodity pattern of East-South trade reflects a rather old type division of labor similar to that existing in West-South trade; i.e., manufactures from the East in exchange for primary goods from the South. Except for the USSR, the CMEA countries' exports to the South are dominated by manufactures. In 1983, the share of manufactures was 49 percent of CMEA-6 exports to the developing countries. In the USSR, the share was only 27 percent. With regard to CMEA imports, the predominance of primary goods can be observed. In 1983 the share of these goods was 93 percent for the CMEA-6 and 90 percent for the Soviet Union.[4]

The commodity pattern of East-South trade when compared with that of East-West trade quite clearly reflects the *intermediate level* of development of the East. As suggested above, the CMEA countries' trade with the South (again with the exception of the USSR whose trade pattern *vis-à-vis* the South is very similar to the typical South-South pattern) exhibits traditional features of the division of labor between a Northern country and a Southern country. This picture, to a considerable extent, repeats itself in the East-West context, where structurally the East plays almost the same role as the South does in the East-South context. One broad key then to an understanding of the underlying forces shaping East-South exchange is *comparative development levels;* more specifically, the *intermediate nature* of Eastern economies.[5]

A more disaggregated analysis is required to discern the sources of comparative advantages and thus specialization patterns in East-South trade. Very limited and partial empirical evidence has been generated in this area. The literature tends to be rather speculative when dealing with sources of comparative advantages in East-South trade.[6] We do not know, due to lack of empirical testing, if there is any trade theory capable of explaining the evolution of specialization patterns over time in the context of East-South exchanges.

To fill at least partially the gap in empirical research, I made a simple test to see if the Hecksher-Ohlin theory of trade is able to explain the pattern of East-South trade. The theory predicts that an economy will specialize in the production and export of commodities that require the relatively intensive application of its more abundant factors of production. Empirical applications of the theory have been moderately successful in explaining the composition of trade of a number of countries.

In the trade literature it is customary to group goods in three groups: goods that require the relatively intensive use of natural resources (Ricardo goods), goods that require high proportions of research and development or employ scientists and engineers fairly intensively (product-cycle or high-technology goods), and goods that use relatively standardized production technologies (Hecksher-Ohlin goods). For the production characteristics categories I adopt the Ricardo and the product cycle groupings and divide the Hecksher-Ohlin group according to relative capital and labor-intensive categories.

As Figure 1 shows, in a broad sense specialization pattern in East-South trade is consistent with the prediction of the Hecksher-Ohlin factor proportions theory. CMEA-6 has been developing a growing comparative advantage *vis-à-vis* the South in mature product-cycle goods and capital-intensive Hecksher-Ohlin goods, while the South has been developing increasing comparative advantage *vis-à-vis* the East in natural-resource intensive goods. These specialization lines are consistent with relative factor endowments among the two groups of countries, as the CMEA-6 is better endowed with both R&D resources and physical capital, while the South is better endowed with natural resources. Figure 1 reveals the strength and persistence of trends in the factor content pattern of East-South trade.

An unexpected aspect of Figure 1 is the trade surplus of CMEA-6 in labor-intensive Hecksher-Ohlin goods. This is contrary to the prediction of factor-proportions theory as developing countries are much better endowed with labor resources than the CMEA countries and, in fact, labor has become a progressively scarce factor input in most of the CMEA-6 countries. This phenomenon seems to indicate "wrong specialization" on the part of the CMEA-6 countries and leads us to the critical problem of the low share of manufactures in CMEA import from the South. More on this follows below.

The share of manufactured goods in the CMEA countries' total imports from the South is especially low in comparison with South-OECD trade. As Table 2 shows, the respective share increased from 6.4 percent in 1970 to 12.9 percent in 1984 in the case of the OECD countries, while it was stagnant at 2.5 percent in the European CMEA countries. Over this period the share of the European CMEA countries in the total manufactured goods exports of the developing countries went down from 3.5 percent to 1.3 percent. The contrast between the OECD and the CMEA countries is especially sharp if one compares the share of manufactures in the total non-fuel exports of the developing countries:

116

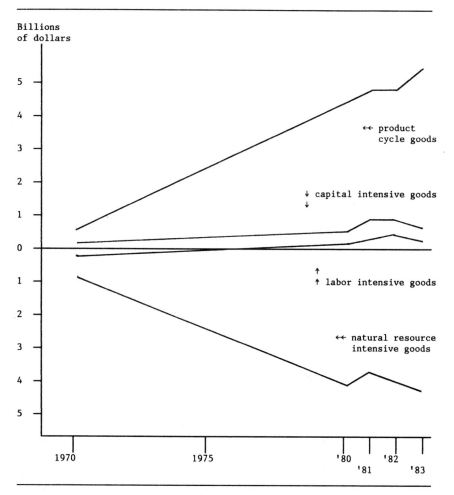

Figure 1. Factor Intensity Pattern in the CMEA6 Trade Balance

vis-à-vis the Third World[a]

a Exports minus imports

Source: United Nations, **Monthly Bulletin of Statistics**, various issues.

Table 2. Share of Developing Countries in the

Total Imports of the OECD and CMEA Countries
(per cent of total imports)

	1970	1975	1980	1981	1982
OECD countries					
Total imports	18.1	25.8	29.2	29.0	26.6
Total non-fuel imports	13.1	12.5	13.1	13.7	13.9
Total manufactures imports[a]	6.4	6.9	9.0	10.1	10.5
CMEA countries					
Total imports	9.9	11.1	11.4	12.4	13.2
Total non-fuel imports	10.2	9.8	10.3	11.8	12.1
Total manufactures imports[a]	2.5	2.2	2.2	2.2	2.0

[a] Manufactures here comprise SITC 5-8.

Source: United Nations, **Monthly Bulletin of Statistics,** May 1981 and May 1984. In Rozália Bogó, "The CMEA Countries and Imports of Manufactures from the Third World," Budapest, 1985 (mimeo).

while this share increased from 34.4 percent in 1970 to 63.8 percent in 1984 in the case of the OECD countries, it decreased from 17.2 percent to 15.6 percent in the CMEA countries.[7]

Even in the case of the relatively open Hungarian economy the share of the South in the total manufactured goods imports was only 2.4 percent in 1983, considerably lower than the share of the South in total imports (13.0 percent).[8]

Why is it that CMEA imports of manufactures from the South is so insignificant and the latter—unlike in its trade with the West—is unable to take advantage of its growing comparative advantage in labor-intensive goods in relation to the CMEA?

The "wrong specialization" in this commodity group reflects the CMEA's persistent internal supply difficulties and slow progress toward selective industrial policy in which the South is assigned a distinct and well-defined role. Developing countries have increasingly been used by the CMEA countries to fill the supply gaps (fuel and food). For example, the growing role of food in Soviet imports from the South can be seen as the result of a series of bad grain harvests in the late 1970s and early 1980s, combined with a diversion of grain imports toward the South as a result of restrictive U.S. policies.[9] Manufactures imports might have thus been "crowded out" by more pressing demands for higher priority primary goods unobtainable within CMEA. The objective of maximizing hard-currency earnings from East-South trade also acted against massive Eastern imports of Southern manufactures. Also, up to the present in the industrial policies of the CMEA countries no substantive structural role has been assigned to developing country imports of manufactures as one way to create a more selective domestic industrial profile. The highly closed domestic manufactures markets of these countries make a more aggressive market penetration by the Southern suppliers very difficult or impossible. Finally, the relative insignificance of manufactures imports is related to the fact that the CMEA countries were not able to integrate themselves into the dynamically unfolding industrial division of labor that exists between some developing countries and the developed Western countries. I am referring, of course, to the NICs (newly industrializing countries), which have been the prime movers on the part of the South to push manufactures exports to the North.

With the partial exception of Brazil, the CMEA countries did not establish strong and organic relations with the NICs. Trading efforts were directed toward lucrative alternative partners (mainly in the Middle East) with primary commodity imports and the maximization of short-term hard-currency export earnings being the primary objective. This situation indicates that the major changes in the manufacturing industrialization which unfolded in the last decade and before in some parts of the South went almost unnoticed by the CMEA countries and, surprisingly enough, the share of these countries in the NICs' exports declined, although it was very insignificant even before. For example, in the case of Hungary's Third World–related imports the share of the ten well-established NICs (Brazil, Argentina, Mexico, Hong Kong, Singapore, South Korea, Taiwan, Philippines, Malaysia, Thailand) went down from 39.2 percent in 1977 to 26.2 percent 1982. This picture is totally distorted by the dominance of Brazil. Basically all the socialist countries import a few important agricultural products from Brazil. So the relatively high share of the NICs in Hungary's overall Third World–related imports does not reflect Hungary's real involvement in the NIC process. As far as the export side is concerned, whereas in 1973 the share of the ten NICs in Hungary's exports to the Third World was 10.7 percent, it went down to less than 3 percent in 1982.[10] The situation is no better for other CMEA countries. The CMEA countries' combined share in the foreign trade of many NICs is lower than that of Austria or the Netherlands.

II. An Open East-South Trade Conflict
in the Western Markets?

While the scope of East-South trade in manufactured goods is very limited, the CMEA countries have met rapidly increasing competition from the NICs in Western markets, particularly in labor-intensive goods. This is also the case in some capital-intensive Hecksher-Ohlin goods and even in some mature product-cycle goods with a high income elasticity of demand as a growing number of NICs successfully upgrade the technological content of manufactures export of the West. The empirical evidence shows an increasingly close resemblance between the pattern of exports of manufactured goods from the CMEA and NICs to Western markets. There is also some evidence that the technological content of CMEA manufactures exported to the West lags behind that of the most advanced group of NICs.[11]

The difficulties posed for the CMEA countries by the competition of NICs can be seen from the fact that the CMEA-6 was unable to widen its share in the total OECD imports of manufactured goods. Instead, it declined from 1.2 percent in 1970 to 1.1 percent in 1983, while a group of eight NICs (Argentina, Brazil, Mexico, Singapore, South Korea, Taiwan and Hong Kong) increased its share from 2.8 percent to 7.4 percent over the same period. The gap in export performance has been particularly drastic in the machinery and transport equipment group, the technologically most complex product category. Here, the CMEA-6's share in the total OECD import demand dropped from the very marginal 0.6 percent in 1970 to 0.4 percent in 1983, compared with a sharp increase from 1.2 percent to 6.6 percent by the NICs.[12] In 1984, Taiwanese machinery exports exceeded by three-fold, South Korean exports by two-fold, and even Malaysian exports exceeded by twenty percent the joint OECD-related machinery exports of the European CMEA countries (including the USSR).[13] As a result of declining CMEA competitiveness in technologically more advanced goods, the socialist countries have no choice but increasingly to compete with the NICs in unsophisticated material and energy-intensive products; an area of competition which contradicts the relative factor endowments of most of the CMEA countries. For the progressive erosion of market share of the European CMEA countries in the OECD market *vis-à-vis* the developing countries as a whole in selected categories of manufactured goods, see Table 3.

Although analyzing the causes behind the eroding Eastern competitiveness and the slow structural transformation of the Eastern export pattern toward technologically more advanced manufactures would go beyond the scope of this chapter, a few broad contributing factors can be indicated: (a) a considerable time lag, as compared with the core

Istvan Dobozi

Table 3. Market Share of the European CMEA Countries and
the Developing Countries in the OECD Total Imports
of Major Manufactured Goods, 1973, 1980, 1984
(in per cent)

	European CMEA Countries			Developing Countries		
	1973	1980	1984	1973	1980	1984
Manufactures total	1.7	1.8	1.3	8.4	10.9	15.2
Chemicals	2.1	2.9	2.6	4.7	5.5	7.2
Manufactures classified chiefly by material	2.3	2.1	2.0	11.2	12.6	17.2
Machinery and transport equipment	1.0	1.0	0.6	3.6	5.8	9.8
Miscellaneous manufactures	2.5	2.2	1.6	17.9	25.1	32.7
Organic and inorganic chemicals	3.0	4.6	3.7	6.5	8.2	10.5
Medicinal and pharmaceutical products	1.0	0.7	0.6	4.6	4.8	4.4
Fertilizers	8.1	8.3	10.9	7.1	6.7	8.4
Plastic materials	0.6	1.5	1.6	0.7	1.6	3.8
Textiles	2.1	1.9	1.5	18.3	21.3	24.7
Leather goods	1.8	1.5	1.0	32.4	31.2	35.4
Rubber manufactures	2.5	2.8	2.8	31.5	26.8	31.3
Iron and steel	3.7	3.2	3.5	5.1	8.1	13.9
Manufactures of metal	1.6	1.3	1.0	4.2	8.8	14.9
Power generating machinery	0.5	1.5	1.2	2.2	5.3	10.3
Office machines and automatic data processing equipment	0.2	0.2	0.0	4.4	4.7	11.4
Telecommunications and sound recording and reproducing apparatus and equipment	0.5	0.3	0.2	16.6	22.7	24.9
Electrical machinery	1.2	0.9	0.6	8.4	15.3	23.6
Clothing	4.0	3.5	2.6	37.2	45.5	57.0
Footwear	3.5	3.3	2.0	21.1	32.5	45.9
Professional, scientific and controlling instruments	0.9	0.5	0.4	2.7	8.4	9.4

Source: Calculated from: **Trade by Commodities**, Series C, Imports, 1973, 1980, 1984, Paris, OECD. Table taken from Inotai Andráa, "Uj irányzatok a nemzetközi ipari munkamegosztásban: magyar szemszögböl" (New Trends in the International Industrial Division of Labour), **Közgazdasági Szemle**, Budapest, No. 9, 1986, p. 1036.

group of NICs, can be observed in the East's switch toward export-oriented growth strategy; (b) a very limited scope for export-oriented foreign direct investments in the socialist economies; (c) too much reliance on inflexible and unattractive trade arrangements such as buy-back agreements; (d) too heavy CMEA reliance on the Western European market which shows a lower propensity to import manufactured goods from all newcomers than does the United States;[14] (e) some well-known disfunctional systemic features of the Eastern economies which act against export orientation and technological-structural transformation at the level of the enterprises.

III. Is the East Using East-South Trade as a Correction Device for Balance-of-Payments Problems?

The foregoing observations suggest a very limited direct role for the South in the manufacturing structural adjustment of CMEA countries other than residual supplier of an *ad hoc* nature. More structural seems to be the role of the South in the balance-of-payments adjustment of the CMEA countries. Such institutional characteristics of the CMEA countries as central planning and the monopoly of foreign trade allows them to take an integrated view of their foreign trade flows and use trade with developing countries as a potential vehicle for an overall balance-of-payments adjustment. There is empirical evidence that, in addition to conventional gains, the CMEA countries derive *special hard-currency gains* from trade with the South, though the precise magnitude of such gains cannot be determined due to data limitations with regard to payment arrangements among socialist and developing countries.

Though some analysts are skeptical about the CMEA countries' ability to reduce their debt towards the West in a significant way by earning hard currency surplus in their trade with developing countries,[15] the newly emerging view attributes a considerable role to the Eastern hard currency surplus *vis-à-vis* the South in offsetting the CMEA countries' hard currency deficits with the West, and in servicing their foreign debts.[16] A shifting combination of export drive, sharp import reduction and re-exports of Middle East and North African oil to the West was consciously used, especially in the first half of the 1980s, to maximize hard currency earnings from trade with the South. This was particularly the case with the oil producing countries of the Middle East and North Africa.

As Table 4 shows, the estimated cumulative trade surplus of CMEA-6 for the period 1980–1986 is US$13.2 billion against $9.1 billion earned in trade with the West. The contribution of surplus with the South is considerable by any measure, but it is especially so given the comparatively marginal share of developing countries in the CMEA-6's overall trade. With the recent collapse of oil prices and the resulting weakness of the OPEC countries' import capacity, the CMEA countries are no longer able to use trade with the Middle East and North Africa as an instrument to offset financial imbalances with the West as effectively as earlier.

Table 4.   Convertible Currency Trade Balance of CMEA6
(in billion dollars)

Year	Market Economies	Developed Market Economies	Developing Market Economies
1980	-2.9	-2.3	-0.6
1981	1.4	-2.0	3.4
1982	5.2	1.7	3.5
1983	6.0	3.7	2.3
1984	7.3	4.7	2.6
1985	4.6	2.7	1.9
1986	0.7	0.6	0.1

Sources: For 1980-81, estimates of the Vienna Institute for Comparative Economic Systems and for trade balances of German Democratic Republic derived from data in United Nations, **Monthly Bulletin of Statistics**, July 1986; for 1982-86, estimates of UN ECE secretariat (**Economic Bulletin for Europe**, Vol. 38, United Nations, 1986). The table is taken from Bartlomiej Kaminski, "External Dimension of Balance of Payments Adjustment in Eastern Europe," University of Maryland, College Park, MD (mimeo).

Before jumping too early to the conclusion that the South has fallen victim to the balance-of-payments adjustment of the CMEA, it must be seen that in the first half of the 1980s an interrelated triangle of international payments emerged whose importance, however, has declined in the most recent period:

Middle East purchases of East bloc goods are paid partly by deliveries of oil and partly by surplus cash earned from oil sales in the developed West. East bloc re-exports of Middle Eastern oil to the developed West augment cash surplus and the entire trade surplus of the East bloc in the Middle East is used to offset the East bloc payments deficit in the developed West; the surplus the developed West earns in its payments transactions with the East bloc is then used to offset its own trade deficit in the Middle East.[17]

IV. Is the East an Underperformer
in Providing Economic Assistance to the South?

Perhaps the most controversial element of East-South economic relations is the aid provided by the CMEA countries to the Third World.

As is well known, in their official statements the socialist countries invariably disclaim any responsibility for the existing conditions of the South and consequently reject all demands for targeted and automatic resource transfer. Since there is no systematic reporting in the socialist countries on aid flows, it has become customary to rely on Western estimates, which are based on highly unsatisfactory and insufficient data. Nevertheless, Western estimates consistently show the CMEA countries as underperformers in aid provision relative to the Western countries and that the overwhelming portion of the aid goes to a few socialist developing countries.

The evaluation of CMEA aid is made difficult not only by the critical nature of the data problem, but also by the fact that the CMEA countries provide assistance in *more complex* forms than is usual among the OECD countries. In addition to the established transfer mechanisms, the CMEA countries, particularly the USSR, provide resource transfer to the socialist developing countries in a variety of ways: pricing arrangements (i.e., price subsidies in the form of selling Soviet oil at lower than the world price or purchasing goods at higher than the prevailing world market price), concessionary terms in the payment for technical assistance provided by the socialist countries, training of Third World students free of charge or at concessionary terms, the provision of favorable maritime transport rates, allowing trade deficits to accumulate, or cancelling or transferring them into concessional loans, etc. Of course, against this have to be set various advantages sometimes obtained by CMEA countries when, for instance, they resell developing country products imported under bilateral agreements on the world market, or acquire fishing rights, etc.[18]

If these forms of aid are also accounted for, the CMEA countries' performance is quite comparable to that of the West. According to official Soviet announcements, the USSR's aid from 1976 to 1980 amounted to 30 billion rubles, allegedly corresponding to 1 percent of the country's GNP over this period. Another official announcement put the 1983 Soviet development assistance at 1.2 percent of the country's GNP. At the 1983 UNCTAD VI session official statements were made by several small CMEA countries. The German Democratic Republic claimed for 1982 total economic assistance equal to 0.79 percent of its national income; Czechoslovakia 0.74 percent, and Bulgaria 0.79 percent. Unfortunately, it is not known how these figures were arrived at and what they exactly include, leaving much room for speculation.[19]

As Table 5 shows, according to OECD estimates based on its Development Assistance Committee (DAC) definitions, total CMEA aid amounted to some US$3 billion a year since the early 1980s. This corresponded to about 0.20 percent of the combined GNP of the member countries. The report of the OECD Development Assistance Committee

Table 5. CMEA Countries' Net Disbursements to
Developing Countries and Multilateral Agencies
(million dollars, current prices and exchange rates)

	1975	1980	1981	1982	1983	1984P
A. Bilateral assistance net of which:						
1. LDCs members of CMEA	1,220	1,822	2,212	2,297	2,347	2,347
2. Other socialist countries	65	456	389	275	411	217
3. Other developing countries	146	97	18	27	-15	-9
4. Scholarships	71	310	360	417	415	415
Total	1,502	2,685	2,979	3,016	3,158	3,024
B. Multilateral contributions	10	14	12	10	9	9
C. Overall total	1,512	2,699	2,991	3,026	3,167	3,033
As % of GNP	0.14	0.17	0.21	0.21	0.21	0.21

P=provisional

Source: OECD/DAC, **Development Cooperation: 1985 Review.** Paris, OECD, 1985, p. 115.

mentions the possibility of underestimation of the CMEA aid flows as it ignores the non-conventional forms of resource transfer. It is quite reasonable to assume that the realistic measure of CMEA aid performance lies somewhere between the downward-biased OECD estimate and the upward-biased official CMEA estimates. On this assumption, CMEA's aid performance does not appear inferior. Even the OECD's downward-biased figure of 0.20 percent compares quite well with the United States (0.24 percent as 1983–84 average), Italy (0.28 percent), or Austria (0.26 percent).[20] This is especially so if one takes into consideration the considerable development and welfare gap between the CMEA and OECD countries, the smaller economic potential and persistent domestic economic difficulties of the CMEA countries, the fact of having its own "Third World" (Soviet Central Asia), the resource requirements of East-West system competition and confrontation, as well as the fact that the CMEA countries do not obtain profit income in their transactions with the South which is comparable in any meaningful way with that of the OECD countries.

V. Main Forces Shaping the Future Evolution
of East-South Economic Interactions

There are a few major forces one can identify which will underlie East-South economic relations over the next 15 years. There is an underlying trend in East European countries for the *labor force to become increasingly scarce and increasingly expensive,* especially if one takes into account the sluggish productivity growth. From this fact one can draw certain conclusions for prospective East-South economic relations. The socialist countries will be increasingly forced to import manufactured goods from the South in order to upgrade and modernize their industrial structure. The structural policy of CMEA countries at the moment is inadequate with respect to needs and requirements. Existing policy tends to result in a situation where a new development amounts to putting one more layer to the existing structure. The industrial structure as a result gets very complex and overly diverse. Such development cannot be very successful as a result of the lack of development resources which hinders the emergence and growth of new sectors and the technological upgrading of the existing ones. This is to a large extent because the socialist economies bear the burden of those enterprises and industries that have been created in the past and, despite their long-term inefficiency, have managed to stay alive and whose assurance of survival is provided at the expense of new sectors.

The South potentially can play a significant role in the adjustment policy of Eastern Europe by freeing resources in those sectors where the socialist countries have clearly lost their comparative advantage. Via conscious structural policy the socialist countries can make room for adjustment by redeploying certain lines of activities to the South and by engaging in accelerated manufactured goods imports from developing countries. This has been the case with respect to Western Europe and North America and it is clear that the structural accommodation of the increased manufactured goods imports from the South has been a painful process, especially for Western Europe. This structural accommodation has not happened so far in the case of Eastern Europe, but it should happen. Otherwise the CMEA countries will find it even more difficult to compete on the world markets because of the inferior quality of the products which results from an overly complex and inflexible economic and industrial structure. The socialist countries have a potential advantage over the market-economy countries that allows them to anticipate structural changes and to implement this adjustment in a planned way. This advantage, however, is not automatically captured. There seems to be a recognition lag on the part of Eastern Europe concerning the importance of industrialization processes in the Third World. There should be a push towards recognizing the need and importance of a structural shift toward less labor- and material-intensive lines of production in Eastern Europe.

A set of "environmental factors" conditioning the prospective evolution of East-South economic interaction is related to changes in the major trading areas of the individual socialist countries. With respect to the CMEA, the important variable will be the *rapidity of the integration process*. One of the major "environmental factors" in the CMEA, which is related to prospective East-South relations, is the natural resource situation. CMEA integration has been to a large extent an extractive industry integration. The *extractive sector* has been the prime mover of the integration process. One can see a deceleration in the integration process as a result of the problems the socialist countries have encountered in the area of extractive industry. The Soviet extractive industry has entered into a new stage in its evolution which cannot be considered dynamic. In some sectors of the Soviet extractive industry there is a significant deceleration of growth and in the case of oil production there is a levelling-off tendency as opposed to a dynamic output increase in the past. This, of course, will be reflected also in the Soviet Union's ability to export natural resources to Eastern Europe. The latter will become increasingly hard commodities within CMEA, almost being the equivalent of hard currency, and they will be difficult to obtain.[21]

This is the current situation. On the basis of the underlying forces in the CMEA I do not foresee any major improvement over the next fifteen years in this area. Actually the situation can get even worse which then may result in serious policy implications for the CMEA-6. Projections indicate that a rise in imports of several major fuels and minerals from non-socialist countries (mainly developing countries) to meet the growing needs of East European countries seems inevitable.[22] Therefore, it is likely that there will continue to be a *competing demand* in the CMEA countries' import of Southern manufactures and primary goods. Earlier I pointed out the necessity of accelerating manufactured goods imports from the South but, on the other hand, the acute problems in the area of natural resource supply can make this evolution towards greater manufactured goods imports very difficult, if not impossible. This depends, of course, on the volume of import needs of the socialist countries with respect to major minerals and fuel. Thus, this is a big question mark, a policy decision dilemma for the East European countries as to how to proceed in this contradictory situation. One possible way to resolve this trade-off in favor of manufactured goods imports would be to decelerate the rate of growth of energy and raw materials consumption, which historically has been excessively rapid as a result of the centrally planned economies' systemic propensity toward over-consumption.[23] There is a considerable potential for decreasing the margin of over-consumption, but this is geared to the reform of the whole institutional set-up, including the incentive structure facing the consumers of these economies.[24] This policy option, then, interrelates the commodity pattern of CMEA imports from the South with domestic economic reform.

The qualitative problems of CMEA integration are most manifest in the area of manufacturing industry integration. The coming period will probably bring a further exacerbation of the problems of intra-CMEA manufacturing export because export growth in every CMEA country will have to be stimulated by the qualitative improvement of manufacturing. "Soft goods" imports from partners, however, will not provide a sufficient base for that.

The crucial condition for the significant qualitative improvement of intra-CMEA manufacturing cooperation is the widespread evolution of direct interfirm cooperation. That, however, requires autonomous enterprises, which in turn means that the future of the whole system of manufacturing cooperation is a function of economic reform in the CMEA countries. However, in most of the member countries the implementation of a reform that is not just symbolic cannot be predicted with certainty. The currently prevailing national economic mechanisms and the mechanism of CMEA-level cooperation reinforce one another and run counter to the widespread development of manufacturing integration. The established system of cooperation fails to stimulate the creation of export capacities producing competitive goods for the world market. In such a situation the more intensive expansion of the division of labor with the non-CMEA countries would be a natural outcome. The South may be one of these partners, particularly in view of the latter's potentially important structural role in creating a more selective and up-graded industrial profile in the CMEA countries.

The expected evolution of *trade between the OECD countries and the developing countries* in the next period will exert a considerable, although indirect, influence on the external conditions of economic cooperation with the developing countries and the criteria of partner choice in the Third World.

In the period up to the year 2000 the manufactures exports of the developing countries are expected to maintain the dynamic growth established in the past decade despite the moderate growth of the world economy and protectionist measures. The developing countries' traditional goods markets may also expand, although under the combined effect of the declining growth of demand and protectionist measures market penetration will be slow. The United States, the EEC, and Japan intend to cut or even abolish their preferences granted to the more advanced developing countries.[25] The above factors will encourage a further diversification and product up-grading in the sphere of manufactures exports on the part of the developing countries. In the case of such labor-intensive goods as china, glassware, and furniture, where the developing countries are represented by a relatively small market share, export to the developed countries will grow dynamically. A rapid export expansion is expected for products characterized by a high income elasticity, such as sporting goods. The export of semifinished goods and parts also provides great opportunities. The share of capital and technology-intensive products will grow at the expense of labor intensive products.

In view of the above, the share of the OECD countries in the overall trade relations of the developing countries will remain decisive up to the turn of the century.

Those developing countries that are most seriously affected by the limiting measures imposed by the OECD countries, or are less competitive than other Third World exporters, might tend to enhance their economic relations with the CMEA in order to diminish their dependence on the markets of the OECD countries and to intensify their exports by market diversification. An eventual *redirection of relations* in favor of the socialist countries greatly depends on the degree to which the CMEA countries open their markets to the products of the developing countrie⌐ and succeed in eliminating, by developing more advanced and long-term forms of cooperation, their own relative disadvantage in the choice of partners by the developing countries.

Within the set of long-term conditions of cooperation with the developing countries, the intensification of an *intra-Third World division of labor* is gaining more importance and, if approached passively, might contribute to the East's relative loss of ground in the Third World. A far-sighted and aggressive marketing policy may temper the possible disadvantageous consequences of the process in question and may even open up new opportunities for cooperation for the CMEA countries.

The strengthening of intra-Third World links has thus far manifested itself first and foremost in the dynamic increase of their trade with one another. In the long run the rate of growth of intra-Third World trade will remain higher than that of world trade and that of the Third World's trade with the other groups of countries. Consequently, an increasing proportion of their exports will go to other developing countries; that is, a growing share of the import demands of the developing countries will be met by exports from other developing countries.

The intensification of South-South economic cooperation has already had a significant impact on the economic relations of the socialist and the developing countries. In the past decade the European CMEA has lost more ground in the export and import markets of the developing countries than the OECD countries, although the socialist countries' share in these markets is very small. Moreover, the greatest loss in the CMEA exports to the developing countries occurred in that very group (machinery and transport equipment) which underwent the most dynamic increase in the intra–Third World trade. Thus the main losers in the expansion of intra-South trade have become the least competitive marginal partners. The promotion of integration into South-South cooperation is a very significant task for the CMEA countries. Otherwise cooperation among developing countries will inevitably exert a permanent negative influence on the CMEA's marketing ability in the Third World, with special regard to manufacturers (especially machines and transport equipment), a sphere where intra–Third World trade is expected to grow fast.

The prospective evolution of *East-West economic exchanges*, as part of the world economic environment indirectly influencing East-South ties, will play an important role in the future. In the 1970s East-West economic relations developed rather rapidly, and the general dynamics of East-West trade was determined by the import needs of the socialist countries. However, the current decade has seen a situation in which the export capabilities of the socialist countries condition the growth of East-West trade. In looking at the CMEA countries' export capabilities objectively and the overall import environment in the OECD countries, one cannot be very optimistic about the prospective potential for growth in East-West trade. There is going to be sluggish growth in this segment of world trade even if the West successfully recovers from the recent recession. The foreign debt situation of most of the East European countries is obviously a constraining factor. Furthermore, to some extent the tendency towards politicization of East-West trade will act as a factor deterring some CMEA countries from East-West relations. The degree of this deterrence will vary with individual socialist countries. The politicization attempts on the part of the United States, which have had some impact on Western Europe and Japan, and the resulting policy uncertainty in the context of East-West economic relations, will not go unnoticed by some of the CMEA countries and potentially may result in a re-direction of efforts to trade with alternative actors. This has been demonstrated, for example, by the USSR with its switch to Southern suppliers for food imports. In the resulting situation the significance of developing countries as alternative export and import markets will probably increase.

An important conditioning factor for East-South exchange will be the prospective evolution of *Third World economic growth*. It is probably correct to suppose that over the next fifteen years the Third World as a whole will develop at a significantly higher rate of growth than the rest of the world. I believe that as the West recovers from the present economic malaise so will most of the South, given the empirically observable strong linkage between growth process in the West and the South. Objective conditions existing in the South will warrant a significantly higher rate of growth for these countries and, by implication, a significantly higher rate of growth of import demand.[26] So, as in the past, during the next fifteen years the developing countries will constitute the most dynamically expanding import markets. There is going to be a continuing shift of economic dynamism towards extra-European territories and the CMEA countries can try to capture the opportunities of growing import demands, although the rapidity of the import increase of the developing countries will not be as strong as it was in the 1970s.

The "push" and "pull" forces discussed above, acting in the foreign and domestic economic environment of the CMEA countries, suggest that in the coming period, the greatest room for maneuver will open up for CMEA economies in relation to the Third World. The combined impact of the above processes in the world economy affecting the long-term economic relations between the East and the South makes it possible and even imperative that the Third World's share in overall CMEA trade be increased significantly.

The intensification of CMEA countries' relations with the developing countries and the exploitation of the inherent opportunities for cooperation require the performance of several foreign economic tasks, the most important of which seem to be the following:

1. Long-term economic strategy and, as part of it, structural policy and foreign economic policy should have clear and definitive aims relating to the developing countries. The Third World should be integrated into a structural policy of the CMEA countries. Treating the Third World as a residual (that is, shortage-eliminating and surplus-discharging) sphere is untenable in the long run.
2. Instead of the prevailing *ad hoc* relations, it would be useful to establish a long-term and stable division of labor corresponding to the aims of the East's long-term structural policy endeavors, to the fundamental economic interests of the developing countries, and to the basic trends of the international division of labor.
3. The excessive fluctuation of trade with the developing countries must be checked by a careful choice of partners and the establishment of more profound division of labor relations.
4. In this context the geographical radius of East-South trade and cooperation relations must be increased, especially in the direction of the steadily and rapidly expanding solvent markets, including the NICs.

5. The present commodity pattern of East-South trade is unsuitable for the dynamic development of mutual economic relations. In Eastern exports a deliberate structural shift is required that would reduce the share of those products for which the developing countries present a growing challenge both in Western and Third World markets. The relatively high proportion of raw material and energy-intensive goods and semifinished products in Eastern exports is in contradiction with both the endowments of most of the CMEA economies and the basic trends of industrialization in the developing countries.

6. Within Eastern imports from the developing countries, the share of nontraditional goods, especially semifinished goods and certain manufactured products (machinery and consumer manufactures among others), should be increased in order to move toward a more selective industrial structure in the East.

7. The organizational forms and mechanisms of cooperation require substantial modernization and the widespread implementation of more flexible, complex, and permanent forms of cooperation, including foreign direct investment ties. Past experience demonstrates that the intensity of cooperation depends, to a great extent, on the chosen institutional form. As opposed to the existing practice, the East should strive to create not only export- but also import-oriented cooperation deals. It would be useful in this respect to redeploy, partially or totally, those domestic productive activities which have lost their competitiveness at home to certain developing countries.

Summary and Conclusions

In the foregoing analysis an attempt has been made to discern the underlying forces shaping East-South exchanges and to identify the nature of an implicit division of labor between the two groups of countries. It was found that the East's middle position between West and South is an important key in explaining the pattern of East-South trade. This trade shows a surprisingly rigid pattern over time and currently reflects a more traditional North-South type division of labor than does West-South trade.

A simple Hecksher-Ohlin framework was applied to explain the sources of comparative advantages in East-South trade and it was found that the specialization pattern is broadly consistent with the prediction of the factor proportions theory of trade: the CMEA-6 has developed a growing comparative advantage *vis-à-vis* the South in mature product-cycle goods and capital-intensive Hecksher-Ohlin goods. Simultaneously, the South has revealed increasing comparative advantage *vis-à-vis* the East in natural-resource intensive commodities. An anomaly has been detected, however, in terms of Eastern trade surplus in labor-intensive Hecksher-Ohlin goods. This area of "wrong specialization" or under-trading reflects such factors as slow progress toward a selective industrial policy in the East in accordance with comparative advantage: manufactures imports being consistently "crowded out" by higher priority primary goods imports; the Eastern objective of hard-currency maximization and lack of involvement in the rapidly unfolding export-oriented industrialization drive of the NICs.

While the CMEA maintains its "Northern" structural profile *vis-à-vis* the South as a whole in direct trade relations, it has been facing a steady erosion of its competitiveness in Western markets for manufactured goods *vis-à-vis* a limited number of NICs. There is evidence that the CMEA countries have started to lose their earlier established technological edge over the most advanced group of NICs, and thus they are being progressively outmatched even in the category of technology-intensive goods. This East-NICs competitive interface in the OECD markets for manufactures, with obvious damaging consequences for the East in terms of potential benefits from trade with the West, constitutes perhaps the most significant dimension of overall East-South interactions in the recent period. This open trade conflict underlies Eastern reservations against West-South trade preferences (not applied in East-West trade) as well as Eastern motives for keeping trade concessions to the South down to a minimum. There are indications that East-South competition has become more generalized and it appears in Western markets for food products, for credit, for technology transfer, and for the favorable attention of Western multinational corporations in the area of foreign direct investments.

There is reasonably strong evidence that, despite the relatively limited scope of overall East-South exchanges in the first half of the 1980s, the CMEA countries have been able to take advantage of an East-West-South payments triangle through which the East has used its hard-currency surplus *vis-à-vis* the South to offset a considerable part of its financial imbalances with the West. The particular circumstances which gave rise to this possibility have largely disappeared by now. Thus, the ability of the CMEA countries to use East-South trade as an important vehicle for overall balance-of-payments adjustment has become rather limited.

In the evaluation of Eastern aid performance the necessity of a complex approach, which takes into consideration East-South resource transfers effected through non-traditional channels, is emphasized. It is concluded that Eastern aid performance is comparable with that of the West, particularly if one takes into account the East-West development gap, the resource requirements of East-West confrontation, and the differences in financial income derived from relations with the South.

Perhaps the most significant generalization that emerges from this chapter is the surprisingly small *autonomous* economic content and rationale behind East-South economic relations. It is suggested that these relations are basically of a residual character and importance for both the East and the South. They can be understood in good part only by reference to the disequilibria occurring in relations with other groups of countries and to domestic and regional supply constraints prevailing in the CMEA. The analysis of the various forces which are expected to influence the prospective environment of East-South exchange suggests, however, the likelihood of a more meaningful and significant future role for East-South trade in the overall foreign economic relations of both groups of countries.

Notes

1. Bulgaria, Czechoslovakia, the German Democratic Republic, Hungary, Poland, Romania, and the Soviet Union. We distinguish a separate group, CMEA-6, which excludes the Soviet Union. For convenience the European CMEA countries are frequently referred to as East and the developing countries as South.

2. See, *inter alia*, Elizabeth Kridl Valkenier, *The Soviet Union and the Third World: An Economic Bind*, New York, Praeger, 1983; Marvin R. Jackson, ed., *East-South Trade. Economics and Political Economics*, A special issue of *Soviet and Eastern European Foreign Trade*, Armonk, N.Y., 1985; Robert Cassen, ed., *Soviet Interests in the Third World*, London, Sage Publications, 1985; Istvan Dobozi, ed., *Economic Cooperation between Socialist and Developing Countries*, Budapest, Hungarian Scientific Council for World Economy, 1978; Leon Zevin, *Economic Cooperation of Socialist and Developing Countries: New Trends*, Moscow, Nauka, 1975; *Sotrudnichestvo sotsialisticheskikh i razvivayushchikhsia stran: novyi tip mezhdunarodnykh otnosenii*, (Cooperation between the Socialist and the Developing Countries: A New Type of International Relations), Moscow, Nauka, 1980; Deepak Nayyar, ed., *Economic Relations between Socialist Countries and the Third World*, London, Macmillian, 1977; Marie Lavigne, *Les Relations Est-Sud dans l'Economie Mondiale*, Paris, Economica, 1986.

3. Thomas A. Wolf has applied gravity models to Soviet-Third World trade to identify the underlying determinants such as complementarity of trade structure, distance, payments mechanism, political orientation and level of development. See "Soviet Trade with the Third World: A Quantitative Assessment," *Osteuropa-Wirtschaft*, No. 4, 1985, pp. 273–295; T.A. Wolf, "An Empirical Analysis of Soviet Economic Relations with Developing Countries," *Soviet Economy*, No. 1, 1986.

4. UN, *Monthly Bulletin of Statistics*, May 1986.

5. This characteristic of the Eastern economies is emphasized, *inter alia,* in G. Adler-Karlsson, *Western Economic Warfare 1947–1967,* Stockholm, Almqvist and Wiksell, 1968; Marie Lavigne, "Consequences of Economic Developments in Eastern Europe for East-West Relations," *Trade and Development,* No. 4, 1983, pp. 129–143; Istvan Dobozi, "Prospects for East-South Economic Interaction in the Changing International Environment," in Marvin R. Jackson, *East-South Trade* . . . , pp. 27–39.

6. See especially Juergen B. Donges, "The North-South-East Competition in the Market for Industrial Products," paper prepared for a GERPI-sponsored Symposium on "The Future of North-South-East Economic Relations," at the *Maison des Sciences de l'Homme,* Paris, January 20–21, 1978; Richard Portes, "East, West, and South: The Role of the Centrally Planned Economies in the International Economy," *Discussion Paper Number 630,* Harvard Institute of Economic Research, Harvard University, Cambridge, Massachusetts, June 1978.

7. Rozalia Bogo, "The CMEA Countries and Imports of Manufactures from the Third World," Budapest, 1985 (mimeo); UN, *Monthly Bulletin of Statistics,* May 1986.

8. Rozalia Bogo, *Ibid.*

9. Thomas A. Wolf, "Soviet Trade . . . ," p. 294.

10. *Külkereskedelmi Statisztikai Evkönyv 1983,* (Foreign Trade Statistical Yearbook 1983), Budapest, Hungarian Statistical Office, 1984.

11. Marie Lavigne, "Consequences . . . ," p. 141; E. Palocz-Nemeth, "Exports of Manufactures of CMEA and Developing Countries to Developed Industrial Countries," *Acta Oeconomica,* No. 12, 1981, p. 105; Kazimierz Poznanski, "Competition between Eastern Europe and Developing Countries in the Western Market for Manufactured Goods," in Joint Economic Committee, Congress of the United States, *East European Economies: Slow Growth in the 1980s,* Volume 2: Foreign Trade and International Finance, Washington, U.S. Government Printing Office, 1986, pp. 62–90. Besides the evolution of relative market shares for the CMEA-6 and the NIC's in the OECD manufactures import market, Poznanski uses export-unit values (i.e., prices per kilogram) to indicate the eroding technological and product quality edge of the CMEA-6 over the NICs. His findings reveal that the NICs very rarely sell manufactures of lowest relative price (calculated per kilogram), whereas CMEA-6 does it quite often. In the ten product categories the lowest export unit price was usually paid to one of the CMEA-6 countries. For instance, Poland obtained only $1.98 per kilogram of its textile and leather machinery, as compared with the $6.25 per paid on the OECD-Europe market to Taiwan (pp. 70–71). The above implies that in some product categories at least, relative competitiveness between the East and the NIC's is increasingly determined by nonprice factors such as product quality and technological sophistication.

12. K. Poznanski, "Competition . . . ," pp. 65–66.

13. Inotai Andras, "Uj iranyzatok a nemzetkozi ipari munkamegosztasban: magyar szemszogbol" (New Trends in the International Industrial Division of Labor: A Hungarian Perspective) *Kozgazdasagi Szemle,* Budapest, No. 9, 1986, p. 1028.

14. In 1980, for instance, the European Community imported 54.8 percent of all manufactured goods purchased by the OECD countries, but only 39.7 percent of those coming from CMEA-6 and NICs combined. In contrast, the share of the U.S. in total OECD manufactured imports was 17.6 percent, but the respective share in the imports from CMEA-6 and the NICs was 50.6 percent. (K. Poznanski, "Competition . . . ," p. 72). The most successful Asian NICs are extremely reliant on the U.S. for their manufactured goods export trade.

15. Marie Lavigne, "Consequences . . . ," p. 139; Daniel Pineye-Georges Sokoloff, "Les echanges Est-Sud," *Economie Prospective Internationale*, No. 1, 1986.

16. Laure Despres, "Eastern Europe and the Third World: Economic Interactions and Policies," paper presented at the Third World Congress for Soviet and East European Studies, Washington, October 30–November 4, 1985; Istvan Dobozi, "Prospects . . . ," pp. 29–30.

17. Jan Vanous, "Soviet and Financial Relations with the Middle East," in Marvin R. Jackson, *East-South Trade* . . . , p. 95.

18. OECD/DAC, *Development Cooperation: 1985 Review*, Paris, OECD 1985, p. 116.

19. Siegfried Schultz and Heinrich Machowski, "CMEA Countries: Economic Relations with the Third World," *Interconomics*, No. 4, 1986, p. 197; Marie Lavigne, "Eastern Europe . . . ," in Joint Economic Committee, p. 45.

20. OECD/DAC, *Development Cooperation* . . . , p. 295.

21. Istvan Dobozi, "Intra-CMEA mineral cooperation. Implications for trade with OECD and Third World countries," *Resources Policy*, September 1986, pp. 187–203.

22. Istvan Dobozi, "World Raw Material Markets until the Year 2000—Implications for Eastern Europe," *Raw Materials Report*, No. 2, 1983, pp. 7–19.

23. My econometric estimation shows that the centrally planned economies as a whole consume considerably more steel, aluminum and primary energy than their market-economy counterparts in the West, after controlling for various non-system influences on resource use. The point estimates show a margin of systemic over-consumption (relative to the Western control group) amounting to 36 percent in steel (both in per capita and per unit of GDP terms), 43 percent in aluminum (per capita) and 63 percent in primary energy (per capita; 84 percent per unit of GDP). See Istvan Dobozi, "Are the Centrally Planned Economies Over-consuming Metals? A Cross-sectional Analysis," *Materials and Society*, No. 3, 1986, pp. 351–367.

24. Istvan Dobozi, "The 'Invisible' Source of 'Alternative' Energy. Comparing Energy Conservation Performance of the East and West," *Natural Resources Forum*, No. 3, 1983, pp. 201–216.

25. Pressure is especially mounting for the discontinuation of U.S. preferential tariffs system for import from the four successful Asian NICs (South Korea, Taiwan, Singapore and Hong Kong). In 1986 the United States already removed fifty-seven Taiwanese items from the list of goods to which preferential tariff rates are applied. Akiyoshi Mori, "Exchange Rate and Export Trends in the Asian NICs," *Tokyo Financial Review*, Bank of Tokyo, September 1986, p. 5.

26. The World Bank projects for the period 1985–95 an average annual growth rate of 4.3 percent (high case) or 2.5 percent (low case) for the industrial countries and 6.4 percent (high case) or 4.0 percent (low case) for the developing countries. The latter's import growth is projected to be 7.7 percent (high) or 3.4 percent (low). See World Bank, *World Development Report 1986*, Oxford University Press, 1986, p. 44.

8

East-South Capital Cooperation: An Unexploited Possibility?*

Jan Monkiewicz and Grazyna Monkiewicz

Introduction

Economic relations between Eastern Europe and the developing countries are characterized by a clear domination of pure trade transactions. Both the size of the cooperation arrangements as well as direct capital linkages are insignificant and apparently do not provide any substantial stimulus to further diversification and enlargement of the traditional trade links.[1]

The lack of institutional innovations in interregional relations, coupled with the development of the general economic situation existing in the two groups of countries and the prevailing international environment have resulted, *inter alia*, in a modest role for interregional trade flows. The share of developing countries in CMEA trade oscillated throughout the period between 1970–1986 at around thirteen to fourteen percent of the total. It has showed only a slight tendency to increase since the beginning of the 1980s. In addition the structure of the bilateral trade has been very traditional, providing no special opportunities for a more dynamic cooperation. Still, in CMEA imports from the South, food (SITC 0+1) and raw materials (SITC 2+3+4) constitute over eighty five percent of the total. In exports on the other hand, around two-thirds of the total are industrial products.[2]

It may be argued that one possible way out of the existing situation would be an intensification of interregional direct capital linkages. This might be taken as a bold statement considering the existing traditions,

---

*The authors are indebted to O. Bagniewski of the University of Hamburg for his helpful comments.

the prevailing infrastructure of the present world economy, and the overall indebtedness of the partners in question. In what follows we shall elaborate more extensively on that, concentrating our attention on the position of the CMEA countries in this respect.

Some Statistics

Official statistics on foreign investments of the CMEA countries do not exist. However, due to the pioneering work of McMillan and, more recently, Zaleski and UNCTAD, the overall picture is now more or less known.[3] According to McMillan, at the end of 1983 there were around 650 enterprises world wide with Eastern European direct capital involvement. Of these around 440 were in the developed market economies and the rest (213) in the developing world. This means that in around a third of all instances they are located in the developing countries; perfectly proportional to their share in extra-CMEA trade (see Table 1). There are quite substantial differences among the three cited sources on the exact number of enterprises operating in the South. McMillan refers to 213 companies, Zaleski to 168, and UNCTAD indicates 152. Whichever figure is taken, however, does not change the basic picture. It is clear that it is by no means a massive phenomenon, either from the point of view of the CMEA or from that of the developing countries. The reported data indicate differing intensities with regard to geographical location of said investments, as well as a differing propensity on the part of individual CMEA member states toward direct capital links with the South.

Africa seems to be the preferred area of capital penetration by the CMEA countries, with roughly half the total operating companies set up there. It is followed by Latin America (around one-fourth) and thereafter by the Middle East (around one-fifth of the total). It may be worthwhile to note that such a geographical pattern of CMEA investment in the South differs significantly from that which is observed in case of the developed capitalist countries. As reported by the United Nations Center on Transnational Corporations, out of the total direct investment stock in developing countries as of the end of 1978, over fifty-seven percent was located in Latin America, over twenty-six percent in Asia (excluding Middle East), 12.6 percent in Africa, and around four percent in the Middle East.[4]

During the 1980s the picture has been undergoing major changes, but again in different directions from that of the CMEA countries. As indicated by recent UNCTC statistics, around forty-five percent of the total inflow of foreign direct investments to developing countries in 1980–85 was destined for Asia (excluding the Middle East), over thirty-

Table 1. Number of enterprises with CMEA capital participation according to McMillan,* Zaleski, and UNCTAD

Region	Bulgaria	Czecho-slovakia	GDR	Hungary	Poland	Romania	Soviet Union	Total
Africa								
McMillan	15	8	-	13	20	33	13	102
Zaleski	6	5	-	5	10	30	14	70
UNCTAD	10	4	-	6	16	26	5	67
Asia								
McMillan	6	3	0	6	8	3	9	36
Zaleski	5	2	1	10	6	2	7	33
UNCTAD	6	5	-	8	-	1	3	23
Latin America								
McMillan	1	24	2	11	6	8	1	52
Zaleski	-	7	2	8	3	7	9	36
UNCTAD	1	20	2	3	7	4	-	37
Middle East								
McMillan	12	3	-	14	3	10	4	46
Zaleski	3	2	-	9	5	6	4	29
UNCTAD	5	1	-	9	1	9	-	25
Total								
McMillan	34	38	2	44	37	54	27	236
Zaleski	14	16	3	32	24	45	34	168
UNCTAD	22	30	2	256	24	40	8	152

Note: *   Of the total number reported by McMillan twenty-three were known to be no longer operational as of the end of 1983.

Source: C.H.McMillan, Multinationals from the Second World ... op.cit. pp. 36-37; E.Zaleski, Socialist Multinationals ... op.cit. p. 157; UNCTAD Data Bank on CMEA investments in developing countries.

four percent to Latin America, around fifteen percent to Africa, and 5.7 percent to the Middle East.[5]

An overwhelming portion of these companies is concentrated in a handful of countries. In the Middle East, Lebanon, Iran, and Egypt hosted around ninety percent of all CMEA companies operating in the region. In Asia, India, Singapore, and Thailand hosted nearly eighty-two percent of all the companies in the region; in Latin America around fifty-six percent of all such companies were located in Peru, Mexico, and Argentina; while in Africa only forty-nine percent were located in Nigeria, Morocco, and Libya.[6] Thus Africa has both the largest number of CMEA companies and, at the same time, has the most even distribution among different countries of all regions. The leading CMEA investor in developing countries is Romania, followed by Hungary, Czechoslovakia, and Bulgaria. The GDR is a clear laggard, with Poland and USSR playing an intermediary role. Poland, Romania, the USSR, and Bulgaria are most active in Africa; Hungary in Middle East and Czechoslovakia in Latin America (see Table 1).

According to both McMillan and Zaleski around half the companies were primarily concerned with production activities and the other half in services. The share of services in overall investments of the socialist states is apparently higher than in cases of investments originating in the developed capitalist countries. According to UNCTC estimates roughly one-third of the total stock of direct investments located in the developing world by the latter was operating in services.[7]

On the other hand the sectoral distribution of CMEA investments is close to the pattern observed in intra-developing countries' investment flows.[8] The recorded picture is in sharp contrast to the pattern of activities of CMEA companies in the West. In those cases less than ten percent of the total number of operating companies is primarily engaged in production.[9] These findings are roughly confirmed by official statistics on Polish companies abroad. At the end of 1985 thirty-six percent of all companies with Polish capital operating in the developing countries were primarily concerned with production, whereas the same figure for the Western countries was five percent.[10] Assembly and manufacturing dominate production activities whereas trading activities are of primary importance in the service sector (see Table 2).

An overwhelming portion of the CMEA companies operating in the South is based on joint equity arrangements with local partners, sometimes also involving Western equity participation. In 1983 wholly owned companies accounted for only about seven percent of the total; this should be distinguished from nearly twenty-three percent in case of CMEA investments in the West. Interestingly enough the same observation was recorded with respect to South-South capital ventures, which is

Table 2. Distribution of CMEA investments in the South by Activity

Activity	McMillan end of 1983 No	%	Zaleski 1984 No	%
1. Trading	60	25.4	25	14.9
2. Production	108	45.8	65	38.7
- manufacturing and assembling	59	25.0	27	16.1
- natural resources, prospecting, and development	20	8.5	14	8.3
- forestry and wood economics	3	1.3	6	3.6
- fishing and fish processing	16	6.8	7	4.2
- agricultural production	10	4.2	11	6.5
3. Services apart from trading	63	26.7	23	13.7
- construction	9	3.8	9	5.4
- banking and insurance	9	3.8	6	3.6
- transportation	26	11.0	7	4.2
4. Unknown	5	2.1	55	32.7
Total	236	100.0	168	100.0

Source: E.Zaleski, **Socialist Multinationals** ... op.cit. p. 162;
C.H.McMillan, **Multinationals from the Second World** ... op.cit. pp.
40-41.

basically interpreted as an indication of the low level of ownership specific advantages of the relevant CMEA investors. The same could be applied to CMEA investments, which are seldom based on technical or managerial superiority and thus need partnership to strengthen their market position. To some extent this could be a result of ideological considerations on the part of the CMEA countries. However, this should not be overestimated. The companies in question are relatively small undertakings, similar to the case of South-South investments. According to McMillan's estimates, total capital investments in 1978 amounted to $270.4 million and total assets reached the sum of $3.9 billion.[11] This means around $1.6 million per company in terms of investments and $23 million in terms of assets.

Using Polish figures as representative we estimate the overall CMEA capital investments for 1984 at around $600 million and assets of around $6.7 billion ($3.5 million and $28 million per company respectively). If this is true that would mean a doubling of the amount reached in 1978 and, consequently, would point to a rapid increase recently in the size of the direct capital involvement of the CMEA countries in the South. Still, however, the relative size of this involvement is insignificant. The total stock of direct investments in developing countries was estimated

Table 3.   Participation role of companies with Polish capital
           in Polish foreign trade

Item	1981	1982	1983	1984	1985
1. Exports via the said companies as a percentage of the total Polish exports to non-socialist world, of which exports to:	32.7	34.0	28.5	36.8	40.9
- developed countries	43.7	48.3	40.7	50.9	54.1
- developing world	16.8	14.4	18.8	17.7	16.9
2. Imports via the said companies as a percentage of the total imports, of which imports from:	10.7	13.8	9.5	12.0	12.4
- developed countries	-	-	-	19.0	15.0
- developing countries	-	-	-	2.0	2.0

Source: Polish Ministry of Foreign Trade.

at \$88.3 billion in 1978 and was increased between 1980–1985 by another \$6 billion.[12] That would mean that less than 0.5 percent of the total foreign capital invested in the developing world is of CMEA origin.

The importance of CMEA capital ventures in the South for the development of East-South economic relationships may be judged, however, not from the figures on capital outlays, but from the relative role of these amounts in East-South trade turnover. Unfortunately, for the time being, no overall statistics for CMEA countries are available. Therefore, we have to rely exclusively on Polish figures to extrapolate. In doing so, we should remember, perhaps, that Poland is among those CMEA countries only moderately involved in East-South capital linkages. Hence, in case of larger investors, like Romania, Hungary, and Bulgaria, the relevant figures might be considerably higher. According to the available Polish data around fifteen to nineteen percent of the country's total exports to the South have been carried out via the above mentioned companies. This is still far behind the level attained by Polish-Western trade, in which case around fifty percent of exports have been arranged through Polish companies located in the West.

As for imports the share of these Polish companies in the developing world is much lower; reaching only two percent. This sharply contrasts with fifteen to nineteen percent in the case of the developed countries (see Table 3). The fact that these companies have lower shares of East-South trade than they do of East-West trade flows is primarily the result of the different pattern of their sectoral distribution. As indicated earlier, in contrast to direct investments in the West, many fewer CMEA companies

Table 4.   Growth pattern of companies with CMEA involvement in the
West and South (per cent of the total)

	Pre-1965	1965-69	1970-74	1975-79	1980-83
1. In the West	14.1	16.1	29.3	29.1	11.2
2. In the South	3.8	12.1	32.9	30.3	20.3

Source: C.H.McMillan, **Multinationals from the Second World ...**
op.cit., pp. 162-163.

in the South were operating in the trade and service related areas and
were significantly more involved in production.

The CMEA's View as to the Role
of Its Investments in the South

CMEA direct investments in the South were practically non-existent
before the mid-sixties. They gained momentum in the first half of the
1970s and thereafter started to decelerate. More than eighty percent of
all such companies operating in the South have been set up since the
beginning of the 1970s. Their growth period coincided largely with the
growth period of CMEA direct investments in the West, which would
indicate, apparently, that the same factors were providing the stimulus.

Those factors were primarily concerned with the attempts on the part
of several CMEA countries to build up their exports and to rationalize
their production structures. These modernization programs were based
on extensive borrowing in the West (see Table 4).

Simultaneously various measures to increase exports, particularly to
the non-socialist world, were undertaken. They included, *inter alia*,
setting up of wholly or jointly owned companies abroad that were mostly
foreign trade-related.[13]

The rapidly expanding markets of the developing countries and their
improved financial position in the 1970s were offering good opportunities
for exports. They too have been explored, *inter alia*, by equity ventures
as an institutional innovation in the foreign economic activities of the
socialist countries. In case of the developing countries this has been
additionally reinforced by their policy of sometimes requesting equity
involvement from the suppliers of equipment and technology as a follow
up to the entire venture. This would to some extent explain the particular
pattern of activities in the South of companies with CMEA involvement.[14]

The hypothesis advanced by McMillan, that the relatively large share in manufacturing related ventures among the CMEA investments is due to redeployment considerations by the investing countries is not very convincing.[15] As indicated by the leading Polish expert on that country's direct investments in the South, it was specific policy throughout the 1970s to set up production oriented equity ventures in the Third World only if a normal export or import of the required products were not possible.[16] This might be well illustrated by the case of fishing and fish processing ventures in the South. A majority of them have been established in response to the creation of exclusive off-shore economic zones by several costal developing countries. Thus they constituted the *condition sine qua non* for a CMEA presence in this sector. This observation may be used to substantiate a hypothesis that the setting up of production oriented ventures in the South was a "forced" process and not a conscious attempt to redeploy or to create constant supply lines for the home markets. It also sounds very logical in view of the CMEA actors involved in foreign investments. By and large they were recruited from among foreign trade companies, with production enterprises clearly playing a secondary role. Logically enough, therefore, the established ventures had primarily trade-related targets.

All in all it seems that present CMEA investments in the South are largely of a defensive, trade supporting nature. The new companies have been set up in order to maintain trade levels already achieved and not to initiate them. If necessary they took the form of production-related ventures, but primarily with a view toward expanding the trade links between the home and host countries. They were not simply to ensure profits for the foreign investor, or to create integrated international production systems aimed at the rationalizations of production activities of the investing companies or at phasing out some outmoded technologies.

Does this mean that the aforementioned investments are of a transitional nature and will disappear in the future, to be replaced by other institutional arrangements?[17] Let us elaborate on that more extensively in the second part of this chapter.

What Is the Future
of East-South Direct Capital Cooperation?

Assuming that the internationalization processes of economic activities is of a continuous and objective nature and that all countries and economic systems are under its influence, the East-South direct capital links in the future will inevitably grow in importance. An open question, however, is when, where, and how.

Table 5. Gross foreign debt of developing
          and CMEA countries, 1986

Country	billions of US dollars
1. Developing countries of which	1035.0
Mexico	104.0
Argentina	53.0
India	41.0
Egypt	38.5
2. CMEA countries of which	110.0
Poland	33.5

Source: **Gospodarka swiatowa i gospodarka
polska** w 1986 r., SGPS, Warszawa 1987, pp.
30 and 64.

On its face the starting point is not very promising for the further development of direct capital involvement by the CMEA countries. Most of them are deeply in debt and suffer from a lack of international liquidity. On the other hand, the same is also true for the majority of the developing countries. This is particularly true with regard to those countries presently having the most CMEA investment.

As indicated in Table 5 the total gross debt of developing countries exceeds US$1 trillion and is still growing. The gross debt of the CMEA countries is a tenth of this figure, but it presents a serious problem, nevertheless, to the countries in question and their management of it is fraught with difficulties. This is particularly true with respect to Poland and Hungary, and to a lesser extent with respect to Romania and the GDR. The financial component, therefore, should be viewed as a clear impediment to the growth of CMEA direct investments. This, however, is true only so long as the hard currency portion cannot be substituted for with in kind contributions. In this case it is the technical competence that matters most.

To determine the scope for possible action a study has been carried out on the investment project proposals by developing countries submitted to the UNIDO Data Bank. The bank, organized and run by the UNIDO Investment Promotion Program, collects official information on investment projects undertaken in the developing countries for which foreign contributions are being sought. The relevant questionaires specify not only the description of the projects, but also the size and type of the foreign

Table 6.   Requested elements of foreign contributions to 327
            investment projects deposited by the developing
            countries in the UNIDO Data Bank as of February 1984

Item	Number of cases	Percentage of the total projects
1. Credits	258	78.9
2. Equity participation	230	70.3
3. Access to export markets	109	33.3
4. Licenses	94	28.7
5. Technical assistance	89	27.2
6. Vocational training	87	26.6
7. Equipment supplies	64	19.6
8. Consulting	20	6.1
9. Subcontracting	7	2.1
10. Marketing	7	2.1
11. Raw materials supply	2	0.6

Source: J. Monkiewicz, Ed., **Zagraniczna polityka techniczna
           Polski w latach 80-tych i 90-tych**, Raport z badan,
           Politechnika Warszawaka, 1984, p. 384.

contribution required. In an empirical study in early 1984 of 327 such investment projects deposited by developing countries in the UNIDO Data Bank, it was found that, apart from credits, a wide spectrum of foreign in kind contributions was requested (see Table 6). They ranged from licences, equipment supplies, access to markets, to consulting, etc. Thus, they were offering sufficient opportunities for CMEA investors, particularly if the necessary know-how were available.

These requests should pose no special difficulties for CMEA based companies, both in terms of their readiness to accept various demands as well as in terms of their capacity to fulfill them. With respect to the first element we can refer to the result of a recent empirical survey carried out by ninety-eight Polish companies on their preferred form of contributions to joint-venture arrangements with developing countries. Nearly sixty percent of the companies declared their interest in supplying know-how and technical documentation; fifty-six percent were interested in supplying technical assistance and training; forty percent expressed their interest in the supply of licences; and thirty-three percent in the supply of the necessary equipment (see Table 7).

With respect to the second element we can refer to the past record of the socialist countries in the export of technology to the developing world. It leaves no doubt as to their technical capacity to meet a good part of the requirements of the developing countries.[18]

Table 7.   Preferred forms of contribution by Polish companies
to joint-ventures with developing countries (per cent
of total)

Item	Percentage
1. Supply of know-how and technical documentation	59
2. Technical assistance and training	56
3. Supply of license	40
4. Supply of equipment	33
5. Design	6
6. Consulting	4
7. Supervision and assembly	3
8. Subcontracting	2
9. Financial contribution	1

Source: T. Golebiowski, **Uwarunkowania wspolpracy przemyslowej
z krajami rozwijajacymi**, Rynki Zagranicze no 95-96,
9-12 September 1986, p. 6.

On the other hand, limited international liquidity on the part of the countries in question could be viewed as a positive factor *per se* for the development of their mutual trade and investment relations. Heavily indebted to the West and faced with the structural problems of increasing their Western export revenues, it may be tempting to try to substitute for Western suppliers at least partially with mutual deliveries.

Existing commodity structures in East-West trade seem to offer such opportunities, as the bulk of Eastern imports from the West constitutes materials and semifinished products. Apparently these are easily supplied by some Third World manufactures. This may require some additional investment which, in turn, might be jointly sponsored by the partners concerned; again supported primarily by in kind arrangements.

Apart from the financial impediments the "Western-bias" of both the CMEA and the Third World countries should be seen as the major constraint on further development of direct CMEA investments. The knowledge of mutual capabilities, habits, traditions, investment, and production conditions; the architecture of logistical lines (communication, transportation, standards, etc.) puts prospective CMEA investors at a disadvantage vis-à-vis Western ones. The same is true for Third World companies in their relationships with CMEA partners.

In the above mentioned empirical survey of Polish companies more than seventeen percent of them mentioned lack of knowledge of the conditions prevailing in the developing countries as one of the major obstacles to possible joint-venture arrangements. An additional constraint is the recent action by the US government to restrict technology exports

to the socialist countries by forcing several industrialized countries to
sign such agreements. That could result in their increased reservation
with regard to any sort of technology-based cooperation with the CMEA
in order to avoid possible tensions with the US Government.

What then are the positive factors? First of all, it is a new approach
towards foreign capital, both in the CMEA as well as in the developing
countries. In the developing countries the period of confrontation with
foreign capital and their carrier-transnational corporations in the 1970s
was replaced by a period of selective cooperation.

The new "balanced" approach towards foreign capital will most
probably be reinforced in the years to come. Apart from the changed
perception with regard to foreign capital among the policy makers in
the developing countries, a perception based on their past experience,
two additional factors seem to be in operation. The first is the continuous
pressure exerted by the United States and other developed countries
upon the developing countries to liberalize further their foreign economic
policies, including policies on foreign investment. The second is the
growing competition in the world economy for foreign investors especially
in view of the growing propensity to invest in the United States and
other developed countries. This might force developing countries to offer
more and more liberal conditions to foreign investors.[19] In the CMEA,
on the other hand, the ideological superstitions were finally removed
and both internal and external investments have become "legalized."
They began to be considered an ordinary economic activity resulting
from the objective process of the internationalization of production.
Particularly important is the growth of internal direct investments as
well as intra-regional direct investment ventures which have begun the
much needed learning process.

Perhaps we should mention that internal foreign investments in the
majority of the CMEA countries were allowed only beginning in the
late 1970s. Only since then has the accumulation of relevant know-how
been initiated.[20] It is a dramatic qualitative shift in the traditional economic
policies of the socialist countries and most probably finds its resonance
also in CMEA investment activities in the South. To indicate the current
state of interests in East-South capital ventures let us recall again the
results of the empirical survey among Polish companies carried out in
1986. When asked to indicate which forms of economic cooperation with
the South were of special interest to them, over nineteen percent
mentioned joint-ventures (capital investments).[21] Interestingly enough the
same ratio for production companies was twenty-seven percent, which
could mean a greater desire for organic forms of cooperation.

Another positive element should be seen in the current evolution of
international trade policies which is characterized by growing protectionist

measures in both the developed as well and the developing countries. This means that to overcome them the CMEA countries have, *inter alia*, to resort to the option of foreign direct investments. In any case this is a traditional adjustment mechanism which has been observed in the world economy under such circumstances. There is no reason for it to be absent in East-South relations, particularly if ideological prejudices are eliminated.

The third positive element is the industrial advancement of several developing countries (especially NICs) which, according to Lindner's theory, provides more opportunities for mutual trade and investment between them and the CMEA countries. These would refer both to trade-related as well as production-related ventures. A good example of such developments is a recent offer by the Soviet Union to set up a large production joint-venture in India to manufacture the Soviet Lada automobile. It is envisaged that the mixed company would manufacture in the future 50,000–100,000 cars per year; twenty to thirty percent could then be exported to the Soviet market. Indians would retain seventy percent and the Soviets thirty percent of the shares.[22] If realized the project would be the largest production venture by a socialist country in the South. Its appearance is undoubtedly the sign of the industrial progress achieved by some of the developing countries.

Last, but not least, among the initiating forces are recent systemic and policy changes introduced in several CMEA countries (Hungary, Poland, the USSR, Bulgaria) which open new possibilities for East-South relations. Systemically, these changes are basically characterized by the growing role and independence of the companies vis-à-vis central authorities, the growing role of economic variables in the companies' decision-making processes, and the growing degree of foreign trade demonopolization (i.e. the grant of foreign trade rights to a much larger number of companies than before, including production companies and private entrepreneurs). In the policy area these changes include, *inter alia*, a new approach towards foreign capital, increased attempts at industrial restructuring, increased attempts to promote exports, and renewed interest in the development of the small scale sector, etc.

It has been argued here that most of these changes create an environment conducive to the further development of East-South capital links. Thus, for example, the granting of foreign trade rights to new economic agents intensifies mutual learning processes and enlarges the base for subsequent direct capital ventures. In Poland, instead of around sixty companies having foreign trade rights in the 1970s, there are currently well over three hundred. This, combined with the greater role of economic variables in the decision processes of CMEA companies, may also result in the restructuring of the already set up capital ventures according to the new criteria. New approaches toward foreign capital open different perspectives for the internationalization process of CMEA-based companies. This may result both in an intensification of their movement abroad, and changes in the pattern of their ventures (apparently more production oriented ventures), as well as the introduction of Third World based investors into the socialist countries. Hence, a one-way street will be transformed, perhaps not into a highway but at least into a two-way street.

Increased efforts by the CMEA towards industrial restructuring, coupled with the new position of its industrial companies in the economic system, may produce a strong stimulus for direct capital investments in the South. It is precisely in a system based on market mechanisms that such spontaneous redeployment may effectively take place. Somehow the current cooperation of the socialist countries with the Third World has been based on the execution of large projects and involvement of large state companies on both sides. It is well known, however, that the majority of the economic institutions in the developing countries are small companies. Renewed interest in the CMEA in promoting small-scale companies along with their entrepreneurial spirit and capacity for risk taking, offers new possibilities for direct capital links between the two regions.

For all these phenomena to materialize requires a certain length of time and a conscious effort to support existing opportunities. It does not seem likely that East-South capital ventures will start to grow immediately as a result of the forces indicated above. It seems, however, that the first signs of revitalization should be able to be observed at the beginning of the 1990s. A particularly important role could be played by the Soviet Union, if the *perestroika* process is successfully completed. This is due both to the USSR's economic potential and its traditional good links to many of the developing countries, as well as its relatively good international financial situation.

Notes

1. J. Monkiewicz and J. Maciejewicz, *Technology Export from the Socialist Countries*, Westview Press, Boulder and London, 1986, pp. 116–149.

2. Z. Wysokińska, "Handel Wschód-Poludnie w latach 1970–1984," *Handel Zagraniczny* No. 3/1987, pp. 21–24.

3. C.H. McMillan, *Multinationals from the Second World: Growth of Foreign Investment by Soviet and East European State Enterprises*, Macmillan Press, London, 1987; E. Zaleski, "Socialist Multinationals in Developing Countries," in: G. Hamilton, *Red Multinationals or Red Herrings: The Activities of Enterprises from Socialist Countries in the West*, Hamilton 1986, pp. 156–184.

4. *Salient Features and Trends in Foreign Direct Investment,* UNCTC, New York 1983, pp. 56–57.

5. "Changes in the Pattern of FDI: An Update," *The CTC Reporter,* No. 23, Spring 1987, p. 3.

6. C.H. McMillan, *Multinationals . . . ,* pp. 38–39.

7. *Salient Features and Trends in Foreign Direct Investment,* UNCTC, New York 1983, pp. 67–68.

8. J. Monkiewicz, *Multinational Production Enterprises: A Preliminary Overview,* UNIDO/P.C. 121, September 1985, pp. 14–15.

9. E. Zaleski, *Socialist Multinationals . . . ,* pp. 158–159.

10. Data supplied by the Polish Ministry of Foreign Trade.

11. C.H. McMillan, "Growth of External Investments by the Comecon Countries," *The World Economy,* No. 3/1979, p. 371.

12. *Salient Features and Trends in Foreign Direct Investment,* UNCTC, New York 1983, p. 56; "Changes in the Pattern of FDI: An Update," *The CTC Reporter,* No. 23, Spring 1987, p. 3.

13. N. N. Voznesenskaya, *Smeshannye predpriyatya kak forma mezhdunarodnogo ekonomitscheskogo sotrudnitschestva,* Nauka, Moskva 1986, pp. 138–144.

14. A. Jung, *Polskie spólki handlowo-produkcyjne w krajach rozwijajacych sie,* SGPS, unpublished Ph.D. dissertation, Warsaw 1980, p. 145.

15. C.H. McMillan, *Multinationals . . . ,* pp. 61–62.

16. A. Jung, *Polskie . . . ,* pp. 145–146.

17. P. Gutman, "Le couple exportation d'ensembles complets/compensation dans les relations Est-Sud, substitut a l'investissement direct? Une hypothèse de travail," paper presented at 5th General Conference of EADI, Amsterdam 1–5 September 1987. A revised version of this paper is also a chapter of this volume.

18. J. Monkiewicz and J. Maciejewicz, *Technology Export. . . .*

19. J. Cieślik, "Developing Countries' Attitudes *vis-à-vis* Transnational Corporations: Time for a Change? " paper presented at 5th General Conference of EADI, Amsterdam, 1–5 September 1987.

20. M. Lebkowski and J. Monkiewicz, "Western Direct Investment in Centrally Planned Economies," *Journal of World Trade Law,* Vol. 20, No. 6, November 1986, pp. 624–638.

21. T. Golebiowski, "Uwarunkowania wspólpracy przemyslowej z krajami rozwijajacymi sie," *Rynki Zagraniczne,* No. 95–96, 9–12 September 1986, p. 6.

22. *Rynki Zagraniczne,* No. 29 (4649) 9 March 1987, p. 5.

9

The Export of "Complete Plants" with Buy-Back Agreements: A Substitute for Direct Investment in East-South Relations?[1]

Patrick Gutman

Introduction

The literature devoted to East-South industrial and technological cooperation virtually ignores any reference to the internationalization of the production process. Is it that the facts, as they pertain to this internationalization between the East and the South, are too marginal or is it the way in which it is presented that minimizes any reference?[2] Other than Carl McMillan's work, carried out as part of the East-West Project of the Institute of Soviet and East European Studies at Carleton University (Ottawa), the study of CMEA direct investment practices in developing countries has not led to many analyses and reflections.[3]

We have no alternative but to ascertain that most analyses of East-South industrial cooperation undertaken by Soviet and Eastern European economists are limited, as a matter of course, simply to enumerating the different forms of cooperation as vectors of technology transfer. Each form is presented, in turn, with concrete examples: the export of isolated machinery and equipment goods, the building of "complete" plants, the transfer of licenses, co-production and subcontracting operations, the creation of joint ventures, tripartite industrial cooperation, the sending of experts, and the training of personnel (manual labor) either in the developing or in the socialist countries.

However, this enumeration, more descriptive than analytical, is only a juxtaposition of the various forms of East-South industrial and technological cooperation and does not take into account their linkage with the internationalization of the production process.[4] It is likely that the explicit lack of reference to the internationalization of the process of production as such, can be attributed to ideological motives. In principle, the difficulty in accepting direct investment, that is—*the export of capital to the developing countries*—is that it would place the East on a par with the West.[5]

Economists from the CMEA countries acknowledge, however, a change in practice: they have emphasized that "New Forms of Cooperation"— the expression frequently used to denote the most elaborate modalities of East-South Industrial Cooperation—have been developed alongside more traditional forms.[6] Are these "New Forms of Cooperation" (NFC) with the East not simply twins of what one refers to as "New Forms of Investment" (NFI) in the West?

Until now East-South industrial and technological cooperation has remained outside the intellectual framework regarding "New Forms of Investment." This could be explained by the fact that, in the West, the debate over NFI usually referred to an implicit North-South relationship in the minds of its promoters[7] even though tripartite industrial coop- eration—within which the socialist Foreign Trade Organizations are involved together with Western firms—is sometimes included.[8]

For the CMEA, which refuses to be compared to the industrial North, it is obvious that a rapprochement between "New Forms of Cooperation" and "New Forms of Investment" would be most undesirable, as such a parallel would tend to situate socialist and capitalist practices on the same level. Hence, the difference in formulation, which is anything but neutral: substituting the term *cooperation* for *investment* in the expression "New Forms of Cooperation" explicitly reflects a refusal to refer to direct investment. One might add that such a change is all the more relevant, as investment does not always occur in NFI, nor does it necessarily have to.

If, quantitatively speaking, "New Forms of Cooperation" have so far been less developed than "New Forms of Investment," the fact remains that the specificity of the NFI concept fits perfectly with the logic behind "New Forms of Cooperation." The juridical and technical breakdown of direct investment and the elimination of control by abolishing the ownership of capital are in fact its most salient features. We feel, therefore, that the CMEA's "New Forms of Cooperation" warrant being part of the debate of "New Forms of Investment."

Given this perspective, this chapter proposes to examine the rela- tionship between two important modalities of East-South industrial cooperation—joint ventures on the one hand, and the building of "complete plants," paid for by buy-back agreements, on the other— each one in relation to the other as well as to the internationalization of the process of production.

Why is it necessary to compare two modalities of East-South industrial cooperation? What is the sense of such a comparison? This question corresponds to the following two objectives.

1. Until now, no study has questioned the fact that each form of cooperation has always been considered separately. Hence, any discussion of their linkage has been ignored. By not putting the modalities into perspective, one implicitly confirms the idea of a neutral recourse to a particular form of cooperation. No explanation is given as to why the CMEA makes wide use of one modality and relatively little of another. A comparative approach should help to explain the choices that have been made.

2. Furthermore, the lack of a theoretical framework limits the scope of these studies by confining them, as a general rule, to a purely descriptive perspective when a more analytical approach is needed. One way would be to undertake a comparative study of "complete plant" exports and East-South joint ventures in connection with the *Direct Investment versus New Forms of Investment* debate. Such a step might serve to add a qualitative dimension to a quantitative valuation: by measuring the acceptance or rejection of direct investment. We will attempt to examine, in particular, the extent to which the coupling of "complete plant" exports with buy-back agreements can take over from, or even act as, a substitute for East-South direct investment which generally takes the form of joint ventures.

It should be understood from the outset that it is not my intention to present a definitive analysis but, rather, a working hypothesis with all the inherent shortcomings of such an exploratory process.

In order to clarify this approach, I have chosen to divide the argument into two parts:

- In the first, we will show that the creation of equity joint ventures by the CMEA is, in fact, a mitigated acceptance of direct investment and reflects, in reality, a shifting towards "New Forms of Investment."
- In the second, we will attempt to demonstrate that the export of "complete plants" provides the CMEA with the opportunity for generating a disguised delocalization of production, without the exportation of capital and, therefore, constitutes a substitute for direct investment.

I. East-South Joint Ventures:
The Mitigated Acceptance of Direct Investment

Before assessing the significance of East-South joint ventures, we should point out that economists from the CMEA or for that matter,

Table 1

Number of East-South Joint-Ventures: Estimates
(number of instances)

	McMillan end 1983[a]	McMillan end 1978[b]	Zaleski April 1984[c]	UNCTAD[d]
Bulgaria	34	21	14	15
Czechoslovakia	38	24	16	25
East Germany	2	1	3	2
Hungary	44	31	32	15-20
Poland	37	34	24	24
Romania	54	49	45	30
Soviet Union	27	25	34	30
CMEA (7)	236[+]	185	168	141-146

[+] Including 23 companies no longer operational as of the end of 1983.
[a] McMillan, 1987, Table 3.4, pp. 36-37.
[b] McMillan, 1979a, Table 2, p. 336.
[c] Zaleski, 1986, Table 6.2, pp. 158-159.
[d] UNCTAD, 1986a, p. 6, §16 (Bulgaria); p. 9, §29 (Chechoslovakia); p. 11, §36 (GDR); p. 13, §44 (Hungary); p. 15, §53 (Poland); p. 17, §58 (Romania); p. 18, §65 (Soviet Union).

Soviet and East European authorities, do not at all appear to be concerned with presenting an exhaustive panorama. Although there is no shortage of declarations of principle, the same cannot be said with regard to statistical information; the vacuum is nearly total. It is, therefore, on the basis of Western data—those of McMillan being the most complete—that we will examine the specificity of East-South joint ventures.

The Importance of East-South Joint Ventures

The number of installations which took place (Tables 1 and 2), clearly shows that East-South direct investment, in the form of joint ventures, has remained quite modest. According to McMillan, at the end of 1978, the number was 185 and grew only to 236 by the end of 1983 (twenty-three of the latter are no longer operational). As such, and even using McMillan's figures which are the highest and the least favorable to our thesis, these data clearly emphasize that joint ventures are not *a priori* the privileged mode of cooperation practiced by the CMEA in the developing countries.

Moreover, the chronological study of the creation of joint ventures as presented by McMillan in his latest book (Figure 1) reveals a relative slowdown in the growth dynamic since 1980. In fact, the emergence of only seventy-five new joint ventures between 1978 and 1986 corresponds to a rough average of ten new cases per year.[9] Such a low figure indicates a weak dynamic.

Table 2

Regional Distribution of East-South Joint-Ventures
(number of instances)

	McMillan end 1983[a]	end 1978[b]	Zaleski April 1984[c]
Africa	102	75	70
Asia	36	34	33
Latin America	52	36	36
Middle East	46	40	29
Total South	236[+]	185	168

[+] Including 23 companies no longer operational as of the end of
1983.
[a] McMillan, 1987, Table 3.4, pp. 36-37.
[b] McMillan, 1979a, Table 2, p. 336.
[c] Zaleski, 1986, Table 6.2, pp. 158-159.

Without putting East-South direct investment and West-South direct investment on a par, and even taking into account the gap between the two, one can still wonder whether the low rate of creation of East-South joint ventures does not reflect a similar tendency observed in the relative decline of direct investment by the OECD countries in the Third World.[10] Does this not point to a certain parallelism? This would seem to be the case when one compares Figure 1 and Table 5 (See Part II). Namely, the relative slowdown noticed in the growth of East-South joint ventures occurs chronologically when the number of "complete plants" installed in the developing countries by the CMEA countries shows a dynamic increase. It is precisely the simultaneity of this slowdown in the growth of direct investment (which takes the form of joint ventures) and the growth of NFC (export of "complete plants") that allows us to draw a parallel between East-South and West-South.[11]

Basically, it seems that the small number of East-South joint ventures corresponds to a certain hostility towards direct investment abroad. The obvious reluctance with which the CMEA views such an important development as the process of internationalization of capital, especially in the Third World, stems in fact from Lenin's analysis of imperialism wherein *the exportation of capital* plays a central role. Also, it is not surprising to see that by the end of 1983, the Soviet Union started up only twenty-seven joint ventures in the developing world; that is to say, less than twelve percent of East-South joint ventures.[12] Despite the latter, this has not prevented an attitudinal evolution from taking place, as Marie Lavigne recently observed: "the creation of joint ventures is regarded quite favorably today in both Soviet publications and in those

Patrick Gutman

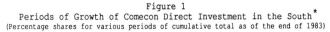

Figure 1
Periods of Growth of Comecon Direct Investment in the South*
(Percentage shares for various periods of cumulative total as of the end of 1983)

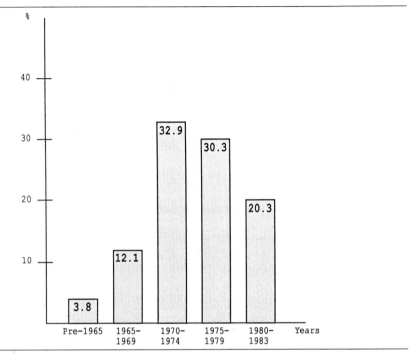

*Based on date of initial Comecon investment in a branch, subsidiary, or other
affiliated company abroad. Sample of 158 cases where date of initial investment
established.
Source: McMillan, 1987, Figure 8.2., p. 163.

of the Comecon Secretariat, . . . as well as in UNCTAD publications.
The documents prepared by the UNCTAD Division of Trade with Socialist
Countries do not differ greatly from viewpoints held in official documents
from these countries themselves. It is therefore possible to consider the
phenomenon as accepted practice."[13]

Nevertheless, the weakness of the flows in question—total CMEA
direct investment in the West and in the South did not represent more
that 0.3 percent of the total world stock of direct investments abroad
in 1978—would lead one to believe that until now, actions have not
been on a par with declarations of principle.[14] The CMEA is still in an
exploratory stage.

Furthermore, there is a discrepancy between direct investment carried
out in the West as opposed to the South:

Table 3
Ownership Structure of Comecon Investments in the South,
End 1983[a]
(number of instances)

East European Country	100% Eastern equity	Joint equity with local partner[b]	Total
Bulgaria	1	16	17
Czechoslovakia	1	19	20
East Germany	0	1	1
Hungary	3	25	28
Romania	2	42	44
Soviet Union	3	15	18
CMEA (7)	11	140	151

[a] Based on data for those companies where basic equity structure known (64 percent of 236 identified cases).

[b] Includes 11 cases where Western equity participation also involved.

Source: McMillan, 1987, Table 3.2, p. 31.

a) On the one hand, the amount of capital invested by the CMEA in the Third World at the end of 1978 attained just slightly over half of what was invested in the OECD countries: $270 million in the South as opposed to $454 million in the West.[15]

b) On the other hand, the statutory distribution of capital in East-South joint ventures between the partners by the end of 1983 shows the extent to which a 100 percent participation by socialist countries is rare (Table 3). Yet, it makes up twenty-three percent of East-West joint ventures in the OECD countries, exclusive of majority participation—the latter representing thirty percent of East-West joint ventures (Table 4).

Whereas the CMEA is setting up a majority direct investment model in the West, the practice in the East-South context is more restrictive. The latter corresponds to an obvious reluctance to make full use of direct investment opportunities that are open abroad. In fact, the specificity of direct investment—the control potential which is acquired through the ownership of capital—is weakened by a shift towards "New Forms of Investment."

Shifting towards "New Forms of Investment"

This mitigated attitude of the CMEA as regard traditional direct investment in the East-South context, constitutes a central point in a

Table 4
Ownership Structure of COMECON Investments in the West,
End of 1983[a]
(percentages)

East European Country	100% Eastern Equity	Majority Eastern Ownership	50-50 Ownership Split	Minority Eastern Ownership	Equity split un-determined[b]	All
Bulgaria	14.6	12.2	17.1	12.1	43.9	100
Czechoslovakia	48.6	18.9	8.1	8.1	16.2	100
East Germany	31.0	24.1	13.8	10.4	20.7	100
Hungary	25.5	15.4	36.3	14.7	8.1	100
Poland	18.9	31.1	8.9	10.0	31.1	100
Romania	5.9	11.8	76.4	5.9	0.0	100
Soviet Union	20.8	55.7	7.5	5.6	10.4	100
CMEA (7)	22.8	30.3	21.2	9.8	15.9	100

[a] Based on data for those instances where at least basic equity structure known (over 90 percent of 484 identified cases).

[b] Cases where joint equity with Western partner established, but exact equity split undetermined.

Source: McMillan, 1987, Table 3.1, p. 31.

"New Forms of Investment versus Direct Investment" perspective. In setting up equity joint enterprises with a 49–51 percent distribution of capital (with the socialist countries owning less) in most cases the CMEA gives majority control to its partners from developing countries. Two factors explain the reasoning behind this distribution of statutory capital between East and South.

On the one hand, there is the desire not to go against the economic sovereignty of the host country so that no comparison can be made between East-South joint ventures and the capitalist transnationals. We should note as well that this mode of action is also in response to internal economic restraints; the difficulty, in terms of resource allocation, and of carrying out a massive export of capital. On the other hand, minority participation is part of an obligation to be enforced by both East and West not to interfere in the process of political indigenization practised by some LDCs (such as Nigeria).

Thus, the model of East-South equity joint ventures introduced by the CMEA should be considered more as a "New Forms of Investment" strategy than a traditional "Direct Investment" policy; the objective is not to take control. We could even argue that East-South equity joint ventures are, in fact, a "New Forms of Investment" when referring to Charles Oman's definition of a joint enterprise in his typology of NFI: "According to our definition, a joint enterprise is categorized as a NFI if the developing country holds at least fifty percent of the social capital. We do not include in NFI those joint enterprises where the foreign associate has majority control."[16]

Moreover, in analyzing the structure of joint ventures in an East-South context, Marie Lavigne stresses their temporary character. In answer to her own question: "Isn't this the start of neo-colonialism?," she replies with the negative, specifying: "The principal argument is that a joint enterprise has a temporary existence which generally dissolves when its Third World partner buys out the socialist country's shares."[17] To emphasize on the short-term aspect of a joint enterprise dissociates it from traditional direct investment and places it squarely in the category of NFI.

The lease formula mentioned by Khaldine in his report to UNCTAD takes this idea one step further: "A long-term lease for enterprises in a developing country which benefits from technical and managerial assistance from Soviet experts and manpower seems to be a formula which is both logical and possible. The counterpart, in this type of operation, would come from a sharing of the production pro-rated to the expenditure incurred by each side. This form of cooperation, while contributing to finding a solution to the problems which exist in the economic relations between the Soviet Union and the developing countries, does not lead to a transfer of property rights. It offers, however, a means to provide each partner with the number of products needed over a period of time."[18] In this manner, Khaldine goes even further in rejecting direct investment. We go from temporary capital holdings with potential transfer of property rights (as with East-South joint ventures) *to no capital holdings at all* by the socialist countries (as with lease formulas).

East-South Joint Ventures and Multinationalization Strategies

Despite their number, which is relatively limited at present, it is important to understand the goals of East-South joint ventures. In this respect, the typology of multinationalization strategies presented by C.A. Michalet[19] is likely to provide a more nuanced view to the mainly sectoral perception we have of joint ventures by helping to clarify the logic of their insertion in the socialist international division of labor.

In fact, almost thirty percent of East-South joint ventures have certain similarities to what Michalet calls, "primary multinationals," the purpose of the latter being the development of a foreign sourcing strategy.[20] A study undertaken by McMillan in 1979 of assets held by the CMEA in joint ventures outlines this perfectly. Not only is the level of fixed assets in the East-South context much higher that in the East-West context ($3.9 billion as opposed to $473.6 million; i.e., almost a factor of eight) but a good ninety-two percent of all fixed assets are directed to "the exploitation of mineral and energy resources."[21]

The fact that a considerable proportion of capital invested by the CMEA (sixty-four percent) and the near total of fixed assets (ninety-two percent) has to do with raw materials and basic commodities underscores the importance for the Eastern countries to build up supplies in order to meet their domestic needs and to procure, if the opportunity arises, foreign currency earnings by marketing the remaining proportion. There is a very definite rationalization behind this type of behavior even if the invested capital remains quite modest: to provide access to the sources of raw materials. Although the levels are not the same, we find here, nevertheless, one of the main objectives of capital export as Lenin himself defines it in *Imperialism, The Highest Stage of Capitalism*. It is this specific characteristic of the activities of East-South joint ventures that defines them, to a certain extent, as having a "neo-colonial" character.

When it comes to those joint ventures having an essentially "commercial" character, they deal, for the most part, in "import-export." These are mainly firms set up abroad to handle foreign trade rather than firms acting in a productive capacity. Their relative share has gone from 17.8 percent by the end of 1978[22] to 26 percent by the end of 1983.[23] Consequently, a double foreign sourcing and marketing strategy is fundamental to explaining the emergence of East-South joint ventures. It emphasizes one of their foremost aspects, that of "circulation."

In fact, even if the joint ventures of the CMEA have a more productive orientation in the developing countries than in the West, industrial production *per se* and assembling involved only 24.3 percent of these firms by the end of 1978 and 25.5 percent by the end of 1983.[24] We should point out, however, that it is more a question of assembling than one of strictly production. In fact, assembling is most often carried out in the LDCs through the incorporation of components coming from the planned economies. Their objective leans more to penetrating the local market in terms of sales rather than to re-exporting production components or the finished product to the CMEA, thanks to the comparative advantage of LDCs in labor costs. Therefore, those East-South production oriented joint ventures are closer to "relay subsidiaries" than to "workshop subsidiaries."[25] It is, thus, difficult to see in the creation of the majority of East-South joint ventures a *well defined* policy of production delocalization by the socialist countries.

Yet, UNCTAD does not hesitate to attribute primacy to the "production" aspect by using as examples the sixty firms among the 113 sample firms whose activities were identified by Eugene Zaleski. The sixty were involved, to different degrees, in productive processes (this included mining, energy, agriculture, and the prospecting and development of natural resources).[26] However, to combine under the label production the various activities mentioned above is misleading because it amalgamates what is known in broad terms as productive phenomenon and *industrial* production in the strictest sense of the word. In particular, it runs the risk of masking the aspect of "circulation" which, given the statistics on the various functions of East-South joint ventures, is at least as important as the production side.

In light of the above, should we conclude that there is really no deliberate delocalization of production in the East-South context?[27] This is not certain and two arguments can be put forth to this effect. In the first place, it simply means that, for the moment, East-South joint ventures have not yet reached this stage of deliberate delocalization. We should not forget that the internationalization of the production process is an evolutionary phenomenon and that the CMEA is only in the exploratory phase. Therefore, it is still not possible to reach a definitive conclusion as to the future. This is so because, as a general rule, the first two strategies of multinationalization (foreign sourcing and marketing) precede, within a certain period of time, production rationalization or technico-financial strategies. In the second place, and of no less importance, even if East-South joint ventures have not yet given rise to a deliberate delocalization of production, this does not prevent its development through organizational modalities other than direct investment.

II. Export of "Complete Plants" or the Possibility of a Disguised Delocalization without Exportation of Capital

In practice, there is a real discrepancy between the importance of East-South joint ventures and that of "complete plants"[28] in East-South Industrial and Technological Cooperation. "Joint enterprises" remain quite limited in relation to the number of plant installations carried out with the assistance of CMEA. According to available estimates, we could only count 230 joint ventures as opposed to a range of 4,200 to 6,400 "complete plants." Such a disparity, which corresponds to a factor of twenty or thirty—depending on the number of estimated projects— emphasizes the fact that the socialist countries have focused their cooperation with the developing countries on technology transfer (by exporting equipment goods and through the setting up of "complete plants") rather than on direct investment through joint ventures. This fact is certainly not neutral when one considers the debate over New Forms of Investment versus Direct Investment. It reveals an obvious choice in favor of NFI which corresponds to a rejection of direct investment in terms of *exportation of capital.*

In this respect, it is clear that the export of "complete plants," as is the case with the export of industrial projects, is nothing other than an *exportation of means of production* (technical means of production) and enters into the sphere of New Forms of Investment (NFI) or of Cooperation (NFC). Both Oman in the West and Khaldine in the East are inclined to agree.[29] Considering that this is, *de facto,* the most widely practiced modality in East-South industrial cooperation, the realization of projects by the CMEA in the developing countries most certainly leaves its mark on East-South relations. However, the lack of in depth analysis in both the East[30] and in the West[31] does not provide the necessary information to delimit precisely the impact of these projects. For this reason we think it opportune to make a tentative assessment, even summarily, of the impact of "complete plants" on economic relations between the USSR and the LDCs.[32] The extent to which the coupling of "complete plants" exports with compensation brings about a disguised delocalization and constitutes, by this very fact, a substitute for direct investment must be appreciated.

Structural Impact of "Complete Plant" Exports
on Economic Relations between the USSR and LDCs

   On the Export Side. Most economists from CMEA countries are unanimous in recognizing that the export of "complete plants" constitutes the central element in East-South technology transfers. It forms the hard core, if not the majority, of total deliveries of machines and equipment from socialist countries destined for the Third World.

   For the Soviet Union, the proportion[33] was at 50 percent in 1960,[34] 52 percent in 1965,[35] almost 65 percent in 1970, 53 percent in 1978,[36] 59 percent in 1979[37] and slightly more than 56 percent in 1980.[38] Taken as a whole—and thus not only for LDCs alone—the same ratio fell to 27.7 percent in 1976,[39] 29 percent in 1978[40] and 33 percent in 1981.[41] Such a difference in the proportions stresses the important structural character of Soviet "complete plant" exports to the Third World.

   For some developing countries, the share of "complete plants" even reaches a much higher percentage: for example, 85.5 percent in 1980 for Algeria, 66 percent for India, 81.9 percent for Iran, 95 percent for Nigeria, 78 percent for Libya, and 74 percent for Turkey.[42] Skatchkov estimates at one hundred the number of projects which have been put into service each year in the Third World over the last two decades, thanks to Soviet support and technical assistance.[43] Comparatively speaking, this represents almost ten times more than the average number of East-South joint ventures which are newly established each year.[44]

   In monetary value, it appears that Soviet delivery of "complete equipment" to the developing countries, in current terms, has practically doubled since the late 1970s (histogram of Figure 2). This doubling can

Figure 2
Complete Enterprises Equipment and Material Export
by Five-Year-Plan Periods (million rubles)

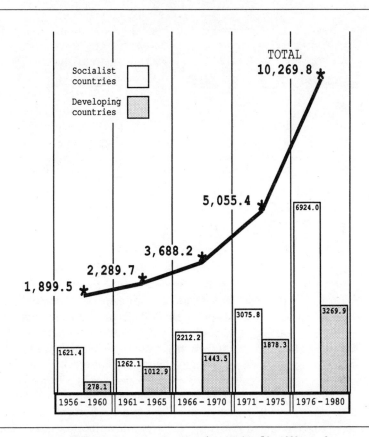

Source: Skatchkov, S., **Foreign Trade**, #6, 1982, p. 8.

be partly explained by an increase in prices which, in fact, corresponds in physical terms to a multiplying factor of 1.6. Moreover, Table 5 shows that if their progression has been less rapid than that of similar exports to the socialist countries, "complete plants" to the Third World nevertheless represent almost a third of total Soviet deliveries of these plants.

In this regard, Egorov and Volkov point out that "complete plant" exports play a decisive role in shaping the course of Soviet exports to the Third World, but also influence the volume and the structure of imports from developing countries owing to compensatory arrangements and flows of resultant products.[45]

Table 5

Export of Equipment and Materials for Complete Projects
Over Five-Year Periods
(thous. million rubles)

	1961–1965	1966–1970	1971–1975	1976–1980
Total Exports	2.29	3.69	5.06	10.22
of which to:				
Socialist countries	1.26	2.21	3.08	6.90
of which CMEA	0.98	1.84	2.51	6.18
Developing countries	1.01	1.44	1.88	3.24

Source: **Foreign Trade**, No. 3, 1981, p. 3 from Egorov & Volkov,
          1982, p. 52.

On the Import Side. From a methodological point of view, one should stress that it is very difficult even to attempt to appraise the impact of the installation of "complete plants" on USSR imports from the Third World, inasmuch as official Soviet statistics do not enable one to isolate the flow of resultant products (taken back as compensation) from the totality of Soviet imports from the developing countries.[46]

The few statistical evaluations which have been gleaned here and there—almost entirely from Soviet sources—do not allow one to measure with precision the exact importance of compensatory flows of all Soviet imports from developing countries. They are simply estimates with definite flaws but which, nevertheless, serve to provide an overall impression. Also, to our knowledge, they make up the only relevant findings that are available at the present time. We can, however, already appreciate the approximate and increasing importance of compensation whether it corresponds to compensatory arrangements,[47] or to flows of resultant products from "complete plants" (buy-back).[48] Teodorovi+ch has indicated that "in 1978 on the basis of various agreements and one-time contracts as much as 670 million rubles' worth of goods made in the projects built with Soviet assistance were delivered to the USSR from the developing countries. These comprised in particular 6.9 million tons of crude oil from Iraq and Syria, 9.5 billion cubic meters of natural gas from Iran and Afghanistan, 90,000 tons of pig iron and 95,000 tons of rolled ferrous metals from India, 2.5 million tons of bauxite from

Guinea, etc. . . . ."[49] The extent of the flow was such that during the five year period between 1976–1980, the Soviet Union supposedly received almost 2.8 billion rubles' worth of resultant products.[50]

Several Soviet economists have estimated the weight of compensation at 20–25 percent of total imports from the Third World. These are, in fact, products which fall either into the category of compensatory arrangements or flows of resultant products from "complete plants."[51] Apart from Soviet sources, UNCTAD estimated the share at 25 percent in 1979,[52] and more recently, the OECD has estimated that the share of operations involving compensation in East-South trade was almost 30 percent, that is a sum of $14.2 billion.[53]

It is obvious that for the Soviet Union it is a question of fulfilling its supply needs on a regular and long-term basis, a point which comes through very clearly in Teodorovitch's analysis: "Construction of enterprises and facilities in foreign countries, the output of which is intended to be either partly or fully used to meet the requirements of the USSR's economy, is another recent trend raising the effectiveness of foreign economic ties. This type of cooperation renders the Soviet Union's foreign economic relations a more diversified, long-term character, and adds to their scope, and at the same time our country's participation in the international division of labor grows even more far reaching, stable, and effective."[54]

In this manner, the export of "complete plants" to the Third World has become, within the function of Soviet foreign trade, a means of overcoming shortfalls in national supply. Besides, in the thinking of Soviet economists with regard to resource allocation, they work from the principle that the granting of credits to developing countries is similar to drawing on the national wealth *in the form of capital intended to yield a return*.[55] Thus, there is an organic link to be established between the granting of credits and their repayment by the developing countries through resultant products.

Marie Lavigne has recently noted: "What we hear said more and more, and most emphatically in the USSR, is that socialist countries should not passively accept simply to buy articles manufactured in the Third World, but rather create, through their cooperation with the South, structures of production adapted to their needs."[56] Lavigne appears to have reached this conclusion on the basis of Bogomolov's analysis:

Today, cooperation in these states (LDCs) centered around the construction of enterprises *oriented to the Comecon market*[57] takes on a particular importance. The extension and deepening of this direction by the IDL (international division of labor) are especially important at present—a time when the Comecon countries are initiating intensive development policies to expand their economies and doing their best to use, as much as possible, their channels of cooperation with the developing countries as a means of improving the efficiency of their own economic activities. In this context, we should mention their interest in obtaining on a long-term basis, certain types of fuels and raw materials, foodstuffs, labor-intensive products (the latter to preempt any tensions that may exist in their own balance of labor), different types of finished products, and these, notably, as a result of buy-back and cooperation agreements.[58]

Considering the barter-type arrangements that existed in the first stages of East-South trade, the compensatory mode has become more than a means of payment. It constitutes, at the present time, an instrument by which the developing countries can be enrolled in the Socialist international division of labor (SIDL).

It has also changed in nature. Although it started out as being strictly commercial, it has become an industrial practice—a subcontracting mechanism—by developing the buy-back flows of resultant products from "complete plants." This compensatory phenomenon, which constitutes a significant share of Soviet imports from the Third World— almost 30 percent—already plays an important role in East-South economic relations. Thus, from an analytical point of view, we must stop thinking of it as a non-monetarized form of payment and accept it as *a mode of disguised delocalization of production without direct investment.* In other words, are we witnessing the emergence of an internationalization *without export of capital,* thanks to the flows of resultant products as reimbursement for "complete plants" built by the CMEA?

The Coupling of "Complete Plant" Exports with
Buy-Back Agreements: A Substitute for Direct Investment?

From an analytical point of view, we will divide the argument into two parts:

First, we will show that buy-back agreements linked to the export of "complete plants" introduce a change in the nature of East-South relations. It transforms punctual sales of equipment goods ("complete plants") into a partnership which binds, on a long-term basis, both buyer and seller, by means of resultant product flows. The coupling of "complete plant" exports with buy-back agreements constitutes therefore a mechanism which gives rise to a disguised delocalization of production. Yet, while it is the necessary condition from a microeconomic perspective, it is not sufficient in itself.

Second, to ensure that the mechanism is, in fact, long lasting and has significant scope, it is essential that this phenomenon becomes at least self-supporting, or better still, grows without exhausting itself. This is the *sufficient* condition from a macroeconomic perspective which will give the mechanism is dynamism by permitting a disguised, but significant, delocalization of production.

The Institutional and Organizational Advantages of the Coupling of "Complete Plant" Exports with Buy-Back Agreements in Relation to Direct Investment

From an institutional point of view, this provides the CMEA countries with the opportunity of being *partners* rather than *associates* with the developing countries. On the one hand, the notion of associate disappears when there is no capital participation, and with this, the eventuality of a control by foreign interests of socialist origin. On the other hand, the traditional relationship of buyer/seller, which prevails in the majority of situations involving the export of equipment goods, becomes blurred to the benefit of the partnership notion. The latter is the result of an interdependent relationship in which the practice of buy-back agreements plays a central function. By the way, it is interesting to note that any reference to direct investment becomes useless. Even if there is disguised, but effective, delocalization of production, the absence of capital flows (direct investment) in the East-South direction does not, as such, prevent the flow of merchandise (resultant products through buy-back agreements) from the LDCs towards the CMEA. In other words, the coupling of "complete plant" exports with buy-back agreements gives the CMEA the opportunity to implement a delocalization *without exportation of capital.*

Thus, we are faced with a contractual mechanism which allows the operators to be juridically independent though economically linked. We leave behind the area of sales, in its simplest form, to partake in a partnership, the third option between "market" and "enterprise" as defined by Patrick Joffre.[59]

From an organizational point of view, the coupling of "complete plant" exports with buy-back agreements has a relative advantage as compared to direct investment. It is less costly in terms of transaction and control costs. This emerges clearly in Figure 3 which compares the different forms of involvement abroad.

The turnkey plant formula ranks below the first bisecting line, whereas the diverse modalities of direct investment[60] are found above. It is, in fact, the coupling of compensation, as an organic link, with the export of "complete plants" which allows for a *pseudo-internationalization.* It introduces a supple and *partial integration* so that the coupling of "complete plant" exports with buy-back agreements distances itself from

Patrick Gutman

Figure 3
Forms of Foreign Participation: Growth of Transaction and Control
Costs in Relation to the Growing Degree of Internalization

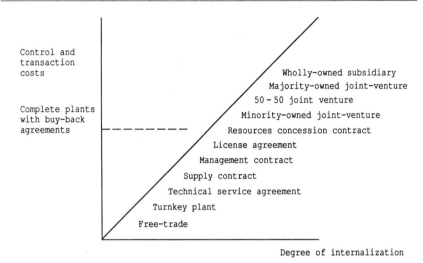

Control and
transaction
costs

Complete plants
with buy-back
agreements

Wholly-owned subsidiary
Majority-owned joint-venture
50 - 50 joint venture
Minority-owned joint-venture
Resources concession contract
License agreement
Management contract
Supply contract
Technical service agreement
Turnkey plant
Free-trade

Degree of internalization

Source: Muchielli, J.L., 1985, p. 209 from R. Hall Mason, "Comments" to J.H. Dunning "Alternative Channels and Modes of International Resource Transmission," pp. 27-36 in T. Sagafi-Mejad, R.W. Moxon & H.V. Perlmutter (eds.), Controlling International Technology Transfer, Issues, Perspectives and Policy Implications, Pergamon Press, New York, 1980.

quasi-market situations in order to move nearer—at an intermediary level on the first bisecting line—to situations of quasi-integration. In fact, the process of internalization does not have to be pushed to the maximum inasmuch as Soviet and East European technology and equipment are not usually characterized by a proprietory rights fee (*rente de situation*) in the final phase of the product.[61]

Without wanting to place buy-back agreements on a par with internalized flows between a transnational corporation and its subsidiaries, from an organizational point of view, it appears that the buy-back mechanism serves as a substitute for the internalization process by favoring a partial integration mechanism.

Although the organizational modalities are quite different,[62] we can find a certain similarity as regards the final purpose, which is to allow a *transfer of value*. From this perspective, the organic link between the building of plants and their payment by means of resultant products is of the utmost importance. Would the installation of "complete plants" not be the necessary condition to ensure that buy-back agreements bring about the transfer of value?

We should stress that we only intend here to advance a hypothesis. Namely, to underline the functional link between a potential transfer of value and the coupling of "complete plant" exports with buy-back agreements. At this point, our objective is simply to present the mechanism and stakes at issue. It is not to quantify the importance of the transfers of value. Moreover, one could easily counter this hypothesis and say that if there is a transfer of value in some CMEA-LDC bilateral relations, then it is very possible that an inverse transfer of value could also take place in other CMEA-LDC bilateral relations. The validity of our hypothesis at a macroeconomic level still needs to be confirmed. Nevertheless, if this should really be the case, then it would have important consequences.

Would this lead to a shift in the "complete plant" exports' objective from its original purpose; i.e., to promote import substitution in developing countries? Might import substitution not run the risk of being transformed into an instrument of "unequal exchange?" Large-scale development of "complete plant/buy-back agreements" in East-South relations would not be neutral but might, on the contrary, become part of a "counter-imperialist" strategy.[63] For this to happen though, our second condition needs still to be fulfilled; namely, that the mechanism has sufficient scope from a macroeconomic perspective.

The Sufficient Condition: A Generalization of the Coupling of "Complete Plant" Exports/Buy-Back Agreements

In order for the mechanism to become generalized, the flow of resultant products cannot stop once the repayment for a given plant has been made. There is a constraint that must be met by the socialist countries to pass from a micro to a macroeconomic level: they must permanently establish new plants to ensure the perpetuation of a regular flow of resultant products. This means the setting up of a *dynamic* process whereby the flow of the most recent resultant products picks up where the last one left off. In fact, this assumes that the mechanism does more than just maintain itself (simply through flow replacements) but undergoes a readily sustainable expansion, failing which the process risks coming to an end.

Is such dynamism regarding the number of "complete plants" built by the CMEA in LDCs plausible? In looking at Table 6, it appears that the number of projects in service has almost tripled between 1973 and 1982, increasing from 1,500 to 4,200.[64] It would seem, therefore, that one could *a priori* consider as plausible the hypothesis of a dynamic

Table 6
Number of Projects Built and to be Built in the Third World
With Soviet and East European Assistance
(Stocks of Projects)

Date of Evaluation	Source and Date of Publication	Number of Projects put into operation[+]	under agreements[++]
End 1965	Vassiley[a] (1967)	1948	
End 1967	Lavigne[b] (1970)	2404	
1971	Zevin[c] (1976)	2653	
January 1973	UNCTAD[d] (1973)	1500	3000
January 1975	Zevin[e] (1976)	1930	2900
January 1976	UNCTAD[f] (1977)	2300	3000
January 1977	UNCTAD[g] (1978)	2700	"several hundreds"
January 1979	UNCTAD[h] (1979)	2900	4000
January 1980	UNCTAD[i] (1980)	3000	1500
January 1981	UNCTAD[j] (1981)	3157	1500
January 1982	UNCTAD[k] (1982)	4200	6400

[+] put into operation means that the production has begun but does not necessarily work at full capacity.

[++] under agreements according to the Soviet and East European habit includes not only the projects already signed but also those the plans of which are established. It thus takes into account planned projects.

[a] pp. 84-85 in Système mondial de l'Economie Socialiste, Vol. 2, Nauka Publishing House, Moscow, 1976.

[b] p. 460 in Les Economies socialistes soviétique et européennes, A. Colin, Paris, 1970.

[c] p. 46 in Economic Cooperation of Socialist and Developing Countries: New Trends, Nauka Publishing House, Moscow, according to I. Ganev, SIV i Tretiyat svyat, Sofia, 1974.

[d] p. 28 in TD/B/458, Supp. 1, §72 according to Foreign Affairs Bulletin, (GDR), No. 7, February 28, 1973 published by the Foreign Affairs Minister of the German Democratic Republic.

[e] p. 48 in Economic Cooperation of Socialist and Developing Countries: New Trends, from Figyelö (Budapest), 1975, No. 13, p. 7.

[f] p. 17 in TD/B/656, §43.

[g] p. 17 in TD/B/708, §40.

[h] p. 17 in TD/B/754, §44.

[i] p. 15 in TD/B/808, §39.

[j] p. 19 in TD/B/859, §39 from Press Bulletin, CMEA Secretariat, Moscow, No. 2, 1981, p. 52 (of the Russian text).

[k] p. 17 in TD/B/912, §56.

process. Nonetheless caution should prevail, as a critical examination of these data reveals its limits. Since we are speaking of stock statistics for projects in service as well as signed projects, to check the accuracy of the orders of magnitude, one can calculate (by subtraction) the annual increases for both categories of projects and compare the results. In so doing, one realizes that these evaluations are, to say the least, questionable. How do we explain, for example, that from 1979 to 1980 the number of signed projects went from 4,000 to 1,500, although the number of operational projects did not increase substantially; here there were only one hundred extra projects. Logically, one would expect that a decrease in the stock of signed projects would bring about a compatible increase in the number of projects in service, even if there is a time gap. This is clearly not the case. Such a discrepancy cannot be explained only by the closing down of obsolete factories.[65]

The second limitation is that one cannot evaluate with precision the proportion of "complete plants" which do or do not give rise to return flows of resultant products. The reason for this is that no distinction has been made to this effect in Soviet statistics on "complete plants." The only available findings for delimiting the relative share of buy-back agreements are actually those estimates presented in the sub-section above, which are expressed in percentages of Soviet imports from the Third World (or in physical data).

In the face of such gaps, and with such inaccurate and unreliable data, how is it possible to verify the effectiveness of this generalization from a quantitative point of view?[66] Considering the present state of available information, we refuse to draw any conclusions even if we could claim with certainty, from an analytical point of view, that the coupling of "complete plants" exports with buy-back agreements does allow an effective generalization.

Conclusions

In fact, our conclusions have to deal more with a few observations than a final conclusion as such. Although this chapter has been limited to a presentation of mechanisms, we will recall in closing the following points:

1. The comparative perspective which we chose enabled us to show that recourse to a specific organizational modality of East-South industrial cooperation is not neutral. The choices implemented are determined by ideological preference and/or economic constraints.

2. The reluctance with which the CMEA views traditional majority direct investment in its East-South relations—especially in the case of the Soviet Union—denotes its unwillingness to develop massive exports of capital. It also reflects a very definite shifting towards "New Forms of Investment" (or Cooperation).

3. The importance of coupling "complete plant" exports with buy-back agreements in relation to direct investment (the latter in the form of joint ventures) underscores the significance in the distinction between "export of capital" and "export of means of production" in an East-South context.

4. Finally, from an analytical point of view, the coupling of "complete plant" exports with buy-back agreements constitutes a substitute for East-South direct investment by favoring a mechanism of

disguised delocalization of production through the flows of resultant products (buy-back).

It appears, nevertheless, that to confirm the hypothesis from a macroeconomic perspective one would run into problems because of inadequate Soviet and East European data. Perhaps, the overhauling of the existing statistical system, which is currently taking place in the USSR, will provide more information on foreign trade, thus making it possible to lift the veil of secrecy and usher in a more open approach thanks to *"glasnost."*

Two research directions would be then worth examining. The first would study the sectoral dimension of coupling "complete plant" exports with buy-back agreements; something which we have not addressed herein. The second would appraise the extent to which coupling of "complete plant" exports with buy-back agreements favors the emergence of a "transfer" policy for the benefit of the CMEA. In other words, one could ask whether such a mechanism serves as a means of "fructifying" capital (in the form of credits granted to the LDCs) and of recovering "revenue" from resultant products themselves, through their price.

Notes

1. From Patrick Gutman, "Le couple exportation d'ensembles complets/ compensation dans les relations Est-Sud, substitut à l'investissement direct? Une hypothèse de travail" *Tiers Monde,* Tome XXIX, No. 113, Janviers-Mars, 1988, pp. 137-164. By permission of Presses Universitaires de France (PUF). Translated by Jokalee Vanderkop. The French version was presented at the Fifth General Conference of E.A.D.I., "Managing the World Economy or Reshaping World Society? Towards a Definition of Europe's Choices," Amsterdam, September 1-5, 1987.

2. For the purposes of this chapter, the terms "East," "CMEA," "socialist countries" are used interchangeably and refer to the six small East European countries and Soviet Union excluding the socialist LDCs, associated or full members of the CMEA.

3. Other than the work of Carl McMillan (1979a, 1979b, and 1987) in the selected bibliography at the end of the chapter, the contribution of Eugene Zaleski can also be cited (Zaleski, 1986). One should also mention the UNCTAD (1986a) monograph and the article by I. Jimenez (1987).

4. A recent Polish study strays somewhat from the usual analysis of East-South joint ventures in that it goes beyond a purely descriptive presentation of organizational modalities to suggest the internationalization process of production as a necessity for CMEA countries within the actual context of the world economy. Monkiewicz, 1987. A slightly revised version of this study appears in this volume.

5. A former Soviet permanent representative to the United Nations declared at the United Nations General Assembly in September 1975: "We will never accept, neither in theory nor in practice, the concept of a divided world between rich and poor, between North and South, placing the socialist states on a par with the capitalist states."

6. See for example the study by Professor Khaldine for UNCTAD (Khaldine 1984, especially paragraphs 27–33 in chapter II) and the articles by Vlasov and Popov, whose analyses are very typical of this evolution (Vlasov, 1983 and Popov, 1987).

7. See particularly Oman, 1984 and Basile, 1985.

8. Basile, 1985, pp. 284–285 as well as *The OECD Observer* No. 112, September 1981, p. 15. On Tripartite Industrial Cooperation itself, see Gutman, 1981 and Ballot-Gutman, 1986.

9. This estimation was obtained on the basis that, by the end of 1986, there were approximately 260 East-South joint ventures. This figure was kindly given by Carl McMillan.

10. This is, in any event, the argument put forth by the supporters of "New Forms of Investment." On this point, see Oman, 1984, pp. 27–33.

11. We should not be mistaken by the meaning of this parallel: the point is not to show that the East and the West are identical, but simply to highlight the similarities as regards the manifestation of certain phenomena. In fact, the differences in degree preclude the placing of them on an equal footing.

12. McMillan, 1987, Table 3.4, pp. 36–37.

13. Lavigne, 1986, p. 113.

14. Andreff, 1987, p. 38.

15. McMillan, 1979a, p. 371.

16. Oman, 1984, pp. 14–15.

17. Lavigne, 1986, p. 113.

18. Khaldine, 1984, p. 8, paragraph 29.

19. C.A. Michalet distinguishes four types of strategies: 1) foreign sourcing, 2) marketing, 3) production rationalization, 4) technico-financial. For a detailed presentation of each of these strategies, see C.A. Michalet, 1985, pp. 56–62.

20. The example of Romania is very significant. By the end of 1978, 60 percent of joint ventures with Romanian participation in developing countries (29 out of 49) were involved in this type of activity. McMillan, 1979a, Table 4, p. 369. For a detailed analysis of the activities of Romanian firms in the mining sector, see Dobozi, 1983a and 1983b as well as Ericsson, 1983.

21. McMillan, 1979a, p. 371, Tables 5, 6.

22. This percentage was reached by adding the three categories "marketing only, marketing and distribution, and marketing and servicing" in Table 4 in McMillan, 1979a, p. 369 (that is: $22 + 5 + 6 = {}^{33}/_{185} = 17.8$ percent).

23. This percentage was taken directly from the "import-export" category in Table 3.6 in McMillan, 1987, pp. 40–41 (that is ${}^{60}/_{231} = 26$ percent).

24. McMillan, 1979a, p. 369 and McMillan, 1987, pp. 40–41.

25. To the extent that we can speak of subsidiaries, the terms equity joint-enterprises/joint ventures seem to be more appropriate because of a shifting towards "New Forms of Investment."

26. UNCTAD, 1986a, p. 28, paragraph 96.

27. This is in any case the opinion of Marie Lavigne: "The economic interests of the Eastern countries in the South are not of the same *nature* as those of the industrialized countries (and their national or multinational corporations). It is not a question of attaining economic ascendancy, nor of conquering markets, nor of delocalizing production. The first economic objective is to obtain from the Third World primary commodities at the lowest possible prices; the second is to use this trade as a means of earning foreign currency," Lavigne, 1986, p. 129.

28. The expressions "complete plants," "complete enterprises," "complete equipment," are currently used in the East, particularly by Soviet economists to designate a realization *which functions autonomously* as opposed to isolated equipment goods or machines that are not necessarily operational. The notion of "complete plant" covers a line of production or a workshop—a subunit—of a factory as well as an enormous industrial complex or any other realizations not connected to industry. Consequently, the notion of "complete plant" is much broader than the notion of "industrial plant." It is in fact synonymous with the term "project." It is nevertheless possible to make an approximation in current practice between the notions of "complete plants" and "turn-key plants" for two reasons: a) the first one, of a quantitative nature, consists in highlighting the relative, preponderant influence of industrial realizations or of the necessary infrastructure (almost 70 percent of all cases); b) the second one, of a qualitative nature, consists in highlighting a certain similarity between "complete plants" and "turn-key plants" when the former are productive units.

29. See Oman, 1984, pp. 16–17 and 20–21 and Khaldine, 1984, pp. 7–8, paragraph 28.

30. In the East, very few studies give a precise picture of "complete plant" exports. Moreover, they use a mainly descriptive and general approach. See Gutman, 1985, pp. 47–49 for more details.

31. In the West, a lack of data banks on "complete plants" installed by the CMEA in developing countries has hindered research on this subject. Furthermore, the Western perception of East-South technology transfer, which is very narrow, is also partly responsible. It is regarded as an autonomous phenomenon within the framework of a strictly bilateral approach between East and South by virtue of the fact that the West is not *directly* involved (excepting tripartite cooperation; see Ballot-Gutman, 1986 on this point). The West is thus failing to analyze East-South technology transfers as part of an overall dynamic which, in fact, goes back to the international division of labor (IDL).

32. It should be understood that the purpose of this chapter is not to present "complete plant" exports in an exhaustive manner but to take a brief look at the mechanisms and stakes involved.

33. This is in fact the ratio of "projects realized under technical assistance/ total delivery of machines and equipment" calculated from Position 10 of the Soviet nomenclature for foreign trade. The total delivery of machines and equipment (A) and the projects built with technical assistance (B) are presented separately. When we calculate the ratio (B)/(A) ourselves, we notice that it is

often slightly less than the estimations of "complete plants" alone which are presented in some articles and studies. The most likely explanation of this slight discrepancy is the fact that a certain proportion of these estimates include *isolated* machinery or equipment.

34. UNCTAD, 1967, p. 17, paragraph 25 and Table 8.
35. *Ibid.*
36. Teodorovitch, 1980, p. 25.
37. Egorov and Volkov, 1982, p. 52.
38. Skatchkov, 1982, p. 10.
39. *Ibid.*, p. 3.
40. Teodorovitch, 1980, p. 25.
41. Skatchkov, 1982, p. 3.
42. *Ibid.*, pp. 10–11.
43. *Ibid.*, p. 3.
44. See Part I of this chapter.
45. Egorov and Volkov, 1982, p. 60.
46. Considering that repayments are not isolated from current trade figures it is totally impossible, through foreign trade statistics, to calculate the exact weight of compensation.
47. The purpose of those agreements with a compensatory basis is to exploit the energy and mineral potential of developing countries. This is made possible through Soviet technical assistance and equipment. In return, the Soviets receive supplies on a regular basis and for a prolonged period of time, which may possibly—and frequently does—continue beyond the phase of repayment. Among agreements of this type, the most important that we could mention are those signed by the USSR with Afghanistan (natural gas, 1963), with Iran (natural gas, 1966), with Guinea (bauxite, 1969), with Syria and Iraq (oil, 1969–75), with Algeria (aluminum, 1976), and with Morocco (phosphates, 1978). See Teodorovitch, 1980, p. 25 and Lavigne, 1986, p. 111.
48. The buy-back agreements foresee a partial or total repayment in the form of resultant products stemming from "complete plants" which have been installed with the help and credit offered by the socialist countries.
49. Teodorovitch, 1980, p. 26.
50. Oulianovski, 1982, p. 123.
51. Particularly Grekov who puts the level of compensatory operations at 20 to 25 percent. Grekov, 1982, p. 2.
52. UNCTAD, 1979, p. 19, paragraph 49 (TD/B/754).
53. OECD, 1985, p. 12.
54. Teodorovitch, 1980, p. 25.
55. On this point, see Vassil Vassilev, 1969, pp. 10–13.
56. Lavigne, 1986, p. 55.
57. Italics in the original.
58. Lavigne, 1986, p. 56 from Bogomolov (ed), 1982, p. 451.
59. In reference to an alternative model which is too restrictive and only leaves an option (or obligation) between market (exchange through export) and

direct regulation of flows inside the enterprise (internalized trade within the transnational corporation). Joffre, 1986, p. 26.

60. Whether these are 100 percent subsidiaries, majority, equity, or minority joint ventures (as with East-South mixed enterprises).

61. See J.L. Mucchielli, 1985, pp. 209–210 who specifies that "the process of internalization and the establishment of a wholly-owned subsidiary are preferred in the hypothesis where the proprietory rights fee is incorporated into the final phase of the product (e.g., as in the case of IBM). On the other hand, if the monopolistic advantage is integrated into an intermediary phase (or an intermediary product), the sale of the technology can take place without the process of internalization and with a less personalized contract which would alleviate the risk of losing any revenue from the secret character of the manufacturing process (as with Coca-Cola, which hands out franchise contracts)."

62. In particular, internalized circulation within the space of a transnational corporation corresponds to captive flows outside the market, whereas the flow of resultant products through buy-back agreements cannot totally escape the market, even if there is partial integration: prices are set by reference to the market whether they are higher, equal, or lower than world market prices.

63. According to the meaning given it by Richard Löwenthal. Löwenthal, 1976.

64. These are according to UNCTAD estimates which are based on figures derived from the CMEA Secretariat.

65. The abandoning of signed projects could actually account for slight variations in the stock of the two project categories (signed and in service) but not to such an extent.

66. As Daniel Pineye has shown, this is a fairly frequent occurrence when it comes to statistical data on East-South commerce and cooperation, Pineye, 1985.

Selected Bibliography

Andreff, W. *Les multinationales,* La Découverte, Paris, Collection Repères, No. 54, 127 pages, 1987.

Ballot, G. and Gutman, P. "Political Economy of East-West-South Industrial Cooperation," pp. 115–146 in: *East European Economies: Slow Growth in the 1980s,* Vol. 2, Foreign Trade and International Finance, Joint Economic Committee, US Congress, March 28, Washington, D.C., USGPO, 354 pages, 1986.

Basile, A. "Les Nouvelles Formes d'Investissement (NFI), Définition, constraintes et perspectives," *Revue d'Economie Politique,* Paris, No. 3, pp. 275–298, 1985.

Bogomolov, O. (ed) *Socialisme et restructuration des relations économiques internationales,* Mezdunarodyne Otnosenija, Moscow, 304 pages, 1982 (in Russian).

CMEA. *Cooperation of the CMEA Member Countries and the Council for Mutual Assistance with the Developing States,* CMEA Secretariat, Moscow, 54 pages, 1982.

Dobozi, I. "Economic Interaction between East and South—the mineral resource dimension," *Raw Materials Report,* Stockholm, Vol. 2, No. 2, pp. 25–41, 1983a.

————. "Arrangements for Mineral Development Cooperation between Socialist Countries and Developing Countries," *Natural Resources Forum*, United Nations, New York, Vol. 7, No. 4, October, pp. 339-350, 1983b.

Egorov, I.A. and Volkov, M.Y. *Structural Changes in the Industry of the USSR and prospects of the Division of labour with developing countries*, UNIDO, ID/WG.357/3, 8 January, Vienna, 87 pages, 1982.

Ericsson, M. "Geomin," *Raw Materials Report*, Stockholm, Vol. 2, No. 2, pp. 21-33, 1983.

Grekov, Y. "L'aide économique de l'URSS aux PVD," *Agence de Presse Novosti*, (APN), No. 3, p. 2, 1982.

Gutman, P. *Le transfer de technologie du CAEM vers le Tiers-Monde, de l'Est-Sud à l'Est-Ouest-Sud—Etat de la question et éléments pour une recherche*, Report submitted to OECD, DSTI, Paris, 155 pages and annexes, 1985.

————. "Tripartite Industrial Cooperation and East Europe," pp. 823-871 in: *East European Economic Assessment, Part 2—Regional Aspects*, Joint Economic Committee, US Congress, July 10, Washington, D.C., USGPO, 886 pages, 1981.

Jimenez, I. "Un exemple d'investissement du CAEM: liste des sociétés mixtes établies dans les pays en développement," *Mondes en Développement*, Tome 15, No. 57, pp. 125-138, 1987.

Joffre, P. "Les Nouvelles relations internationales inter-entreprises," *Problèmes Economiques*, Paris, 13 August 1986, pp. 25-29.

Khaldine, M. *Les pays en développement et l'URSS: formes nouvelles de coopération commerciale et économique*, UNCTAD, 11 April, TD/B/AC.38/2/Add.1, Geneva, 18 pages, 1984.

Lavigne, M. (ed) *Les Relations Est-Sud dans l'Economie Mondiale*, Economica, Paris, 346 pages, 1986.

Löwenthal, R. "Soviet Counter-Imperialism," *Problems of Communism*, Washington, D.C., Vol. 25, No. 6, November-December, pp. 52-63, 1976.

McMillan, C.H. *Multinationals from the Second World—Growth of Foreign Investment by Soviet and East European State Enterprises*, Macmillan Press, London, 220 pages, 1987.

————. "Growth of external investments by the Comecon Countries," *The World Economy*, Amsterdam, Vol. 2, No. 3, September, pp. 363-386, 1979a.

————. "Soviet investment in the industrialized Western economies and in the developing economies of the Third World," pp. 625-647 in: *Soviet Economy in a Time of Change*, Vol. 2, Joint Economic Committee, US Congress, October 10, Washington, D.C., USGPO, 677 pages, 1979.

Michalet, C.A. *Le Capitalisme Mondial*, PUF, Paris, 386 pages, second edition, Collection Economie en Liberté, 1985.

Monkiewicz, J. and Monkiewicz, G. *East-South Capital Cooperation—An unexploited possibility?* Paper presented at the 5th EADI General Conference, Amsterdam, September 1-5, 1987. This article also appears in the present volume.

Mucchielli, J.L. *Les Firmes multinationales: mutations et nouvelles perspectives*, Economica, Paris, 310 pages, 1985.

OECD. *Countertrade: developing country practices*, OECD, Paris, 1985.

Oman, C. *New Forms of International Investment in Developing Countries*, Development Centre, OECD, Paris, 140 pages, 1982.

Oulianovski, R. "Les résultats de la coopération entre l'URSS at les pays en développement," *Socialisme: Théorie et Pratique*, Moscow, (105), pp. 119–124, 1982.

Pineye, D. "Evolution dans les relations économiques Est-Sud," *Le Courrier des Pays de l'Est*, Paris, No. 292, pp. 3–38, 1985.

Popov, V.D. "Pays du CAEM et pays en développement: une analyse soviétique du commerce et de la coopération," *Mondes en Développement*, Paris, Tome 15, No. 57, pp. 19–35, 1987, (translation in French of Popov's Article: "The New Forms of Economic Cooperation of CMEA Member Countries with Developing Countries," *Izvestija Akademii Nauk*, Moscow, (series on economy), 1985, No. 5, pp. 105–116 (in Russian).

Skatchkov, S. "USSR Economic and Technical Cooperation with Foreign Countries," *Foreign Trade*, Moscow, No. 6, pp. 2–13, 1982.

Teodorovitch, T. "Cooperation Between the USSR and Developing Countries," *Foreign Trade*, Moscow, No. 5, pp. 25–27, 1980.

UNCTAD. *Joint ventures with the participation of enterprises of the socialist countries of Eastern Europe*, UNCTAD/ST/TSC/5, 20 June, Geneva, 44 pages, 1986a.

———. *Echanges compensés*, TD/B/C.7/82, 28 August, Geneva, 16 pages, 1986b.

———. *Trade relations among countries having different economic and social systems and all trade flows resulting therefrom*, "Trends and policies in trade among countries having different economic and social systems," TD/B/754, 30 August, Geneva, 24 pages and annexes, 1979.

———. *Review of trade relations among countries having different economic and social systems*, Part 2, "Trade between the socialist and developing countries," TD/B/128/Add.2, 21 July 1967, Geneva, 85 pages, 1967.

Vassilev, V. *Policy in the Soviet Bloc on Aid to Developing Countries*, Development Centre, OECD, Paris, 114 pages, 1969.

Vlasov, A. "New Forms of Economic Relations of CMEA Member-Countries with Developing Nations," *Foreign Trade*, Moscow, No. 12, pp. 14–16, 1983.

Zaleski, E. "Socialist multinationals in developing countries," pp. 156–184 in Hamilton, G. (ed) *Red Multinationals or Red Herrings? The Activities of Enterprises from Socialist Countries in the West*, Frances Pinter, London, 202 pages, 1986.

Zevin, L.Z. *Economic Cooperation of Socialist and Developing Countries: New Trends*, Nauka Publishing House, Moscow, 240 pages, 1976.

10

Nkomati and Soviet Policy on Africa in the Eighties: The End of Ideological Expansion?

Winrich Kühne

Introduction

Three decades of Soviet involvement in Africa have seen a remarkable growth in "normal" interstate relations with African countries. Starting almost from zero Moscow now has diplomatic ties with more than forty African states. For the Soviets as well as for their East European allies, decolonization turned out to be the road to widespread acceptance in the international arena. It was this acceptance, and not merely military gains made in Europe during the Second World War, which brought Soviet Russia the status of a great power.

The record, however, is quite different concerning Moscow's quest for ideological expansion; i.e., the world wide establishment of Marxism-Leninism under Soviet leadership. In Africa, a continual pattern of ups and downs has evolved. Those African states that became close allies of the socialist camp remained in that position for a while and then broke off again (Ghana, Guinea, Mali, Sudan, Egypt, Somalia, etc.). There is no "growth rate" in this area comparable to the one achieved in the field of diplomatic relations. Obviously a clear line of distinction has to be drawn between advances in taking up normal interstate relations and the ability to secure lasting pro-Soviet positions. This is what the history of Soviet involvement in Africa teaches with remarkable clarity.

In the mid-seventies, far-reaching ideological and military gains in Mozambique, Angola, and Ethiopia prompted another rise in Eastern bloc hopes for more influence. In the meantime, however, Soviet hopes as well as Western fears for communist domination in Southern Africa received serious blows. In March 1984 the People's Republic of Mozambique under President Samora Machel and the ideological archenemy of revolutionary socialism in Africa, the white minority regime in South Africa led by Pieter Botha, signed a "Treaty of Non-Aggression and Good Neighbourliness" (Nkomati Accord) in a ceremony that was broadcasted world-wide. This treaty led to the expulsion from Mozambique of another important Soviet ally, the South Africa liberation organization, the African National Congress (ANC). (Only a small group of about ten people was allowed to stay on, but strictly prohibited from engaging in any activities that could lead to unrest and violence against the apartheid regime.) Furthermore, only a few weeks before Nkomati the Marxist-Leninist oriented regime in Angola, the MPLA, had changed it relations with Pretoria by agreeing to an armistice (Lusaka Agreement) without the Namibia issue being resolved.

Nkomati and the Lusaka Agreement, of course, have not dealt the final blow to Soviet activities in Southern Africa. However, the Nkomati Accord in particular was paralleled by an "opening to the West," as the media called it, not only in the economic but also in the political, ideological, and to some extent, even the military field.

The thesis of this chapter is that developments in Southern Africa in the spring of 1984 are an expression of a more fundamental crisis in Soviet Africa policy. As an American analyst put it, in the mid-eighties the fundamental "modus operandi" of Eastern bloc Third World policy appears to be challenged.[1] Also there is probably some truth in the statement by Mittelman: ". . . if Mozambique fails to consummate the transition, socialism is unlikely to flourish anywhere in Africa in the near future. If Mozambique succeeds in stamping out underdevelopment, the experience will herald new possibilities for the Third World."[2]

An analysis of the sequence of events in the Mozambican–South African relationship seems to confirm the view that Pretoria's destabilization policy was crucial for bringing about FRELIMO's rapprochement with the West. This is, however, a very simple-minded, one-dimensional perception of events. If we take into account another dimension of Mozambique's policy—its relations with the East—the picture becomes very different and much more complicated. In this dimension it is not South Africa's stepped up destabilization efforts in 1980–81 which were decisive to Mozambique's re-orientation to the West, but another event: In 1980 FRELIMO leaders tried hard to achieve full membership for Mozambique in the CMEA, but were turned down by Moscow.[3] Like Ethiopia and a few other socialist-oriented countries, Mozambique kept only its previous observer status.

Space does not permit here a discussion of this refusal in detail. The financial burden that Vietnam, Laos, and Cuba are to the rest of the

CMEA is one obvious reason. Integrational problems are another. For Machel and probably for other FRELIMO leaders also, the consequences of this refusal were clear: the comprehensive socialist, Marxist-Leninist orientation of FRELIMO's Third Party Programme could no longer be continued as before. Integration into the Eastern Bloc economic system had been too important a pillar of this orientation.[4]

Thus, as early as 1980 Machel had to look for new partners and a new outlook. Various events in 1982 show that this resulted in rapprochement with the West and consequently also with South Africa:

1. To the surprise of many FRELIMO concluded in April, 1982 a treaty of military cooperation with its former colonial oppressor, Portugal; there were also rumors of military cooperation with France and Great Britain which, however, did not materialize.

2. In August, 1982 FRELIMO for the first time accepted the so-called "Berlin Clause" in an agreement on food aid with the Federal Republic of Germany. This was a highly symbolic step in terms of FRELIMO's position in questions concerning the East-West conflict. For years FRELIMO had cut itself off from the flow of bilateral West German and multilateral EC development aid in favor of practicing "socialist solidarity" with the GDR. Because the "Berlin clause" has no relevance at all for Mozambique's national interests, but is of utmost importance to both Germanies in their struggle regarding the legal and political status of the city of Berlin, FRELIMO's long time refusal to accede to the West German formulation may be the reason the GDR is reported to have been the only CMEA member country to support Mozambique's application for full membership.

3. In fall, 1982 Maputo publicly declared its decision to take part in the Lome III negotiations, thereby beginning *de jure* its re-integration into the Western economic system. Since then Mozambique has become a full member of Lome and the IMF.

4. In August, 1982 Mozambique also concluded its first trade agreement with the People's Republic of China, thereby revitalizing its relations with another great power fighting Soviet influence in Southern Africa. When FRELIMO was still a guerilla movement, its relations to Peking were most amicable.

5. Finally, in April, 1983 the 4th Congress of the FRELIMO Party ended with very significant decisions concerning the country's further political and economic orientation. Compared with earlier documents, there was a clear tendency to de-emphasize the importance of "proletarian class struggle" as the ideological justification for FRELIMO's leadership, although the dominant role of

the party and the centralized leadership were clearly strengthened. FRELIMO was moving in the direction of Afro-socialist one party systems. More important, however, were the modifications, or better to say, the corrections of orthodox Marxist-Leninist elements of Mozambique's economic policy. First, more decentralization of economic planning and implementation and, second, a re-orientation of agricultural development away from the state farms to more support for small scale family farming was advocated. Eastern Bloc type state farms, so far getting the bulk of governmental financial support, had, in most cases, proved to be costly failures in terms of productivity. This new line of the 4th Party Congress to encourage private initiatives and private capital was probably accelerated by the Nkomati process and Mozambique's hope to end its economic disaster by attracting South African and international capital into the country. On September 6, 1984, a new investment code came into force which not only advocates and facilitates private capital, but which—a more dramatic change considering the original ideological line—allows for the establishment of wholly foreign-owned companies, giving them every guarantee to work profitably and take their profits out of the country in hard currency.

FRELIMO's Disenchantment with Soviet Military Assistance

South Africa's destabilization policy and the steady deterioration of Mozambique's security situation brings up another fundamental question in Mozambique's relationship with the East: Why was the Kremlin either unwilling or unable to take advantage of this situation in the sense of increasing FRELIMO's dependence on Eastern Bloc military assistance (weapons, advisors, training, etc.)? Here is a classic situation of conflict and instability, in which, according to conventional wisdom in the West, Moscow would not hesitate to use to its advantage.

Article 4 of the Treaty of Friendship and Cooperation, concluded in March, 1977, provides for long-term military cooperation between Mozambique and the Soviet Union. It aims at "reinforcing defense potentials of the high contracting parties." Quite similar clauses of military cooperation became part of the treaties with other Eastern Bloc countries; for example Article 4 of the Treaty of Friendship, Cooperation and Mutual Assistance between Mozambique and Cuba of October, 1977 and Article 5 of the treaty with the GDR of February, 1979. As with economic cooperation, Machel and others in FRELIMO's leadership gradually became disenchanted with the usefulness of the close military alliance with Eastern Bloc countries. The chronology of events, however, was different.[5]

In February, 1981, about two weeks after the attack by South African commandos on ANC buildings in Matola, one cruiser and three smaller units of the Soviet Indian Ocean Fleet visited Maputo and Beira. Soviet Ambassador Vodovin in Maputo told the press that these ships were meant to demonstrate "Soviet solidarity with socialist Mozambique" against further attacks by South Africa. His public remarks created the impression that Moscow had decided to take a much tougher stand concerning South Africa's aggressiveness.[6] However, apart from further regular visits by Soviet warships (for instance in September, 1981), little happened in the following months.

In May–June, 1982, however, the number of Soviet-Mozambican visits and talks on security questions increased significantly, triggered by Mozambique's security situation, which now had become precarious indeed. At short intervals, Marcellino Dos Santos, number two in FRELIMO leadership, and then Sebastio Mabote, Defense Minister and Chief of the Mozambican General Staff, travelled to Moscow. In the first week of June, 1982, their visits were countered by a high-ranking Soviet military delegation, led by General Yepishev, head of the main political directorate of the Soviet Army and Navy.[7]

In terms of a substantial increase in military assistance, however, this delegation seems not to have been very forthcoming, although Yepishev in very general terms stated the Soviet Union's willingness to intensify military cooperation.[8] (Western monitoring agencies do not report a significant increase in Soviet arms deliveries after this visit. In US dollars their value in 1982 and 1983 was less than in 1978, when Soviet deliveries reached their peak, and also less than in 1979–1980.[9]) Yepishev, however, is reported to have brought forward in strong terms the Soviet displeasure with the agreement on military cooperation with Portugal of April, 1982.[10] In hindsight, however, and considering that until today nothing substantial has come out of this agreement, one may well speculate whether it was not concluded by Machel merely to push the Soviets towards a more active military support.

In November, 1982 Samora Machel himself went to Moscow to attend Leonid Brezhnev's funeral. He and Defense Minister Mabote had at least one meeting with Soviet Defense Minister Ustinov, Marshal Ogarkov, Deputy Defense Minister Marshal Sokolov, and other leading Soviet military personnel.[11] The concrete results of these talks were not published. Only a few weeks later, however, South African Foreign Minister Pik Botha felt compelled to warn Fidel Castro in public not to send Cuban troops to Mozambique. Such an eventuality would not be tolerated by South Africa.[12] Furthermore, Frank Wisner, United States Deputy Under

Secretary of State for African Affairs, who was in Maputo the same month, advised President Machel not to internationalize the war,[13] South African and United States intelligence obviously had come to the conclusion that the Soviet and Cuban leadership were considering a step up in Mozambican defense.

No additional Cuban advisers or combat troops showed up in Mozambique. Instead, from February 28 to March 5, Machel paid another visit to Moscow. This time he was accompanied by Foreign Minister Chissano, not by Defense Minister Mabote. They met with Andropov, Gromyko and Ustinov to inform the Soviet side about FRELIMO's preparations for its 4th Party Congress and—most probably, although not reported in public—Mozambique's decision now to seek an accommodation with South Africa, as there was no military option left.[14] About two weeks later, Machel for the first time went public about ongoing talks between a Mozambican and a South African delegation to find such an accommodation.[15]

There is little official information available as to why the Soviets and Mozambicans failed to agree on a level of military cooperation which would have saved them both the "errand" to Nkomati. The reluctance shown by the Soviets does, of course, confirm views held by many Western analysts, that Southern Africa, in terms of "Realpolitik," is only of second or even third rate importance to the Kremlin.[16] In contrast to Angola, Mozambique had no hard currency to pay for modern and effective Soviet weapons, whereas on the other hand, the risk of a direct confrontation between Eastern Bloc advisers and South African combat troops was much greater than in Angola. After all, South Africa's threat to invade Mozambique in case of Cuban troops being deployed had to be taken seriously. Most certainly the Reagan administration would have backed such a move politically and, in case of direct Soviet intervention to save the Cubans from defeat by the South Africans, also militarily.

The Mozambicans also had good reasons not to push too hard for closer ties with the Soviets in the military field. Strong misgivings about the effectiveness of Soviet military assistance already existed, as Isaacman has pointed out: "Soviet weapons—with the exception of a handful of MIG-21s, MI-24 helicopter gun ships, and some SAM-7s—were out of date and costly, a fact not lost on the Mozambicans. Moreover, there was growing dissatisfaction with the quality of the conventional military training provided by Eastern Bloc advisers, which proved ineffectual against the MNR guerrillas."[17] Therefore Machel probably did not see much sense in making farreaching concessions to the Soviets concerning basing rights, the only way by which he probably could have motivated the Soviet leadership to transfer more weapons and advisers to Mozambique under acceptable terms of payment.

In short, the process which led to Mozambique's rapprochement with the West apparently was a product of the general weaknesses of Soviet policy toward Africa and the Third World in both the economic and military field. A glance back on the history of Soviet involvement in Africa helps to understand how these weaknesses have impaired Soviet expectations, hampering further expansion of Marxism-Leninism in Africa and in other parts of the Third World.

Socialist Orientation in the Eighties: A Failing Doctrine?

The prime importance which Soviet doctrine attaches to single-party systems along Marxist-Leninist lines has led many in the West—especially those who tend to reduce the complexity of global East-West competition in the Third World to a one-dimensional, zero-sum game—to believe that the existence of such a party is a reliable indicator of that country's having been drawn irreversibly into the Soviet orbit. Reactions to the long expected founding of the Worker's Party of Ethiopia (WPE) in September 1984 are a recent case in point. Moscow's propaganda was, of course, jubilant and quite a few commentators in the West saw their fears confirmed. In their view Ethiopia has become another Soviet vassal state.

People familiar with the details of the founding process of this party, however, came to quite different conclusions. They pointed out that Mengistu and the military loyal to him have been remarkably successful in satisfying Soviet propaganda needs on the one hand, and in turning the party into a tool for their personal and rather nationalistic ambitions on the other.[18] More or less all the important functions in the WPE are kept by military or civilians who are known to be loyal to Mengistu. It is by no means inconceivable that the consolidation of Mengistu's power through a single-party system will actually one day make it easier for him to loosen his ties with the Eastern Bloc, once the military situation has improved. Quite obviously that is the lesson of Mozambique as well as those of the Congo and Benin in their rapprochement with the West. All three have singly-party systems organized along Marxist-Leninist lines: the FRELIMO Party since 1977, the "Mouvement Nationale de la Revolution (MNR)" in the Congo since 1969 and the "Parti de la Revolution Populaire du Benin (PRPB)" since 1975. It is not the single-party system which keeps Mengistu close to the Soviet Union, but the stalemated and bloody civil war in Eritrea, Tigre, and other parts of the country and the consequent undiminished need for military assistance.

Those who take single-party systems in Marxist-Leninist disguise as a reliable indicator of Soviet influence overlook a simple fact of African reality: apart from military rule, single-party rule is the "normal" form of government in post-colonial Africa. The reasons for this tendency, well known to all Africanists, are complex and cannot be elaborated here. However, to readers not familiar with Africa it should be pointed out that even in such indisputably pro-Western countries with single-party systems as Zaire or Zambia, "Politbureaus" and "Central Committees" do exist.

In the eighties the fact that single-party systems do not assure lasting Soviet influence can be stated with much more certainty than for earlier decades for two reasons:

1. Eastern Bloc military and security co-operation with socialist-oriented regimes did not prove to generate the long-term influence hoped for by Moscow, although in the seventies arms sales to African countries reached a level unknown before.
2. Marxist-Leninist models which—after the disappointing performance of Afro-socialist models—had become very attractive to all those Africans who were sincerely interested in bringing about socialism as a better way of life for their peoples, are losing their appeal. As one African journal recently put it: "Socialism has not proved to be a quick way to development."

Military co-operation does generate influence in the short- and medium term, especially if the client-states are involved in a severe internal or external conflict. However, there is a marked *structural discontinuity* between *short, medium,* and *long-term effects.* With regard to long-term influence, the Soviet dilemma can be stated in a very simplified manner as follows: To gain time for building up ideological and political structures and ties that are strong enough to guarantee the permanence of a close anti-Western alliance with the Socialist camp, a protracted conflict is desirable, whereas conflict solution—after a short phase of gratitude for Soviet support—will very soon give prominence to the limitations of the Soviets and East Europeans as economic partners. Even a protracted conflict will develop a dynamism that the Soviets have little capacity to control and that will eventually destroy the client state's exclusive alliance with the Eastern Bloc. In the course of the conflict, the client state loses every perspective of development; the unsatiable need for spare parts and new weapons leads to a heavy drain of capital, urgently needed for social and economic programs. Economic development declines because of permanent fighting and the resulting destruction. In the end it has to be realized that the war for which so many weapons were bought and so many human lives spent cannot be won. It is in this phase that the regime most probably will be confronted with rising resentment among its own populace and élite against the close ties with Moscow and Marxist-Leninist orientation. In Ethiopia as well as in Angola this phenomenon has already been clearly visible to Western observers for quite a while.

On the whole, a close, one-sided alliance with the Soviet Union in the long run tends to bring to the fore two fundamental questions for almost any socialist-oriented regime in Africa:

1. how much sense does it make to continue a very intensive military alliance with the Soviet Union to win a war;
2. to what extent does it make sense to pursue further orthodox Marxist-Leninist models of development? This is a question which today all socialist-oriented regimes face, no matter how close their military ties with Moscow. (It is hardly necessary to mention that, of course, there also exists and has always existed a very critical debate with regard to the utility of capitalist models of development.)

The Crisis of Marxist-Leninist Models of Development: State Farming and the Problem of Agricultural Productivity

In an article published in a Soviet journal in the fall of 1984, A. Kiva, a well-known Soviet expert on developing countries, made a very revealing remark: "One of the major problems looming large on the developing countries' horizon is what can be called the problem of creating an operational socio-economic model of a socialist-oriented country."[19] For all experienced readers of Soviet publications on Third World problems, this immediately raised the question: What does he really want to tell us? For obviously Eastern Bloc authors, including Kava, under the heading of *non-capitalist way of development with a socialist orientation* have always maintained that they firmly believed Marxism-Leninism to be in the possession of such a model, superior to all other theoretical and practical approaches to development. As late as 1981, Nikolai Kosukhin, for instance, wrote: "Today, revolutionary democrats view scientific socialism as a theory capable not only of becoming a world outlook for the broad masses of the working people, but also of providing them with a real program for building a new progressive society."[20] Why, then, does Kiva in 1984 talk about the necessity of "creating" an operational socio-economic order for socialist orientation? This can only be interpreted as an admission that in the eyes of at least some Soviet analysts the model of non-capitalist development has failed and they are prepared to discuss this fact.

The crisis of orthodox Marxist-Leninist thinking in the field of development, however, should not be seen in isolation from the more general crisis of development theories and policies. This crisis focusses mainly on the dominant role of the state, or, more precisely, the role of overcentralized, bureaucratic government and of more or less urban-based élites, as an "agent for development." As Elsenhans and others have pointed out, the state, together with foreign capital, dominates the economy and consequently development in the majority of Third World countries, especially Africa.[21] The choice of a socialist or capitalist orientation has only limited influence on the extent of this dominance. The Soviet model of non-capitalist development for obvious ideological reasons attributes prime importance to the dominant role of the state. E.M. Primakov, referring to Lenin, saw the interruption of the capitalist path of development and the formation of a strong state sector as the cornerstone for any further development toward socialism.[22] Brezhnev, in his report to the 24th Congress of the CPSU in March 1971, left no doubt that for the Soviets the state sector is the economic basis for a truly revolutionary democratic policy.[23]

Very early, however, the Soviets had to make concessions concerning the application of this dogma in practice. There was little capital and technical know-how to be found in most Third World countries and the limits of the CMEA countries to provide these "commodities" soon became manifest. Already in the sixties, Moscow had to tell friends like Egypt, Algeria, Guinea, and Mali that they had to look for capital and know-how on the capitalist world market.[24] Pointing out the experience in Soviet Russia during Lenin's New Economic Policy (NEP), this was not seen as an unsurmountable obstacle to the successful implementation of a non-capitalist way of development. In order to limit the ideologically negative influence of domestic and foreign private capital, Soviet academics as well as politicians postulated absolute control by the state of all important economic sectors, including nationalizing foreign firms, the gradual cooperativization of agriculture and the handicrafts, establishment of state farms in the countryside, and for the state to hold a foreign-trade monopoly.

By the mid-eighties it had become virtually an irrefutable fact (see Kiva's admission) that this state-centered approach for bypassing private initiative has failed in the most important socio-economic sector of African states; agriculture. (In most black African countries about eighty per cent of the population still lives in the rural areas.) Eastern Bloc type state farms and state controlled cooperatives have proved to be especially costly failures. In Mali, the Congo, and other socialist-oriented countries this was already realized in the sixties and seventies. FRELIMO was ready to admit to this fact at its 4th Party Congress in 1983. The leadership in Angola came to a similar conclusion in 1984, when the Minister of Finance stressed the important role of the peasant farmer. In a significant policy reversal he announced that greater financial and technical support, as well as material incentives would be provided to small-scale producers to increase their output.[25] In Ethiopia the resistance of peasants against collective and state farming is considerable and had already forced the government in 1980/81 to slow down its program. Soviet specialists did not refrain from mentioning these difficulties in their writings: "The state farms ran into considerable difficulties as soon as they were set up, . . . production on most farms went down to half of the pre-revolutionary level."[26] Contrary to Mozambique and Angola, however, Mengistu's government is not yet prepared to admit the failure of state farms in comparison with peasant farming. In view of the actual terrible shortage of food, it seems to be only a matter of time, not of principle, before Mengistu will have to make the same adjustments in agricultural policy as have FRELIMO and MPLA.

The *failure of state farming* can be traced back to different causes:

1. An erroneous assumption by Eastern Bloc experts and their African counterparts with regard to the nature of traditional peasant farming. This method was held to be capable of subsistence production only and thus unable to raise production to a level which would satisfy the needs of the growing urban population and the need of the state to earn hard currency though agricultural exports.[27] Therefore the state, i.e., the urban élite, had to take care of raising productivity by organizing new forms of production and providing them with capital, technological know-how, etc.
2. State farming has consumed more capital than had been anticipated. As Lofchie and others have pointed out, it is the irony of socialist-oriented state farming that it has tended to exacerbate the very dependency on foreign capital it was meant to remove. Heightened levels of financial and material aid from Western donors became necessary.[28] Sweden, for example, was at one time providing over eighty per cent of all foreign exchange investment in the state farms of Mozambique. In Ethiopia the Mengistu regime channels ninety per cent of agricultural investment into state farms that only produce six per cent of the nation's grain.
3. The participation of peasants in collective and state farming has been reluctant. There was little confidence among them in state-bureaucratic structures being able to take care of their subsistence needs. This distrust often turned into open refusal and sometimes even active resistance when mismanagement and corruption became rampant.

It was A.P. Butenko, Head of Department in the Institute for the Economy of the Socialist World System, who already in 1982 (i.e. one year before the 4th FRELIMO Party Congress) quite openly discussed the necessity of changing the agricultural development policy in countries of socialist orientation. Two statements from his article, which first appeared in Russian and later in German, may serve as a demonstration of new and significant tendencies in Soviet thinking in this field:

> Neither the collective organization of labor nor the application of technology—unavoidably very simple due to limited capacities—can compensate for a loss of interest on the part of the majority of producers. . . . A reliable way of vitalizing the agricultural sector, and the economy as a whole, . . . consists in a policy which attributes top priority to the personal factors of production in this phase; i.e., in stimulating the individual work of the peasant and, by virtue of its close connection, that of the craftsman and merchant.[29]

Soviet experts and African Marxist-Leninist politicians, therefore, again have to face a basic problem of Marxism-Leninism in African and other developing countries: "to call the ideology of the party 'proletarian' can only hide that the development problems of the present society are caused by and should be solved in a revolutionary relation with the traditional agrarian structure, which determines the material basis of the society."[30] Economic realities in Africa are pushing hard the abandonment of rigid and highly abstract ideological differentiations between Afro-Socialism, Marxism-Leninism, or so-called Afrocommunism, and capitalist approaches to development. Machel, once a fierce opponent of a "Third-way" between capitalism and Marxism, more and more turned back to Afro-socialist rhetoric.

Conclusions

One conclusion of this short study on recent developments and present problems in Soviet Africa policy is obvious. A rising number of Soviet specialists is deeply worried about the future outlook for the expansion of Marxism-Leninism in developing countries.[31] Some of them almost seem to be ready to conclude that it makes little sense to invest further in this goal. Even among GDR academics, who in the past were often much more ideologically orthodox in their writing on developing countries than their Soviet counterparts, a fierce debate is going on as to the circumstances under which there is still hope for a successful implementation of socialism.[32] However, frustrations exist not only in the ideological field. Objective economic factors have forced Eastern Bloc economists into an even more far-reaching change of mind about the character of the present global economy. To continue an uncompromising antagonistic policy against this economic world order and its main protagonists, the Western industrialized countries, may prove to be more dangerous to the CMEA countries than to anyone else. Thus there is hope that the East-West conflict, whose treatment as antagonistic has already become outdated in the field of security because of the mutual capacity for assured nuclear destruction, will also become less antagonistic in the Third World because of economic forces.

Developments in Mozambique are already an interesting case in point. Although there is no doubt that Nkomati was seen by the Soviets as a heavy blow to their policy, Moscow did not retaliate by cutting aid or calling back advisors from Mozambique. On December 26, 1983, with Nkomati already *ante portas*, the Soviet Ambassador in Maputo, Sepelev, made quite clear in a public statement that it was essential to understand that Mozambique was an independent country and "nobody's puppet." The Soviet Union fully understood Mozambique's desire to improve its relations "in all directions."[33] To prove that this was not just a rhetorical position the Soviet Ambassador announced that more shiploads of rice and oil would arrive and also drew attention to the trade agreement of US$300 million in value which had been signed shortly before. Only a few days after the signing of the Nkomati Treaty Sepelev announced further Soviet loans. Furthermore, the USSR was the first creditor to agree to reschedule Mozambique's debt, after a world wide appeal by FRELIMO. Moscow's willingness to move away from long-held positions even in the case of white-dominated South Africa, the long time arch-enemy of Soviet Africa policy and African revolutionary movements, is also demonstrated by an announcement of Radio Maputo: In January 1985 an official delegation from the Soviet Union and from South Africa met in Beira for joint discussion with the state-owned Mozambican fishing company, Emopesca. They discussed future Soviet and South African technical assistance for Mozambique's fishing industry.[34]

In the military field Maputo is trying to diversify its relations. Although the Soviets still provide most of Mozambique's military hardware it is the Zimbabweans who now have become the dominant force in the fight against RENAMO. Some troops from Tanzania are stationed in Northern Mozambique for the same reasons. Furthermore, the government has continued in its efforts to establish or increase military cooperation with Portugal, Britain, and the United States. Unfortunately, in 1985 Capitol Hill turned down a request by the State Department to give Mozambique US$1.15 million in non-lethal military aid.

The need, however, to get away from the strictly antagonistic outlook on the world, raises a very difficult question for Soviet politicians and scholars: To what extent is the *legitimacy* of the Soviet regime based on the pursuit of expansionist ideological goals, as Christoph Royan has concluded in a comprehensive study?[35] Is this dogma so deeply embedded in the Soviet system that it precluded profound learning processes as to the limit of ideological expansion? Western sovietologists do not agree in their answer to this question. On the Soviet side there also seems to be considerable controversy about this point, if one takes as an example the diversity of views concerning the future outlook of Soviet Africa policy. For instance, two authors, L. Alexandrovskaya and V. Vigland, did not even once mention the Soviet Union and the other CMEA countries when asking, "Where do Africans place their hopes in this decade?"[36] This, however, is not typical for all Soviet writers. There are others, like N. Kapchenko, Deputy Editor in Chief of *International Affairs*, who in 1985 still held it to be of great importance to repeat traditional ideological slogans: "The growing scale and intensity of the ideological battle in the international arena make it imperative to step up the efforts of the socialist countries and all revolutionary forces of modern times in exposing and checking the political and ideological subversion of imperialism. . . ."[37] Kapchenko argues from the standpoint of an ideological generalist, or "globalist" as one would say in Western terminology, and not of a Third World specialist. There are, of course, strong tendencies in the Soviet Union, not least in the military, *not to give up positions easily*, because the *credibility* of the Soviet Union *as a super power is at stake*. Case studies on *Soviet-Ethiopian* and *Soviet-Angolan* relations would bring this aspect of Soviet Third World policy more unmistakably into perspective than the analysis of Soviet-Mozambican relations can. However, there is little doubt that by and large Soviet relations with these two countries suffer from the same deep structural weaknesses which have led to Mozambique's rapprochement with the West.

Thus, the conclusion of this analysis is not that the Soviet system is about to give up its dogma regarding the world revolutionary expansion of Marxism-Leninism. However, the extent to which it is put into question as a realistic option by Soviet Third World specialists is remarkable. By referring to Lenin's New Economic Policy as a model for problem-ridden socialist-oriented countries of today, Soviet ideologues have found a way to discuss openly and frankly all kinds of fundamental problems facing Marxism-Leninism, not only in developing countries.

Notes

1. See Thomas J. Zamostny, "Moscow and the Third World: Recent Trade Trends in Soviet Thinking," in: *Soviet Studies*, Vol. 36, No. 2, April 1984, pp.

223–235. For a general analysis of recent trends in Soviet Africa policy see David E. Albright, "New Trends in Soviet Policy toward Africa," in: *CSIS-Africa Notes*, No. 27, April 29, 1984.

2. James H. Mittelman, *Underdevelopment and the Transition to Socialism: Mozambique and Tanzania*, New York: Academic Press, 1981, p. 122.

3. See Norman MacQueen, "Mozambique's Widening Foreign Policy," in: *The World Today*, Vol. 40, No. 1, January 1984, pp. 22–28; Christopher Coker, "The Soviet Union, Eastern Europe and the New International Economic Order," *The Washington Papers*, No. 111, published with The Center for Strategic and International Studies, Georgetown University, Washington, 1984, p. 92.

4. See Wolfgang Schoeller, *Aussenwirtschaftliche Neuorientierung Mozambiques, Gründe und allgemeine Bedeutung*, Ebenhausen: Stiftung Wissenschaft und Politik, SWP-AP 2421, 1985.

5. I am grateful to Prof. Michael Clough, from the U.S. Naval Postgraduate School in Monterey, CA, for pointing out this difference to me.

6. *Frankfurter Allgemeine Zeitung*, February 24, 1984 and *SWB/Monitoring Report*, ME/6843/ii, October 2, 1981.

7. *Monitor-Dienst* (Afrika), June 1, 1982, p. 3 and *SWB/Monitoring Report*, ME/7043/ii, June 4, 1982.

8. *SWB/Monitoring Report*, ME/7043/ii, June 4, 1982.

9. See U.S. Arms Control and Disarmament Agency (ACDA), *World Military Expenditures and Arms Transfers 1972–1982*, Washington, April 1982, pp. 80/95; and Joachim Krause, "Soviet Arms Transfers to Sub-Saharan Africa," in: R. Craig Nation and Mark V. Kauppi (Eds.), *The Soviet Impact on Africa*, Lexington, MA.: Lexington Books, 1984, pp. 125–145.

10. See MacQueen, "Mozambique's Widening Foreign Policy," p. 23.

11. *USSR and Third World*, Vol. 13, No. 182, 1983, p. 21.

12. *SWB/Monitoring Report*, ME/7201/B/3, December 6, 1982.

13. *Guardian*, January 13, 1983.

14. *USSR and Third World*, p. 22.

15. *Süddeutsche Zeitung*, March 20, 1983.

16. See Winrich Kühne, *Die Politik der Sowjetunion in Afrika, Bedingungen und Dynamik ihres ideologischen, ökonomischen und politischen Engagements*, Baden-Baden: Nomos Verlag, 1983, p. 163.

17. See Allen Isaacman, "After the Nkomati Accord," in: *Africa Report*, Vol. 30, No. 1, January–February 1985, pp. 10–13.

18. See *Africa Confidential*, Vol. 25, No. 19, September 19, 1984; *Ibid.*, No. 20, October 3, 1984; Gerald A. Funk, "Can Ethiopia Survive Both Communism and Drought?" in: *CSIS-Africa Notes*, No. 40, March 15, 1985.

19. A. Kiva, "Socialist-Oriented Countries: Some Development Problems," in: *International Affairs*, Moscow, No. 10, October 1984, pp. 22–29.

20. Nikolai Kosukhin, *Dissemination of the Concept of Scientific Socialism in Africa*, No. 6, 1981, pp. 4–7.

21. Hartmut Elsenhans, *Abhängiger Kapitalismus oder bürokratische Entwicklungsgesellschaft—Versuch über den Staat in der Dritten Welt*, Frankfurt/Main: Campus Verlag, 1981.

22. E. M. Primakov, "Länder mit sozialistischer Orientierung: ein schwieringer, aber realer Übergang zum Sozialismus," in: *Asien, Afrika, Lateinamerika*, Vol. 9, No. 6, 1981, pp. 965–978.

23. Leonid Brezhnev, *Über die Politik der Sowjetunion und die internationale Lage*, Cologne, 1973, pp. 62–99.

24. See Kühne, *Die Politik der Sowjetuion in Afrika*, p. 54.

25. See Margaret A. Novicki, "Angola—Against All Odds," in: *Africa Report*, Vol. 30, No. 1, January–February 1985, pp. 4–9.

26. Georgi Galperin, "Ethiopia—Strategies of Agrarian Revolution," in: *Asia and Africa Today*, No. 6, 1981, pp. 37–40.

27. See Barbara Munslow, "State Intervention in Agriculture: The Mozambican Experience," in: *The Journal of Modern African Studies*, Vol. 22, No. 2, 1984, pp. 199–221; see also Wolfgang Schoeller, "Mozambique—Struktur und Krise einer Dienstleistungsökonomie im südlichen Afrika," in: *Africa-Spektrum*, Vol. 16, No. 3, 1981, pp. 345–368.

28. Michael F. Lofchie and Stephen Commins, "Food Deficits and Agricultural Policies in Tropical Africa," in: *The Journal of Modern African Studies*, Cambridge, Vol. 20, No. 1, March 1982, pp. 7–25.

29. See A.P. Butenko, "Der Übergang zum Sozialismus in Ländern mit unterentwickleter Wirtschaft," in: *Sowjetwissenschaft, Gesellschaftswissenschaftliche Beiträge*, Vol. 36, No. 3, 1983, pp. 395–407.

30. Peter Aaby, "The State of Guinea-Bissau, African Socialism or Socialism in Africa?," *Research Report No. 45* (The Scandinavian Institute of African Studies), Uppsala 1978, p. 18.

31. For an analysis of Soviet Policy in other Third World regions see for instance: Augusto Varas, "Moscow's double-track Policy, Ideology and Politics in American-USSR Relations," in: *Problems of Communism*, Vol. 33, No. 1, 1984, pp. 35–47. George W. Breslauer, "Soviet Policy in the Middle East 1967–1972: Unalterable Antagonism or Collaborative Competition?," in: Alexander L. George (Ed.), *Managing U.S.-Soviet Rivalry: Problems of Crisis Prevention*, Boulder, Colorado: Westview, 1983, pp. 65–105; Donald S. Zagoria, "The USSR and Africa in 1984," in: *Asian Survey*, January 1985, pp. 21–32.

32. See for instance Gerhard Brehme, "Sozialistische Orientierung und Sozialistischer Entwicklungsweg in Afrika und Nahost—Die Erfahrungen der Sechziger und Siebziger Jahre," in: *Asien, Afrika, Lateinamerika*, Vol. 11, No. 5, 1983, pp. 858–867.

33. See *Monitor-Dienst* (Africa), December 28, 1983.

34. See *Monitor-Dienst* (Africa), January 10, 1985.

35. See Christoph Royen, "Die sowjetische Koexistenzpolitik gegenüber Westeuropa. Voraussetzungen, Ziele, Dilemmata," Stiftung Wissenschaft und Politik. ed., *Internationale Politik und Sicherheit*, Baden-Baden: Nomos Verlag, 1978.

36. Lyudmila Alexandrovskaya/Vladimir Vigand, "Africa—A Hard Decade," in: *Asia and Africa Today*, No. 1, 1985, pp. 6–8.

37. N. Kapchenko, "Foreign Policy and Ideological Struggle Today," in: *International Affairs*, No. 3, 1985, pp. 45–54.

11

Romania: Boundary Disintegration between East and South

Robin Alison Remington

There are many things that can be said about the Romanian–Third World connection, but as so often with Romanian politics that connection is not as straightforward as it seems at first. That is partly because calculated ambiguity is standard practice in Bucharest's foreign policy; a conscious tactic designed to maximize options. Indeed, one could say that Nicolae Ceausescu has a certain Emersonian disregard for "foolish consistencies." However, even if such propensities did not exist, untangling Romanian ties with the South would be a complex task by virtue of the fact that the Third World itself represents a wide range of political, ideological, and economic opportunities to Romanian policymakers. Given that the G-77 has grown to 120 countries and that 101 member-states attended the 1986 8th nonaligned summit, in-depth, country-specific analysis is out of the question.

Nonetheless, since Romania is clearly one end of a spectrum of East-South relations, it is useful to look at the general pattern. In doing so I am assuming: (1) that, although Romanian-South relations are in part a function of political/ideological imperatives flowing from Bucharest's maverick position within the intra-bloc (Warsaw Pact) arena and the intra-Communist subsystem of ruling and non-ruling parties, the extent of that involvement reflects psychological/political needs stemming from Ceausescu's personality cult, (2) that individual targets of Romanian activity in the South may be chosen for reasons of ideology, economics or political culture either together or separately and (3) that Romanian capabilities in the South are subject to objective economic/political restraints. Based on these assumptions, I would put forward two tentative hypotheses: first, that Bucharest is overextended in the South and, unless the Romanian economy does substantially better in the second half of the 1980s that it has done to date, the predicted Ceausescu succession could mean a decline in the absolute amount of Romanian–Third World activity; secondly, that the political economy of the East will interact with lack of coherence in the intra-Communist arena to make it most unlikely that even given such a decline the process of boundary disintegration between East and South symbolized by Romania will be reversed.[1] To evaluate these positions it is necessary to consider them in the context of events that pushed Romania into that country's recognized deviant position within the Soviet-East European alliance structures, the Council for Mutual Economic Assistance (CMEA) and the Warsaw Pact.

The World Socialist Economy

The notion of a world socialist economy is deeply ingrained in the ideological underpinnings of the world Communist movement. It is implicit in Marx's concept of proletarian internationalism and organizational efforts that go back to the League of Communists of 1847.[2] With the Russian revolution of 1917, the power configuration of the international Communist movement changed from that of a loose cluster of non-ruling parties attempting to spur their respective proletariats into revolutionary action to the Soviet Union as the first surviving socialist state surrounded by non-ruling parties whose number one task in terms of proletarian internationalism became seeing that the Russian revolution was not strangled in its cradle.

One dimension of the intense debate between Trotsky and Stalin over permanent revolution versus socialism in one country was precisely their conflicting interpretations of what constituted a viable socialist economy. Even Stalin had moments of doubt as to whether or not the organization of socialist production in a peasant country like Russia was indeed possible.[3] Nonetheless, for a host of political and psychological reasons, the concept of socialism in one country triumphed; Stalin opted for Russian self-sufficiency and economic autarky. Proletarian internationalism was transformed into blatant Russian national Communism. Furthermore, to whatever extent one thought of a world socialist economy, it was synonymous with the Soviet Economy.

With the emergence of ruling parties in Eastern Europe and Asia after World War II, Soviet leadership/domination of the Communist world subtly began to change. Despite the virtues of the Soviet model and love of Comrade Stalin, the CPSU was no longer the *only* ruling party. Those Communist leaders socialized into the Stalin cult, accustomed to blind obedience, financially tied to Moscow, and psychologically tied to Soviet revolutionary myths, acquired real estate and the apparatuses of power, along with hostile populations, and a totally unfamiliar set of problems and pressures. They became national actors subject to the lure of what Brzezinski called "domesticism": that temptation to put domestic concerns above the international obligations dictated by Soviet priorities.[4] At the same time the commitment to the Soviet model meant restructuring East European economies along Soviet lines, i.e., crash programs of industrialization and economic autarky. There was no world socialist economy that was more than the sum of its parts. Although the Council for Mutual Economic Assistance was set up in 1949 symbolically to counter the Marshall Plan, in fact CMEA was largely a conduit for East European resources siphoned off into the Soviet reconstruction effort.[5]

It is generally agreed that the Stalinist economic model benefited the less developed among those East European countries tentatively setting out on the route to socialism. That was certainly true for Romania, where by the mid-1950s the transformation of the economy had resulted in rapid economic growth, urbanization, and relative modernization.[6] The New Course designed to rally the Soviet consumer to the post-Stalin leadership had negative implications for Romanian industrialization as well as Gheorghe Gheorghui-Dej's political style. Moreover, by the 1960s Khrushchev's proposed "socialist international division of labor" was a direct threat to building Romanian socialism as the Romanian leadership intended to build it.

Khrushchev raised his "vital questions" for the world socialist system in the context of an effort to restructure the world socialist economy so as to overcome "the exclusiveness inherited from the past."[7] The problem for the Romanians was that acquiescence to any such socialist division of labor would put a sudden end to Romanian industrialization plans; Khrushchev's vision of a world socialist economy would relegate Romania to being a supplier of raw materials for the more industrialized members of that system. In short, Romanian differences with Moscow were a function of Gheorghui-Dej's refusal to allow Romania to be turned into a de facto internal colony of the socialist camp.

Bucharest responded with delaying tactics and skillfully manipulated the Sino-Soviet split so as to gain both time and room for independent political maneuver. Although efforts to broker that increasingly intransigent conflict failed to budge either Moscow or Beijing, the very attempt provided a vehicle for putting forward Romanian views on Khrushchev's vital questions:

Even when socialism has triumphed on a world scale or at least in most countries, the diversity of the peculiarities of these countries, of the distinctive national and state features, which as Lenin pointed out, will prevail for a long time even after the victory of the proletariat on a world scale, will make it an extremely complex task to find the organizational forms of economic cooperation. Life experience will shape these forms, then the concrete methods of cooperation. To establish now these forms linked to the setting up a single world economy, a problem of a future historical stage, lacks a real basis.

The trend toward the creation of a single world economy as indicated by Lenin is an objective factor in the development of society, one manifest in present day conditions, but this fact can not operate by violating the objective laws characteristic of the present stage of the socialist world economic system, which comprises the national economies of sovereign and independent countries.[8]

There followed what might be considered the Romanian package for relations among socialist countries, those principles that should be seen as an "immutable law" to guarantee the development of the entire world socialist system: national independence, sovereignty, equal rights, mutual advantage, comradely assistance, non-interference in internal affairs, observance of territorial integrity.[9] Clearly these principles of socialist internationalism were a far cry from what Moscow had in mind.

One might say that by rejecting the Soviet preferred world socialist economy the Romanians were refusing to become the South of the world socialist system. And there is no small irony in the fact that an unintended consequence of that refusal has been to emphasize Romania's "developing" as opposed to the country's socialist identity.

Who Is Romania?

In my view, it is helpful to keep in mind that although they are often referred to that way, East and South are by no means mutually exclusive categories. Eastern Europe does not exist as an historical or geographical region. Rather in current usage East Europe refers to ideological/political boundaries separating those East Central European countries that underwent Communist revolutions following World War II from those that did not. The concept of Eastern Europe is shorthand for European socialist states, usually connoting priority for their socialist as opposed to European identities. Objectively, however, these countries vary dramatically in size, natural resources, levels of economic development, political culture and historical experience. Within Eastern Europe the underdeveloped countries of the Balkans were and are by any nonideological criteria, a part of the South.

Moreover, while there is no doubt that Mikhail Gorbachev continues to believe in an implicitly leading role for Moscow within the intra-Communist arena—what I have referred to elsewhere as "the contradictions of real socialism" Soviet style[10]—this has worked to undermine Soviet hegemony. References to general laws of socialist development *are* a euphemism for the Soviet model. Yet, as the recent 27th CPSU Congress so graphically demonstrated, that model is undergoing agonizing reappraisal, the outcome of which remains to be seen. No matter what he means by "radical reform,"[11] Gorbachev's rhetorical commitment to that process strengthens reformist forces throughout Eastern Europe. More importantly from the perspective of Romania, where it is most unlikely that the climate of reform would have any immediate spillover, that climate in itself reinforces what Kevin Delvin has called the "institutionalization of diversity" within the Communist world.[12] It sanctions the socialist pluralism implicit in the 1976 Berlin Conference of Communist and Workers Parties' reinterpretation of proletarian internationalism as "voluntary cooperation" among equal parties engaged in "creative interpretation" of Marxism-Leninism on their national road to socialism.[13]

In these circumstances Soviet control over the substance of just what is "real socialism" has visibly slipped. The formula "national in form and socialist in content" has taken a 180 degree turn to become increasingly socialist in form, national in content; thereby legitimizing socialist patriotism at the expense of Soviet defined proletarian internationalism. In short, the configuration of the world Communist movement that became bipolar with the Sino-Soviet dispute has become increasingly polycentric.

The consequence of what we could call a systemic transformation of the Communist subsystem (or perhaps adolescence on the part of the former children in the family of socialist nations) has been to erode the coherence of the World Communist movement. Communists may agree that both tactically and strategically there is a right solution at any given time. There is less and less agreement on *what* that solution is in specific instances or even on procedures for finding it.

On the one hand, this has made the Romanian insistence on the validity of its identity as a socialist developing country possible. On the other, it allows for considerable ambiguity about just what that means in circumstances where the South is seen to include countries of "socialist orientation," what my Indian friends would call on the byroad rather than the highway of socialist construction, so to speak.

Although in the Romanian case that concept is in some sense a logical consequence of Bucharest's call for a abolition of military blocs, it was not an official part of the Romanian self-image until spelled out by Ceausescu himself at the 1972 National Conference of the Romanian Communist Party.[14] From the Romanian perspective there is some dispute over what "developing" means that has centered around the tendency since the late 1970s for Romanian commentators to distinguish between "developing countries" and nonaligned states. Michael Radu has speculated that this might imply that in the Romanian view only the radical countries of the South, those tilting towards socialism, can be considered developing, while nonaligned is a much more limited category.[15] If so, this would tend to blur Ceausescu's original distinction substantially. However, I am not persuaded; largely because that interpretation would go beyond the Cuban position that there is a natural alliance between the nonaligned and socialist countries, which the Romanians have skillfully avoided. I do agree with Radu's provocative analysis on the fundamental importance of Romania's claim to be *structurally* similar to the developing countries of the South. Not only is that claim the basis for Bucharest's unique de facto membership in the Nonaligned Political Movement (NAM), it has specific implications for what constitutes acceptable mutual advantage in terms of Romanian relations with the political economy of the East and participation in CMEA joint projects.

Ideologically Romanian arguments against the distinction between "progressive" and "moderate" regimes in the South[16] has been used to reiterate Bucharest's commitment to self-determination as an essential component of peaceful coexistence of countries with different social/political systems, rejection of spheres of influence, and Ceausescu's conviction that membership in military blocs does not exempt a country from the obligation to follow the rules of international law; i.e., a distinct slap at the Brezhnev Doctrine of limited sovereignty within the Socialist Commonwealth. In this sense, polemics centered on the South become a way of asserting the Romanian position that international norms supercede intra-bloc convenience. At the same time the South provides an alternative for national initiatives lacking in the East. When it comes to actions in this regard, they are considerably less ambiguous than Romanian rhetoric.

Nonaligned Networking

Romania first managed to get a foot in the door by attending as a guest the Nonaligned Foreign Ministers Meeting in Lima (1975) followed by the 1976 NAM summit in Colombo. Subsequently, Romanian guests have become a permanent feature at nonaligned summits, Foreign Minister meetings, and other ad hoc sessions. Romanian speeches appear in conference proceedings, and Romanian authored articles are published in *The Nonaligned World*, an international journal devoted to the nonaligned movement published in New Delhi.

Since the second NAM Summit (Cairo 1964), it has been the practice for the Romanian head of state to send personal messages to each summit conference; i.e., a practice begun by Gheorghiu-Dej and turned into a fine art by Ceausescu. Indeed, according to Romanian data, between 1965 and 1982 Ceausescu personally visited seventy-seven nonaligned states, while Heads of State of forty-three nonaligned nations paid eighty-five official visits to Romania; thereby creating a substantial political/legal infrastructure. By 1982 this amounted to twelve treaties of friendship and cooperation/collaboration, three formal statements, 137 communiques, and 269 instruments of mutual collaboration in areas of mutual interest.[17]

Another unique political objective can be seen in Bucharest's sustained efforts to assist in peaceful settlements of disputes that wrack the nonaligned movement.[18] Although the attempt to play a mediating role in the Iran-Iraq War have apparently fallen on deaf ears, Romanian shuttle diplomacy designed to de-escalate the Lebanese civil war received considerable international recognition and appreciation. Bucharest's peace initiatives in the Middle East serve the practical purpose of allowing Romania to maintain good relations with Israel as well as with the PLO and its Arab supporters. Such a political balancing act is no mean trick.

This is not to imply that Romanian–Third World engagement has no ideological agenda. There appears to have been relatively substantial military involvement with those African states of "socialist orientation" in the 1970s; even reports that Romanian officers trained tank crews in Mozambique in the use of Soviet made T-34 and T-54 tanks.[19] However, if we consider the implications of the fact that Romania reportedly supplied weapons to all three of the liberation movements in Angola, and the 1978 Treaty of Friendship and Cooperation with the Khmer Rouge, that agenda takes on a Byzantine complexity. To sort it out would require case by case analysis that is beyond the scope of this chapter. In the most general terms, we can only say that Romania appears to take both its "socialist" and "developing" identities seriously and that Bucharest's behavior in the South reflects a desire to maintain intra-Communist credibility while gaining acceptance of Romania as a developing country.

It is also quite possible that a range of Romanian–Third World involvement is motivated by the need for pro-Soviet trade-offs in the intra-bloc political game that Romania plays by virtue of its East European identity. In short, the South may well be still another arena in which Bucharest's political objective is to blur the line between anti-Soviet, autonomous, and supportive activity so as to prevent polarization that would increase the risk of Moscow's retaliation.[20]

As to the extent of this activity, Ceausescu appears to take pride in his conceptualization of Romania as a developing socialist country and to find his flourishing summit diplomacy in the South gratifying, enhancing his own personality cult as well as Romanian visibility as an independent national actor rather than a Soviet proxy. There can be little doubt that the Romanian leader views his prestige in the South as an important card in the game of Soviet-East European alliance politics.

In playing that card, the Romanians have targeted some areas for political/ideological reasons, others for economic payoffs, and, in some cases, become involved based on a sense of affinity stemming from specifically Romanian political culture. Radu alludes to this in his discussion of Bucharest's substantial commitment in Latin America.[21] Romanian is a Romance language. It is quite possible that the Romanian perception of itself as a Latin culture played a role in Romanian-South collaboration in the Western Hemisphere, or conversely facilitated Latin American receptivity to such contacts, or both.

There is some question as to whether Ceausescu's contribution to Marxist theory in the form of a "developing socialist" milestone on the road to socialism would survive the eventual succession even if he succeeds in his somewhat tactless efforts to establish "socialism in one family" via a Ceausescu dynasty. That question in itself has tangled the economic dilemmas that have increasingly strained the Romanian-South ties in recent years.

The Political Economy of Eastern Europe

In the West there has been a tendency to minimize the extent to which East European options are a function not only of the Soviet shadow across East Europe but of international trends and Western policy as well. Yet in the economic dimension, the importance of the big picture and Western input is inescapable.

The 1970s were a time of deceptive plenty. East European economies appeared stronger than they were. Western bankers needed markets to recycle OPEC petro-dollars. East European planners faced increasing energy costs and declining Soviet willingness to foot the bill. The political climate was encouraging. However ultimately illusory, détente legitimized more independent East European foreign policies and facilitated East-West economic deals. The loans were available. It was less painful to live on borrowed money than to cut back domestic consumption or investment.

In retrospect, the temptation of that economic strategy was much like that of the biblical apple in the Garden of Eden. Subsequent Western economic recession, high interest rates, and economic insecurity was bad news for East European policymakers and ordinary citizens alike. Whatever pleasure Party ideologues took in the ideological implications,

Table 1

East European Annual Growth Rates 1971 - 1985

	1971-1975	1976-1980	1981-1985*
Bulgaria	7.8	6.1	4.1
Czechoslovakia	5.6	3.7	1.7
German Democratic Republic	5.4	4.1	3.4
Hungary	6.2	3.2	2.0
Poland	9.8	1.6	-3.3
Romania	11.3	7.3	3.1

*Project Source: Wharton Econometric Forecasting Associates, Jan Vanous, "East European Economic Slowdown," **Problems of Communism** (July-August, 1982):3.

East European countries, increasingly dependent on new loans, suffered from these "contradictions" of capitalism. When the political climate soured in the aftermath of the Soviet intervention in Afghanistan, access to Western credits declined even for Romania. The hard choices could no longer be avoided.

Paul Marer is undoubtedly right that a substantial part of the problem was economic mismanagement on the part of East European planners, that borrowed funds were used less effectively than they might have been.[22] It is also true that even if economic management had been much better than it was, the East European options in the 1980s would be bleak, for small and medium-sized countries—Communist and non-Communist alike—are visibly not masters of their fate in the international economic system. Furthermore, although Romania is less subject than its neighbors to the spillover of U.S.-Soviet hostilities, the dismal Romanian record on human rights does not help matters in this regard. The bottom line is that Western credit is harder to get and depends on potentially politically destabilizing austerity programs.

The receptivity, or lack of it, of the West to Romanian economic needs, in turn, has led to increased trade with the Soviet Union. However, even if the Romanians were willing to slide into a politically sensitive economic dependence on Moscow, it is not clear that option is actually available.

Ever since the change in CMEA pricing mechanisms in the mid-1970s to a moving average based on world prices, it has been apparent that the Soviets intended to cut perceived losses, especially in the realm of energy subsidies to Eastern Europe. Whether this is because their energy resources will peak in the 1980s as predicted, because Moscow needs hard currency from energy sales for other more global commitments, or for some other reason, does not change the consequence.[23] In general,

Table 2

Billion US $
East European Gross Hard Currency Debt to the West: 1971-1983

Year	1971	1975	1980	1981	1982	1983
Bulgaria	.7	2.6	3.5	3.5	2.7	2.4
Czechoslovakia	.4	1.1	9.2*	4.5	4.0	3.7
East Germany	1.4	5.3	14.1	14.9	13.0	12.6
Hungary	1.0	3.1	9.0	8.7	7.7	8.2
Poland	1.1	8.0	25.0	25.5	24.8	26.5
Romania	1.2	2.9	9.4	10.1	9.7	9.0

Source: **CIA Handbook of Economic Statistics,** (September 1984) p. 48.

*Note the figure for Czechoslovakia 1980 seems completely out of line. The Wharton Econometrics figure of 4.9 billion would appear more likely.

Table 3

Eastern Europe Estimated Debt Service Rations (Percent)

Year	1970	1975	1980	1981	1982
Bulgaria	30	44	30	24	20
Czechoslovakia	9	11	23	26	24
East Germany	13	24	36	35	29
Hungary	14	20	26	42	38
Poland	19	32	107	102	64
Romania	36	21	38	43	46

Source: Paul Marer, "East European Economies," in: Teresa Rakowska-Harmstone, (ed). **Communism in Eastern Europe,** 2nd ed., Bloomington, IN: I.U. Press, 1984, p. 316.

East Europeans, never mind Romanians, will have to pay more and look elsewhere if they hope to meet their own projected energy consumption levels. In this sense, the declining availability of Soviet resources becomes a constraint to be reckoned with in the 1980s.

Earlier Western assumptions to the contrary notwithstanding, Soviet response to recent debt-servicing crises makes quite clear that neither East European borrowers nor Western lenders can count on a Soviet "umbrella" to protect them from the fallout of potential defaults. Considering Soviet preoccupation with its own economic problems, so evident at the 1986 27th CPSU Party Congress,[24] the basic conclusion in Moscow that the Soviet Union can not be responsible for East European bad debts is unlikely to be reversed.

Thus, despite the continued Soviet dominance of intra-CMEA economic options, Soviet policy itself is making it more and more essential for all East Europeans to seek other economic alternatives, suppliers and markets. Whatever the formal commitment to increased integration and coordination of national plans within the CMEA, the reality is that of less Soviet assistance, always less than a sure thing for Bucharest. This reality was reflected in the 1984 CMEA Moscow Summit Declaration's insistence that CMEA countries have been "consistent opponents of economic isolationism"; that they have given support for "increased exploitation of the potential for the development of business cooperation with capitalist states and also with their businesses and companies."[25]

This means that with substantial Western credits unlikely in view of the Reagan administration's order of priorities and the state of most West European economies, economic imperatives will provide incentive to continue Romania's search for targets of economic opportunity in the South with or without Ceausescu. Romanian joint ventures frequently focus on the development of vital raw materials, while the much lauded peace efforts often have a dual task, i.e., conflict resolution and preventing interruption of desperately needed resources.

Whether we take Romanian or Western figures, Bucharest's foreign trade with the South increased from ten per cent in 1970 to almost thirty per cent by the 1980s. It is a reasonably good bet that the reportedly more than 130 economic projects that have been commissioned or are now under construction with Romanian technical assistance reflect mutual economic advantage as calculated in Bucharest. Indeed, the "approximately 15,000" Romanian engineering specialists working in the South are probably doing so as much for hard cash as for solidarity.[26]

This does not mean that there would not be a hard look at both the extent and nature of Romanian-South activity in any post-Ceausescu era. Given the burden of Romanian debt-service obligation and the country's declining growth rate, by the late 1970s there was growing internal criticism. Ceausescu personally responded with a reminder of the political importance of the Romanian-South connection.[27] Consequently, as of 1984 Romanian trade turnover with the South remained considerably higher than that of other East European countries.

Conclusions

In terms of rough cost-benefit analysis, the political payoffs from Bucharest's extensive involvement in the South have been substantial. These benefits accrue to Ceausescu psychologically and politically, to Romania as a national actor in the intra-bloc arena and with spillover into the Romanian position in the intra-communist area and in the

Table 4

Million US $
East European Imports from Less Developed Countries: 1960-1980

1960		1970		1980	
Czechoslovakia	161	Czechoslovakia	214	Romania	3,841
Poland	99	Poland	196	Poland	1,798
East Germany	90	East Germany	182	East Germany	1,288
Hungary	58	Hungary	177	Hungary	848
Romania	20	Romania	117	Czechoslovakia	829
Bulgaria	13	Bulgaria	81	Bulgaria	278

East European Exports to Less Developed Countries: 1960-1980

1960		1970		1980	
Czechoslovakia	200	Czechoslovakia	331	Romania	2,508
Poland	93	Poland	258	Poland	1,649
East Germany	89	East Germany	183	Bulgaria	1,383
Hungary	58	Romania	153	East Germany	1,356
Romania	40	Hungary	137	Czechoslovakia	1,302
Bulgaria	18	Bulgaria	125	Hungary	848

Source: **CIA Handbook of Economic Statistics, 1983,** OPAS 83-10006, (September 1983), pp. 100 and 101.

international system as well. The political/ideological boundary disintegration symbolized by Romania's self-proclaimed status as a socialist developing country has maximized Romanian opportunities in the South,[28] whether or not it is accepted in Moscow, in the West, or for that matter with across the board credibility in the South. The resulting ambiguity has expanded Bucharest's freedom of maneuver vis-à-vis Romania's Warsaw Pact allies.

The cost comes in what since 1980 has been a consistently unfavorable balance of trade between Romania and the South. This means that whereas in general East European countries are exceedingly careful not to operate at a loss in terms of their import-export ratio with the South, Ceausescu has been willing to do so for political advantage. The trade off is increasingly controversial in light of Romania's debt service problem and the punishing austerity programs endured by the long-suffering Romanian citizens who pay the bills.

As long as Ceausescu personally dominates the Romanian political scene, there is every reason to think he will continue the present order of political/economic priorities, with perhaps some attention to making Romanian resources expended in the South somewhat more economically efficient. Notwithstanding declining Romanian economic capabilities, in my view, his successors will not have as much leeway in this regard

Table 5

Million US$

East European Imports from Less Developed Countries: 1981-1983

1981		1982		1983*	
Romania	3,540	Romania	2,881	Romania	2,500
Poland	924	East Germany	965	Hungary	1,102
Hungary	845	Hungary	913	East Germany	1,000
East Germany	762	Czechoslovakia	725	Bulgaria	742
Czechoslovakia	758	Bulgaria	723	Poland	713
Bulgaria	492	Poland	598	Czechoslovakia	663

East European Exports to Less Developed Countries: 1981-1983

1981		1982		1983*	
Romania	3,498	Romania	2,634	Romania	2,800
Bulgaria	1,844	Bulgaria	2,010	East Germany	1,700
Czechoslovakia	1,410	East Germany	1,797	Bulgaria	1,601
East Germany	1,268	Poland	1,550	Czechoslovakia	1,462
Poland	1,174	Czechoslovakia	1,395	Poland	1,227
Hungary	1,015	Hungary	1,198	Hungary	1,133

Source: **CIA Handbook of Economic Statistics, 1984,** CP AS 84-1002, September 1984, pp. 103 and 104.

*Preliminary

as is sometimes supposed. This is so because economic imperatives flowing from both the international economic system and the political economy of the East will push Romania to seek economic advantages in the South. In short, with or without Ceausescu, the emphasis of Romanian-South activity will be increasingly governed by the fact that willy-nilly economic boundary disintegration has followed on heels of the blurred ideological/political distinctions that Bucharest worked so hard to achieve. Unless there is a change of heart in Moscow, Romania will have no choice but to draw closer to the South economically on the road to becoming a "multilaterally developed socialist society."

Finally I would caution against writing Nicolae Ceausescu off so soon. Ceausescu is one of the youngest leaders in Eastern Europe who has built an effective political machine, skillfully utilizing Romanian political culture. Perhaps because it is less frustrating to speculate about the future than to deal with the present, Western academics spend a great deal of intellectual energy in "after Tito, after Hoxha, after Brezhnev, etc." Remember that Tito remained the Godfather of Yugoslav Communism for another ten years after such speculation became the common denominator of those writing on Yugoslavia. "After Ceausescu" depends very much on what happens in the meantime.

Notes

1. This chapter expands upon an earlier, more comprehensive analysis, "Eastern Europe and the Third World: Interest, Capabilities and Objectives," presented to The Wilson Center Seminar Series, "The Third World and International Security: Competing East-West Perspectives and Policies," January 30, 1985.

2. See Günther Nollau, *International Communism and World and Revolution: History and Methods*, New York: Praeger, 1961.

3. J. Stalin, *Problems of Leninism*, Moscow: 1945, p. 157. For analysis, Isaac Deutscher, *Stalin: A Political Biography*, 2nd edition, New York: Oxford University Press, 1949, pp. 282ff.

4. Z.K. Brzezinski, *The Soviet Bloc: Unity and Conflict*, 4th rev. edition, Cambridge, MA: Harvard University Press, 1971, p. 51.

5. Paul Marer, "Has Eastern Europe Become a Liability to the Soviet Union? (III) The Economic Aspect," in Charles Gati, ed., *The International Relations of Eastern Europe*, New York: Praeger, 1976, p. 61.

6. See John Michael Montias, *Economic Development in Communist Rumania*, Cambridge, MA: The MIT Press, 1967; and Kenneth Jowitt, *Revolutionary Breakthrough and National Development: The Case of Romania, 1944–1965*, Berkeley and Los Angeles: The University of California Press, 1971. More recently, Walter M. Bacon, Jr., "Romania," in Teresa Rakowska-Harmstone, ed., *Communism in Eastern Europe*, 2nd ed., Bloomington, IN: Indiana University Press, 1984, pp. 171–173.

7. N.S. Khrushchev, "Vital Questions of Development of the World Socialist System," *World Marxist Review*, 5, no. 9 (September 1962).

8. "Statement on the Stand of the Rumanian Workers' Party Concerning the Problems of the International Communist and Working Class Movement," adopted at an enlarged Plenum of the RWP help in April 1964. Complete text in W.E. Griffith, ed., *Sino-Soviet Relations 1964–1965*, Cambridge, MA: The MIT Press, 1967, p. 283. For analysis of the Romanian "Road to Independence" see Stephen Fischer-Galati, *The New Rumanian: From People's Democracy to Socialist Republic*, Cambridge, MA: The MIT Press, 1967.

9. Griffith, *Sino-Soviet Relations* . . . , pp. 284–285.

10. Robin Alison Remington, "The Political Environment of Eastern Europe: Sources of Tension and Possible Futures," paper delivered at the American Political Science Association national meeting in Washington, D.C., September 2, 1984.

11. *Christian Science Monitor*, March 11, 1986.

12. Kevin Delvin, "The Interparty Drama," *Problems of Communism* 24 (July-August 1975): pp. 18–35.

13. Text of the Berlin Conference final document, *New Times* (Moscow) 28 (July 1976): pp. 17–32.

14. Nicolae Ceausescu, "Report on the National Conference of the Romanian Communist party, July 12, 1972," in Nicolae Ceausescu, *Romania on the Way of Building Up the Multilaterally Developed Socialist Society*, Vol. 7 (Bucharest, 1973) p. 428.

15. Michael Radu, "Romania and the Third World: The Dilemmas of a 'Free Rider,'" in his edited collection, *Eastern Europe and the Third World: East vs South*, New York: Praeger, 1981, p. 241.

16. Marcel Dinu, "The Developing Countries: Unity in Action," *Lumea*, April 7, 1979. Quoted, *ibid.*, p. 240.

17. See Constantine Vlad and Nicolae Calina, "The Nonaligned Movement, the International System, and Romanian Foreign Policy," *The Nonaligned World* (New Delhi) (April-June 1984): 260–272.

18. Christian Popisteanu, "A Few Remarks Concerning Non-Alignment Policy and Movement in the Struggle for Ensuring International Peace, for Promoting Security in the World, for Solving the Problems in the 80s," *Nonalignment in the Eighties*, Belgrade, 1982, pp. 77–85.

19. Trond Gilberg, "East European Military Assistance to the Third World," in John F. Copper and Daniel S. Papp, eds., *Communist Nations' Military Assistance*, Boulder, CO: Westview Press, 1983, p. 87.

20. See Kenneth Jowitt's comments on Romanian "identity referents" in Sylva Sinanian, Istvan Deak, and Peter C. Ludz, eds., *Eastern Europe in the 1970s*, New York: Praeger, 1972, pp. 180–184. My own view goes slightly beyond his "safety in numbers" theory.

21. Radu, "Romania . . . ," p. 241.

22. Paul Marer, "East Europe's Current Indebtedness Causes and Consequences," paper presented to the American Historical Association, annual meeting in San Francisco, December 28–30, 1983.

23. *Ibid.* For a more comprehensive treatment see Marer's "The Political Economy of Soviet Relations with Eastern Europe," in Sarah Meiklejohn Terry, ed., *Soviet Policy in Eastern Europe*, New Haven and London: Yale University Press, 1984, pp. 155–188.

24. Gorbachev Report to the CPSU 27th Congress, February 25, 1986 (unofficial translation).

25. *Pravda*, June 16, 1984.

26. Vlad and Calina, "The Non-Aligned Movement . . . ," p. 271.

27. *Scinteia*, August 3, 1978; quoted by Radu, "Romania . . . ," p. 2157.

28. This interpretation is substantially more optimistic than Andrzej Korbonski's provocative paper, "Eastern Europe and the Third World, Or 'Limited Regret Strategy' Revisited," in Andrzej Korbondski and Francis Fukuyama (eds.), *The Soviet Union and the Third World: The Last Three Decades*, Ithaca and London: Cornell University Press, 1987, pp. 94–122.

12

The German Democratic Republic and Sub-Saharan Africa: The Limits of East-South Economic Relations

Brigitte H. Schulz

Introduction

In this chapter we will look at economic relations between the GDR and the Third World, with a particular emphasis on sub-Saharan Africa. It is with that continent that the GDR has enjoyed the closest political relations. Sub-Saharan Africa is also the least developed area of the so-called Third World and suffers from all of the classical symptoms of underdevelopment: low levels of industrialization, export-oriented agricultural production of mono-crops with a simultaneous high level of malnourishment of the population, high birth rates, high infant mortality rates, etc. Since independence various African governments have sought, at least at the rhetorical level, to overcome underdevelopment and dependence. While in the sixties it was such countries as Ghana, Mali, Guinea, and Tanzania, in the seventies it was newly independent Lusophone Africa as well as Ethiopia which adopted the most radical course on the African continent. Close ties with the socialist East were always part of this strategy of attempting to embark on a path of economic and social development.

As is pointed out in various chapters of this book, particularly by Helmut Faulwetter, an East German economist, the East's position in explaining the poverty of the South is that it is the direct consequence of colonial as well as neocolonial exploitation on the part of the West. The East therefore has presented itself in the postcolonial era as a real alternative to the Western imperialist countries, not just in terms of political and social organization but also in terms of economic development. Since among the Eastern European countries the GDR is by far the most successful economically[1] its ties with developing countries are of particular interest in this regard. As will be argued in this chapter, however, the East simply does not have the economic resources to help in the development of the South. In fact, it looks to the South for the satisfaction of its own economic needs, from exporting finished goods to importing vital raw materials. "Proletarian internationalism" between a highly industrialized and a poor agrarian country thus appears to be little more than lipservice when the dominating principle for the relatively richer partner is one of so-called "mutual advantage." This chapter thus shows that East-South economic relations differ more in scope than in substance from those between West and South. If anything, differences between the economic relations of East and West in the South have become even less pronounced during the last decade, a trend which surely will continue in the future.

Economic Relations with Developing Countries

The GDR includes under the rubric of economic relations with developing countries not only trade but also so-called scientific and technical cooperation. These relations are carried out almost exclusively on a bilateral basis between the GDR and the respective "partner" and are claimed by the GDR to operate on the basis of "mutual advantage."[2] Bilateral trade takes up the major share of these economic relations, although the component of scientific and technical cooperation is growing. Included in the latter category are:

- the exchange of scientific information, technological know-how, and scientific or technical expertise;
- joint projects at research institutions;
- assistance in education and training;
- sending experts and scientists; and
- the transfer of licenses.[3]

Discussed first will be bilateral trade, followed by more complex forms of economic cooperation such as compensation agreements and tripartite cooperation. Finally, the various activities subsumed under the rubric of scientific and technical cooperation will be analyzed.

Bilateral trade

Traditionally, trade has been the main instrument of economic interaction with developing countries. The GDR claims that this constitutes an important element of its "aid" relations with these countries as well.

Table 1
Trade with Africa, 1970-1985
(in million US $)

	Imports	Exports
1970	52	60
1975	124	172
1980	276	332
1981	190	342
1982	113	431
1983	119	271
1984	137	327
1985	262	324

Source: UN Monthly Bulletin of Statistics, July 1984, 1986, 1987.

The GDR argues that its economic relations with developing countries are of a "new type" and therefore by nature different from those between advanced capitalist and third world countries. Even trade relations become an expression of "the international class struggle between socialism and capitalism."[4] As this chapter will show, however, this assertation is more an article of faith than the reflection of objective empirical analysis.

The GDR has a marked trade emphasis on only a few developing countries, many of which are important trading partners for Western countries also. For example, in 1980 seventy-three percent of all GDR exports to the Third World went to only fifteen LDCs (Angola, Mozambique, Ethiopia, Nigeria, India, Brazil, Columbia, Argentina, Mexico, Egypt, Syria, Libya, Iraq, and Iran). Angola, Mozambique, and Ethiopia accounted for 15.9 percent of trade within that group, while the oil-exporting countries of Algeria, Iraq, Iran, Libya and Nigeria accounted for almost half, clearly reflecting the GDR's dependence on imported oil from these countries.[5] Most developing countries appear to be of little economic interest to the GDR, however, particularly the resource-poor least developed ones. Table 1 shows East German trade, broken down into separate figures for imports and exports, with the African continent between 1970 and 1985.

These figures confirm the general trend in the GDR's foreign economic policy since the early seventies. At that point it, like those all over Eastern Europe, embarked on an economic program based on increased investments in productive capacity. The money was to come through loans from the West, which would be repaid from the hard-currency earnings made by selling the products to the West. The conception was as elegant in its simplicity as it was wrong in its predictive capacity.

Changed economic circumstances in the West coupled with growing
exports from the newly industrializing countries, in addition to a de-
teriorating political climate which seriously affected East-West trade,
meant that the expected exports of industrial goods did not take place
to any appreciable degree. Repayments of hard currency loans, on the
other hand, continued to become due. These developments forced changes
in the foreign economic strategy of the GDR in the eighties:

(1) a dramatic increase in exports, even at the expense of domestic
    consumption in certain products;
(2) an increase of hard-currency sales to LDCs and the aggressive
    opening up of sales markets, particularly of complete plants, to
    these countries;
(3) replacing hard-currency imports such as grain from the United
    States with barter trade involving LDCs, and reducing imports
    from NATO countries to products which cannot be gotten on any
    other market, mainly high technology and industrial goods.

In the case of Africa, 1984 was clearly the most dramatic manifestion
of this shift away from a reasonably balanced trade relationship to one
confined mainly to finding export markets and reducing imports to a
bare minimum. The East German government does not publish country-
by-country import and export statistics and it is thus impossible to
determine the precise trade relationship with any particular sub-Saharan
African country. What the government does, instead, is to publish
"aggregate" trade data on "selected" countries, without telling the reader
the relative importance of these countries within its overall foreign trade
relations. Table 2 shows this data as published by Berlin on trade with
selected sub-Saharan African countries.

What is striking about this table is how large the fluctuations are in
the trade volume with individual countries. Rather than rising continuously, they show for most countries an up-and-down pattern one would
not expect in trade which is regulated by official bilateral trade agreements.
What does it mean, for example, if a long-term economic cooperation
agreement is ratified between the GDR and Mozambique in 1979 and
covering the period up to 1990, states that the two countries

> will make every effort to expand their mutually advantageous co-operation
> and exchange of experience in the fields of industry, agriculture, fishing,
> communications, training of personnel, etc. The two countries will continue
> to develop their cooperation in the field of trade on the basis of the
> principles of equality, mutual advantage and preferential treatment.[6]

Table 2

Trade Volume with Selected Countries in Sub-Saharan Africa
1960-1985
(in million Valuta-Marks and current prices)

Country	1960	1965	1970	1975	1980	1981	1982	1983	1984	1985
Angola	-	-	-	-	275.0	198.5	264.3	255.2	797.8	844.0
PR Congo	2.8	0.2	0.3	0.1	3.6	14.2	28.6	11.9	6.8	5.0
Ethiopia	0.3	0.4	0.6	0.2	132.3	62.4	129.1	193.9	93.7	112.0
Ghana	7.0	53.0	2.2	13.7	49.5	46.4	74.7	115.7	112.5	189.8
Guinea	38.4	18.9	8.9	6.6	3.8	n.a.	n.a.	32.2	25.2	8.5
Mozambique	-	-	-	-	274.5	368.0	411.8	222.7	109.0	93.3
Nigeria	0.9	13.4	12.9	3.3	47.5	148.3	137.9	14.6	9.5	13.2
Sudan	11.1	9.9	25.0	33.3	26.7	6.2	16.0	79.3	96.8	36.6
Tanzania	-	2.0	6.6	6.3	49.1	3.5	2.6	2.4	2.0	0.6
Zambia	-	-	0.3	0.1	95.5	n.a.	n.a.	33.8	33.7	1.7
Zimbabwe*	-	-	-	-	-	-	-	37.4	53.8	106.6

* Prior to 1980 Rhodesia

Source: Statistisches Jahrbuch der DDR, 1987, p. 242.

Since this agreement was worked out, the trade volume with Mozambique has dropped from a high of M411.8 million in 1982 to a mere M93.3 million in 1985. The figures for Ethiopia also indicate a sharp drop since 1983. Of the three countries with "socialist orientation" in Africa, only the trading volume with Angola has increased steadily. In fact, the trade volume jumped over 300 percent from 1983 to 1984, again not necessarily a sign of planned and thus "stable" foreign economic relations![7]

Data broken down into exports and imports is no longer available from official East German sources. What little statistical information is available from African sources seems to indicate that the GDR in fact enjoys a considerable trade surplus with all of sub-Saharan Africa. Too little information is available on the conditions of this trade to determine conclusively, however, whether the GDR is using this surplus to balance its hard currency commitments to the West. Istvan Dobozi argues that this is in fact the economic strategy pursued by the East European countries.[8] If this is the case for the GDR, money made in the developing countries is thus spent in the West rather than on purchases from the South.

The *structure* of trade between the GDR and its trading partners in the Third World shows the usual pattern between a highly industrialized country and LDCs. According to an UNCTAD manual on trading with socialist countries, the GDR's

> Exports to developing countries consist mainly of machinery and equipment, especially for transport and communications, electrification, building and construction, the textile industry, machine building, printing and the processing of agricultural products. . . . Imports from developing countries consist mainly of raw materials, including crude oil, hard coal, rubber, ferrous and non-ferrous metals, phosphate, cotton, cotton fabrics, protein fodder, vegetable oil, coffee, tea, cocoa, and tropical fruits.[9]

Although the GDR attacks the nature of West-South trade as a manifestation of imperialist exploitation, it sees its own trade in a rather more favorable light, even finding praise for the lopsided nature of this trade with developing countries. In discussing Angolan/East German trade, for example, a prominent East German economist notes that, "Due to the dissimilarity of their economic structure it opens up promising prospects."[10] The prospects Scharschmidt is talking about is that the GDR is now able to import Angolan coffee in exchange for its industrial goods, primarily from the machinery sector. This seems hardly a convincing argument that a new type of relationship between a developed and an underdeveloped nation is emerging!

According to West German analysts, at the beginning of the eighties, finished products constituted over ninety percent of the exports of the GDR to the Third World, while over eighty percent of all imports were agricultural products plus oil and raw materials of all types.[11] Published GDR sources paint a much more optimistic picture, generally maintaining that "roughly" forty percent of imports from developing countries are in the form of semi-finished or finished products.[12] Trusting these figures from the GDR essentially amounts to a matter of faith, however, because no detailed data is published that would substantiate the claim. The author's own data collected in the GDR essentially confirms the lower West German figures cited above and indicates that, if anything, the share of imported raw materials is expected to go up even higher, naturally at the expense of more imported manufactured goods.

In seeking to locate the impetus behind the GDR's foreign trade relations, the traditional argument to explain the need for this trade has been the need to "create conditions for the steady purchase from these countries of such products as crude oil, cotton, cotton fabrics, protein fodder, vegetable oil, coffee, cocoa and tropical fruits."[13] The very high dependence of the East German economy on these products is certainly a fact. Since overall energy self-sufficiency in the CMEA is going down and the Soviets are also seeking to diversify their exports to earn more hard currency themselves, GDR imports from non-CMEA sources will become correspondingly more important in the decades to come.[14] Thus raw materials from Africa will play an even greater role for the GDR in the years ahead.

The need to pay for these imports with East German products is not the only, nor necessarily the most important reason, however. In fact, it is argued here that these markets are important to the GDR in any case because of the need to sell its industrial goods. The LDCs provide a market for East German goods which would be difficult, if not impossible, to sell in another part of the world. This is so because the industrial products manufactured in the GDR, with few exceptions, do not meet the international technical standards to make them competitive in the West.[15] Thus the Third World offers a market for socialist countries in "capital goods and manufactured consumer goods which they could not sell in the advanced capitalist countries because of their low quality. It is well known that the great majority of capital goods exported to non-socialist markets go to developing countries and, in particular, to the African countries."[16] Despite past attempts at integration of the East European economies, they essentially remain similar rather than complementary in structure and thus offer insufficient opportunities for exporting industrial products to one another.[17] Since the GDR has only a limited internal market for these goods, the CMEA market does not absorb all of them, and its manufactured goods are largely uncompetitive on Western markets, the importance of Africa in this regard is certainly not insignificant and, it is argued here, will be growing. This would of course change again were the GDR able to produce technically more advanced products which would then become more competitive on Western markets. As it stands, however, it urgently needs to sell these goods in order to earn the hard currency to purchase technologically advanced products from the West.

As part of the official bilateral trade agreements between the GDR and its partner countries in the Third World, various payment mechanisms have been established. Until the early seventies, the primary mechanism for trade with the Third World was through *clearing agreements.* In the early years of bilateral trade, this was considered the preferred method of payment because it enabled both partners to avoid hard currency transactions. In the early seventies, as economic priorities changed inside Eastern Europe, the need for hard currency to pay for imports from the West began to influence payment arrangements with the Third World. Hard currency payments became the preferred choice of the GDR in its trade with the South, although other payment arrangments were also possible.[18] As the debt crisis has worsened inside the Third World in the eighties, many of these countries are again looking for partners willing to circumvent hard currency transactions. It remains to be seen to what extent the GDR and the other socialist countries will be willing to return to this type of payment arrangement, considering their own economic priorities in the coming decade.

No precise data is available on the prices at which these goods are exchanged, although they appear to be based on current world market prices. Competition sometimes drives down the price of certain goods just as it does in trade between Western countries and LDCs. For the GDR this means competing not only with Western firms but also with fellow CMEA countries equally eager to sell their goods on these hard-currency markets. One suspects that one reason for the GDR's insistence on secrecy lies in that fact that it does not want to give critics a chance to admonish it for using prices set on the imperialist world market, prices which the GDR insisted until recently served as a vehicle of resource extraction from the Third World on the part of the capitalist countries. As the most respected economist of this "school," Gunther Kohlmey, phrased it in 1968:

Marx was the first theoretician of foreign trade who explained the class nature of the capitalist world economy by proving that foreign trade is not only circulation but also distribution of national surplus and thus an instrument of exploitation of one nation by another. It was thus that Marx could explain scientifically the great tragedy of the capitalist world economy.[19]

As the GDR has become more integrated into the capitalist world economy via trade, the ideological adjustment to the above position soon followed. Hans-Peter Krueger, in sharp contrast to the analyses of his predecessors, by the mid-eighties argued that in the Marxist view, exploitation can only occur at the point of production and not in the sphere of circulation; emphasizing that capitalism is essentially an exploitative relationship between capital and labor. Thus trade itself cannot be exploitative.[20] It should be noted, however, that Krueger's book has not muted East German criticisms of Western trade relations with the Third World. It has simply provided a convenient ideological rebuttal to Western and Third World criticisms of the East's trading practices with the South.

If the structure of trade is very similar to that between capitalist industrial countries and LDCs, and the prices underlying the sales transactions likewise do not differ from those with capitalist countries, it is difficult to accept the logic advanced by the GDR that trading with it is *a priori* more beneficial for a developing country than trading with any capitalist enterprise. Nor does it look like trade relations between the GDR and LDCs, including Angola, Mozambique, and Ethiopia, will change drastically in the decade to come. Dobozi and Inotai have projected a commodity composition between the CMEA countries and LDCs to 1990 to be roughly the same as at present,[21] and an analysis of the types of long-term economic agreements ratified between the GDR and Angola, Mozambique and Ethiopia over the past years confirms this projection. The pattern of trade between the GDR and LDCs of whatever political variety thus does little to alter the existing division of labor but merely shifts the geographical distribution of this trade from one part of the world to another. However, as Deepak Nayyar has pointed out, "such traditional patterns of trade can neither transform the structure of production in the South nor make for a new international division of labor."[22]

Compensation Agreements

In this form of economic cooperation, the GDR generally provides the experts and the necessary industrial equipment for which it gets compensated in future production from the investment project. The East German involvement in the coal-mining operations in Mozambique is an example of this type of arrangement, in which the GDR was scheduled to receive much of the coal mined at Moatize in return for the material and technical assistance it rendered there. Mozambican tantalum mining is another example: the GDR supplies the investment goods plus the experts in exchange for the exclusive right to this tantalum, with the option to resell it on hard-currency markets. The mines themselves, however, stay in the possession of the Mozambican state and do not themselves become the property of the GDR.[23] One further example of this type of transaction, which is also one of the few cases of multilateral cooperation within the CMEA in developing countries, is the textile plant in Kombolcha, Ethiopia, built jointly by the GDR and the CSSR. While Ethiopia presently exports raw cotton, the operation of this plant will enable it to export cotton fabrics to the GDR in the future.

These buy-back agreements normally are part of the export of "complete," or "turn-key," plants. This means that the GDR installs a complete plant, trains local labor to run it, and normally gets compensated for this economic transaction with the finished products, usually one year after the start-up of the operation. Between 1950 and 1984, the GDR exported more than eight hundred of these complete plants to developing countries.[24] GDR sources praise this as a particularly important aspect of its economic cooperation with the Third World. In terms of the GDR literature, this a clear case of helping a country on a much-needed path of industrialization without any of the disadvantages involved in dealing with Western multinationals because ownership of the plant is in the hands of the local government.

As usual, however, the case is not as clear cut as it may seem, particularly if one looks upon this not simply as a sales transaction, but instead within the framework of the internationalization of production within a single changing global division of labor. Thus these transactions must be viewed as more than simple imports and exports but instead represent a shift of certain (particularly labor-intensive) production from East to South. What the GDR is apparently seeking to accomplish is the establishment of long-term economic relations in which production inside the country is increasingly coordinated with that of the partner in the Third World. In this way, the GDR is able not only to satisfy its urgent raw materials requirements, but also to shift some of its production outside its own borders.

Tripartite Cooperation

This type of cooperation involves a company from Eastern Europe cooperating with a Western partner in a third country. The first such venture took place in 1962, involving a joint Austrian-Hungarian project in India. As Henrik Bischof has pointed out, until the late seventies this type of cooperation tended to be initiated by a Western firm, which, in effect, subcontracted the delivery of parts or services from a partner in the East. In the beginning, the Soviet Union and the GDR showed a great deal of ideological reservation about this type of venture, but since the late seventies have themselves actively pursued them, particularly the Soviet Union.[25] The role of the developing countries in all of this is mainly limited to being the "purchasers of goods and services jointly provided by enterprises in the East and West."[26]

Since ideological reservations[27] have once again given way to the demands of its economy, the projects underway on this basis in which the GDR was taking part in mid-1984 were twice the total number of those completed in all previous years.[28] Projects undertaken by the GDR on this basis in sub-Saharan Africa until the mid-eighties can be found in Tanzania, Sudan, Mauritania, Nigeria, Cameroun, and Ethiopia.[29]

One of the more interesting cases concerning tripartite cooperation occurred in 1977, when the East German enterprise "Unitechna-Textimaprojekt" and West Germany's Krupp steel-exporting works decided to cooperate in the construction of a textile plant in Addis Ababa, Ethiopia. While Krupp initially had been awarded the contract, this changed after the Ethiopian government moved closer to the GDR and handed overall management responsibility to the East German firm for the completion of the project in 1981.[30]

The primary motivation on the part of the East in pursuing tripartite cooperation appears to be that "in most cases, the CMEA countries themselves do not have the technology necessary for the projects and thus hope to gain technological advantages from cooperating with Western firms."[31] It reflects increasing interest in economic activities in the South in which it is handicapped by the low level of technology and poor quality of its manufactured goods. Overall, tripartite economic cooperation tends to take place with countries not on a path of "socialist orientation" and thus not as closely allied with the GDR politically. One wonders if Schöller's characterization of "comparative disadvantage" in East-South trade also applies to this situation. As long as comrades in the South are willing, for ideological or other reasons, to deal exclusively with the East on a particular project, it is not necessary to involve a Western firm and thus lose some of the business. If, on the other hand, a Third World country not *a priori* inclined to deal with the East will only do so by insisting on products meeting world (viz. *Western*) standards, then the East seems very willing to include a Western firm in order to get at least a part of the pie.

Scientific and Technical Cooperation

It is in this category that the distinction between trade and aid becomes most difficult to make. The main emphasis here is on the training of personnel from, and sending of experts to, the developing countries. Other areas included under this rubric also are non-material items such as licensing, patents, consulting services, etc.

Cooperation in this sphere, like all other types of economic transactions, are regulated on the basis of bilateral government agreements. By 1985, twenty-nine formal bilateral agreements were in effect concerning scientific/technical cooperation between the GDR and various developing countries.[32]

Although the GDR likes to present cooperation in the field of expert services and apprenticeship training as part of its "solidarity" activities, they normally closely complement commercial relations between the GDR and developing countries. The sending of experts and training of cadres usually is part of a sales transaction of GDR machines and equipment to these countries. According to one East German analysis, the "non-material" component of sales transactions, particularly in the case of the export of complete plants, by the mid-eighties amounted "to as many [sic] as 50 per cent of the contract price."[33] These services "may include the granting of production rights, provision of technological and construction designs, assembly supervision, training of personnel, preparation of organizational plans, preparation of production and initial running of the plant by GDR experts."[34]

For example, the commercial agreement with the East German enterprise "Schwarze Pumpe" to help in the operation of the coal mine in Moatize was accompanied by the sending of GDR experts under the scientific and technical cooperation agreement between the GDR and Mozambique. Since one of the main export items of the GDR is complete plants (turnkey or product-in-hand) as discussed above, and this is an area in which international competition is particularly keen, East Germans consider the training programs which they can offer in conjunction with the sale of such plants as a real competitive advantage over capitalist firms,[35] particularly since they lack an extensive international service and maintenance network. It is thus imperative that follow-up service be provided by training personnel inside the third world to perform that role.

This commercial motivation is actually openly admitted in the GDR. As stated by Gerhard Scharschmidt in discussing the GDR's relations with Angola:

> The development of long-term and stable export ties requires that all the necessary after-sale services are provided to the importer. This is no easy task in the case of Angola which is facing a difficult situation regarding its economic development and where the provider of such services is exposed to severe competition with captalist firms. Such an aftersale

services scheme, which additionally trains young Angolans to become motor mechanics, was set up in Angola by the GDR for its truck exports.[36]

According to East German sources, the purpose of the training inside the less developed country itself is to allow local labor to acquire the necessary skills as quickly as possible to operate a particular plant. For example, in order to train the staff of the Kombolcha textile plant in Ethiopia, forty plumbers and twenty electricians were trained in Addis Ababa for eight months. These men then were sent back to Kombolcha in order to train the other personnel of the textile plant.[37] The GDR thus argues that it actually does not sell turnkey projects, meaning simply the installation of the plant and then leaving untrained local personnel to staff it. Rather, it supplies *product in hand* installations, which means that the GDR is involved with the plant beyond its physical completion until a trained staff can actually manage the production process. Training of personnel is not included in the price of the plant, however, and the GDR charges for this program separately.[38] Since 1970, more than 45,000 people inside developing countries have received vocational and technical training.[39]

The training at both the vocational and university levels inside the GDR is another important element of cooperation in the scientific and technical sphere. By the end of 1985, a total of more than 65,000 people from developing countries had received either vocational/technical or university training inside the GDR itself. Between 1977 and 1982, more than 400 Ethiopians alone were trained at East German universities.[40] This training takes place either on the basis of bilateral agreements on scientific-technical cooperation, purely commercial arrangements, or under so-called solidarity activities.

Training inside the country on a commercial basis has become of increasing interest to the GDR since this enables it to make hard currency earnings. The *Institut für berufliche Entwicklung* (ibe), in conjunction with the state-owned foreign trade company, *Intercoop*, looks for trainees from abroad on a commercial basis. This now also includes helping foreigners with the necessary cash in hard currency gain admission into an East German university. *Intercoop* has its own booth at the Leipzig Spring Fair, the GDR's most important trade fair.[41]

A three-year technical apprenticeship program inside the GDR by the mid-eighties cost a minimum of M20,000. In 1984, roughly 3,500 trainees from thirty-four different countries were in the GDR for vocational training under the terms of scientific/technical or commercial cooperation, or under the auspices of the Solidarity Committee. Roughly one thousand of these trainees were in the GDR under the terms of purely commercial agreements, such as with Libya, for example.[42] According to *Neues*

Deutschland, in 1986 2,500 citizens of the Third World were receiving vocational/technical training in the GDR as part of solidarity, scientific/technical, or commercial agreements.[43]

Two points of caution concerning these figures seem in order. *Firstly,* since the GDR does not publish regular data concerning these training programs and the exact number of students enrolled in them, it is difficult to say anything with precision. Furthermore, numbers given in various publications often give widely divergent statistical data.

Secondly, statistics concerning the number of foreigners being trained in the country are normally presented as part of the GDR's active solidarity with the South. However, some of the young people studying in the GDR are there on a regular commercial basis, with their home country paying their tuition expenses as well as providing the students with a monthly stipend. In these cases, the East German government accepts the payments in hard currency and gives the students a monthly stipend in its own non-convertible currency. This would thus appear to be more a straight-forward economic transaction, certainly also working to the advantage of the GDR, than an act of "solidarity." For example, a large contingent of Libyans is in the GDR receiving vocational training on this basis. The author also met several students from sub-Saharan Africa (e.g., Zambia and Zimbabwe) who were studying in the country under such terms. Thus it is often difficult to determine the precise nature of the relationships existing between the GDR and developing countries in this regard.

Before concluding, agricultural cooperation deserves a few separate comments because of the enormous importance this sector has in the economies of developing countries. Cooperation here is mainly in the area of promoting cooperatives and state farms.[44] The GDR supplies agricultural equipment, fertilizers, and experts in exchange for agricultural products. As developments over the past few years have shown, however, this East German agricultural model based on the use of machines and cooperative farming on large state farms is not necessarily applicable to the conditions prevailing in sub-Saharan Africa. To begin with, these machines are not only expensive but they continue to require funds for replacement parts as well as to purchase fuel, something very few developing countries have as a domestic resource. In addition, they require a skilled workforce which is able to operate as well as service the equipment. Thus borrowing the East German model is fraught with potential problems for the South.

There are sociological problems in the transfer of the Eastern agricultural model as well. Even today, most African peasants produce mainly for their own subsistence, while in Eastern Europe commodity production was generalized even at the rural village level by the beginning of this century. Even in Cuba, the country which often serves as the model of successful socialist development in the Third World, at the time of its revolution, sixty-four percent of all people involved in agriculture were wage laborers on big estates and another thirty percent were small-hold tenants or owners involved in commodity production. In addition, fifty-seven percent of the population already lived in urban areas.[45] Thus, in addition to economies distorted to meet foreign needs, African governments, no matter how Marxist-Leninist in their persuasion, have to take into account populations that as a whole are still far removed from their "homo economicus" counterparts in both East and West.

The East's model also overlooks another key sociological factor in Africa: most agricultural work is traditionally performed by women and most Africans still live in extended family settings.[46] This is not to say that women cannot be taught to operate tractors and other big agricultural equipment, nor that extended families cannot also be incorporated into rural cooperatives. It is argued, however, that any successful rural development strategy in Africa must take these factors into account. The simple transfer of models which does not take into consideration these real sociological differences does not necessarily bring "development."[47] The negative experiences made on Mozambican state farms in recent years, for example, have shown that establishing such an operation takes more than importing a few experts and tractors from the GDR. FRELIMO basically admitted this at its Fourth Party Congress in 1983, arguing self-critically that the agricultural model it pursued after independence was doomed to failure because it sought to emulate Eastern Europe and thus failed to take account of the specific conditions prevailing in the country at that time.[48]

Toward a Tentative Assessment: Eleven Theses

With published materials as scantily available as discussed above, reaching more than tentative conclusions concerning the nature of the GDR's economic relations with the South becomes a daunting task indeed. The following concluding comments are thus advanced to make only some preliminary judgements concerning the GDR's relations with the developing countries:

1. The East's commitment to help in the economic development of the South appears limited. Of all funds available to the Third world at concessional terms, only six percent were granted by the East in 1981.[49] Even membership in the CMEA has apparently been closed off to additional developing countries. Only Mongolia, Vietnam and Cuba have been admitted as non-European powers and thus able to gain certain benefits which membership in that organization entails. Both Angola's

and Mozambique's requests for membership, on the other hand, were denied and they have simple observer status only.[50]

2. An examination of East-South relations shows that there is only one international economic system, in which West, East and the South form an integral part. Within this global system, both West and East behave as advanced industrialized countries *vis-à-vis* the South and both have economic interests there. East German prescriptions that developing countries slowly free themselves from the capitalist world economy and gradually integrate themselves "into the socialist world economic system as an objective requirement of a socialist development path"[51] thus appear to mean nothing more than shifting some of their existing economic relations from West to East. There is no indication that the GDR is pursuing a Third World policy intent on a radical restructuring of the existing international division of labor. Its trade relations with the developing countries follow the traditional North-South pattern, exporting finished goods for primary commodities. Since the prices are also based on those prevailing on the world market, this aspect of East-South relations does not differ fundamentally from those between West and South, official utterances to the contrary notwithstanding.[52]

3. Even if the East's programs were aimed at helping third world countries overcome their level of underdevelopment by radically restructing their economies toward the satisfaction of domestic needs rather than producing for export, the *ability* of the East to do so would be severely limited. The GDR, just like the other socialist countries, simply lacks the economic resources to help underdeveloped countries in a sustained development drive independent of the advanced market economies. On top of that, the East itself is more integrated into the world capitalist economy than ever before and thus its own economic well-being now dependends on the continuation of the international economic status quo.

4. Bilateral trade relations between the GDR and developing countries thus do not differ significantly from those between West and South, except in absolute volumes. This applies both to the *structure of trade* as well as to the *transfer of value* involved in this trade. The economic strategy of the GDR pursued throughout the seventies has led to its deeper incorporation into the capitalist world economy, putting essentially the same pressures on "socialist" as on "capitalist" firms. Thus "the pressures of costsaving and Marx's law of value operate on both."[53] This has led to increasingly economic considerations in relations with the Third World at the expense of "solidarity." The GDR's oft repeated claim that its trade relations constitute "aid" to these countries can thus not be empirically substantiated. Ricardian notions of comparative ad-

vantage work equally well, or fail equally miserably, depending on one's viewpoint, in East-South as in West-South trade. The fact that one of the trading partners calls itself "socialist" does nothing to make the transition itself more fair or equitable for the developing country.

5. "Mutual advantage" as the basis of economic relations between East and South does not offer a prescription for the successful transformation of underdevelopment. If the GDR seeks the best possible economic deal for itself then it will at best offer an alternative market for the products of the South, but not a long-term solution to the structural problems of underdevelopment. With increasing competition among the developing countries themselves for markets for their tropical goods being able to sell some of these items to the GDR obviously helps in the short-term but there is little evidence to suggest that this measure in itself leads to *qualitatively new relations*.[54]

6. Even in the case of training of personnel under the rubric of scientific/technical cooperation, the claim that this purely constitutes aid can not be substantiated.[55] As shown in this chapter, the training of personnel, particularly inside the developing country itself, mainly follows trade relations and is usually part of the sales package. Even if the training takes place at concessional terms (as it probably often does), as long as it takes place in order to enable an East German firm to make a sale in the face of stiff competition from a Western multinational corporation, the aid label is misplaced, unless one wishes to count this as aid to the East German firm in making the sale.

7. According to UNCTAD, the socialist countries as a whole have directed most of their economic cooperation agreements with African countries—a full 79 percent—toward the industrial sector and only 5.2 percent toward agriculture.[56] This does not show a deep understanding of the primary problem facing sub-Saharan Africa; i.e., how to transform peasant-based agricultural production in order attain food sufficiency. It shows that the East seeks to apply its own model of economic growth in the South, even when conditions there are vastly different. It also seems to confirm that an important motivation of the East (and particularly of a highly industrialized country such as the GDR) is to export machinery and import primary commodities. Helping peasants attain food self-sufficiency does not generate this type of economic activity, at least not in the immediate future.

8. By concentrating its "trade and aid" relations in the agricultural sector mainly on state farms, the GDR does little to help alleviate the lot of the peasantry as a whole. Ethiopia, for example, has committed about ninety percent of its agricultural investments to state farms, which now produce roughly five percent of agricultural output.[57] This dovetails neatly with the demands of a highly centralized government for a high

level of control, which in turn dovetails nicely with the GDR's own ideas about economic and political organization. The burden of proof is on the GDR, however, to show how support for highly capital-intensive, mechanized, and inefficient state farms serves the interests of the masses of peasants living at or below subsistence level.

9. If, in addition, the agricultural goods produced on the state farm, such as coffee, for example, are earmarked for export to the GDR, the neocolonial nature of the relationship is even more pronounced. This arrangement does not alter the "dualistic" nature of domestic agriculture, with large production units (now state farms but in colonial times large foreign owned plantations) produce for export while the peasant sector is unable to provide sufficient nutritional means for the local population.[58]

10. The logic of the dual model advanced by the GDR; i.e., building socialism at the superstructural level while gradually gaining concessions from imperialism, assumes that imperialism is vitally interested in *all* developing countries and that the latter have considerable leverage over the interests of foreign capital. Yet as the situation in both Mozambique and Angola has shown, for example, the power of a very poor and economically backward country to harness imperialism for its own advantage is actually extremely limited.[59] Transnational corporations simply move elsewhere if the conditions imposed on them by a "progressive" country are not to their liking. Even the signing of the Nkomati accord with South Africa in early 1984 did not bring the foreign investors the FRELIMO government had hoped for. The CMEA countries, on the other hand, have shown themselves unable to fill the gap economically and, like the GDR, have pursued a strategy of self-interest in dealing with this country in the economic sphere.

11. By aiding in the transformation of Third World societies at the *political* (superstructural) level without helping to change the problem at the economic base; i.e., the substructural level, the GDR's policies *vis-à-vis* the South are self-defeating. Helping in the construction of socialism in the periphery by establishing a costly and inefficient political and military superstructure while offering no real solutions to the economic problems of the Third World, the GDR thus becomes part of the problem rather than a possible solution.

To conclude in the words of Michael Barratt Brown:

> These are harsh judgements, but the evidence is inescapable, in the growing dependence of the Soviet Union and of Eastern Europe on Western capitalism, technology and grain supplies, even more in the attempt to emulate capitalist production, "catching up with the West," and not building a new society. . . . The Soviet Union was not itself able to offer an alternative world system but only an Eastern bloc and a military bloc.[60]

Nowhere is this more apparent than in the economic relations between East and South, of which the GDR's relations with sub-Saharan Africa as outlined in this chapter are but one example.

Notes

1. With less than four percent of the total population and roughly one-half percent of the land within the CMEA community, the GDR's share of total CMEA trade is 13.4 percent and per capita production is 176 percent of the CMEA average. *Zahlenspiegel Bundesrepublik/Deutsche Demokratische Republik*, third edition, Bonn: Bundesministerium für innerdeutsche Beziehungen, first edition September 1985, p. 43.

2. See, for example, Friedmar Clausnitzer, "Prinzipien und Praxis der Aussenhandelspolitik der DDR gegenüber Entwicklungsländern," in: *Asien, Afrika, Lateinamerika*, No. 5, 1974; Jürgen Nitz and Paul Freiberg, "Ökonomische Zusammenarbeit zwischen RGW-Staaten und national befreiten Ländern," in: *Deutsche Aussenpolitik*, 4/80, and "Zur ökonomischen Zusammenarbeit zwischen der DDR und befreiten Ländern," in: *Deutsche Aussenpolitik*, 8/81. For a fuller discussion of the trade between the GDR and LDCs from a West German perspective, see, for example, Bernard von Plate, "Die Handelsbeziehungen der DDR mit den Entwicklungsländern," in: *Deutschland Archiv*, Vol. 13, August 1980; Hans Siegfried Lamm and Siegfried Kupper, *DDR und Dritte Welt*, Munich and Vienna: R. Oldenbourg Verlag, 1976, pp. 100–107.

3. UNCTAD/TD/280, *Trade Relations Among Countries Having Different Economic and Social Systems and All Trade Flows Resulting Therefrom*, UNCTAD VI (Belgrade, June 1983), Item 3d–Policy Paper, p. 24.

4. Gerhard Scharschmidt/Wolfgang Spröte, "DDR an der Seite der Entwicklungsländer im Kampf um demokratische Umgestaltung der internationalen Wirtschaftsbeziehungen," in: *IPW-Berichte*, Vol. 13, Nr. 9, 1984, p. 19.

5. Information obtained during the author's research visit to the GDR during 1983/84 and in the summer of 1985.

6. Quoted in Scharschmidt, "Economic Cooperation between the German Democratic Republic and developing countries," in: *Economic Quarterly*, Berlin (East), Vol. 19, Nr. 4, 1984, p. 8.

7. For an East German perspective of the nature of economic cooperation between the socialist countries and "socialist-oriented" third world nations, see Gerhard Scharschmidt/Manfred Stelter, "Bedingungen und Tendenzen der ökonomischen und wissenschaftlich-technischen Zusammenarbiet zwischen Mitgliedsländern des RGW and Ländern Asiens, Afrikas und Lateinamerikas mit sozialistischem Entwicklungsweg," in: *Asien, Afrika, Lateinamerika*, Vol. 13, Nr. 5, 1984, pp. 802–812; Jörg Jeran, "Zur ökonomischen Zusammenarbeit der DDR und der sozialistischen Länder mit Entwicklungsländern," in: *Wissenschaftliche Zeitung*, Hochschule für Verkehrswesen, Nr. 2, 1986, pp. 217–223.

8. Istvan Dobozi, "Ost-Süd Wirtschaftsbeziehungen: Ungesund," in: *Entwicklungspolitik*, Bonn, Nr. 22, 1984, p. 13. Also see his chapter in this volume.

9. UNCTAD, *Manual on Trading with the Socialist Countries of Eastern Europe*, UNCTAD/ST/TSC/1/Rev.1, 1987, pp. 38–39.

10. Gerhard Scharschmidt, "Economic Cooperation . . . ," p. 12.

11. Heinrich Machowski and Siegfried Schultz, "Die Beziehungen zwischen den sozialistischen Planwirtschaften und der Dritten Welt," in: *Deutschland Archiv*, Vol. 14, July 1981, p. 739.

12. Ralf Schaarschmidt, "DDR/Entwicklungsländer. Traditionelle und neue Formen der wirtschaftlichen Zusammenarbeit," in: *Horizont*, Vol. 17, Nr. 7, July 1984, p. 23.

13. UNCTAD, *Prospects in Trade* . . . , p. 14.

14. For a thorough treatment of the energy and raw materials situation in the CMEA and cooperative ventures between it and LDCs, see Istvan Dobozi, "Arrangements for Mineral Development Cooperation between Socialist Countries and Developing Countries," in: *Natural Resources Forum* (United Nations, New York 1983), pp. 339–350; also *Intra-CMEA Mineral Cooperation: Implications for Trade with OECD and Third World Countries*, paper presented at the Workshop on East-West Mineral Trade, IIASA, 5–7 March 1984.

15. East German products are of very high quality for CMEA standards but still not good enough to compete with products from advanced capitalist countries and lately also of the newly industrialized countries such as Singapore, Taiwan, Hong Kong, and South Korea. The latter group has industrialized in a highly export-dependent mode and is able to sell its products very competitively due to cheap labor and a level of technology far exceeding that of the socialist countries. Imports from these four "little tigers" now constitute roughly forty percent of the total import volume of the United States, for example. *Die Rheinpfalz*, 19 March 1988.

16. T. Bartkowski, "The Conditions for Effective Economic Relations of the Socialist Countries with the African States," in: *Economic Relations of Africa with the Socialist Countries*, Vol. III, Budapest, 1978, p. 43. See also Tibor Kiss, "Einige Fragen der internationalen Arbeitsteilung und des Wirtschaftswachstums," in: Gunther Kohlmey, ed., *Aussenwirtschaft und Wachstum: Theoretische Probleme des ökonomischen Wachstums im Sozialismus und Kapitalismus*, Berlin: Akademie-Verlag, 1968, pp. 256–281. The Kiss contribution is interesting because it addressed these questions a full two decades ago.

17. Under the leadership of Mikhail Gorbachev, the Soviet Union is once again attempting to move "socialist economic integration" forward. The hope is that such mechanisms as "direct ties" between Soviet and Eastern European firms will move cooperation and economic activity between individual CMEA members beyond the mainly rhetorical level. For a full discussion of these developments inside the CMEA, see *USSR: New Management Mechanism in Foreign Economic Relations*, UNCTAD/ST/TSC/10, 2 October 1987.

18. For an elaboration of these various payment methods, see *Payments Arrangements among Countries Having Different Economic and Social Systems*, UNCTAD/ST/TSC/3, 18 April 1986. Ironically, now that the socialist countries have switched their trading practices from clearing arragements to hard currency transactions, Western firms have "discovered" clearing and are increasingly

looking for barter agreements with Third World countries to improve their sales opportunities. For a very useful overview of these developments in trade between the West and the South, see John E. Parsons, *A Theory of Countertrade Financing of International Business*, Working Paper Nr. 1632-85, MIT Sloan School of Management, March 1985. See also "Third World Debt is Encumbering U.S. Trade," *International Herald Tribune*, 28 December 1987.

19. Kohlmey, *Aussenwirtschaft und Wachstum* . . . , p. 8.

20. Hans-Peter Krueger, *Werte und Weltmarkt: Zur Bildung und Realisierung internationaler Werte*, Berlin, 1984, for which the young author immediately received highest academic recognition in the country. The argument itself is not new, of course. Some Western Marxists have used the same line of reasoning in works published over the last two decades. See, *inter alia*, Bill Warren, *Imperialism: Pioneer of Capitalism*, London: Verso, 1980, and Robert Brenner, "On the Origins of Capitalist Development: A Critique of Neo-Smithian Marxism," in: *New Left Review*, Nr. 104, July/August 1977, in the so-called "articulation debate" to attack the dependency, world system, and unequal exchange perspectives of writers such as Frank, Rodney, Wallerstein, Amin, Emmanuel, etc.

21. Istvan Dobozi and Andreas Inotai, "Prospects of Economic Cooperation between CMEA Countries and Developing Countries," in: Christopher T. Saunders, ed., *East-West-South: Economic Interactions between Three Worlds*, New York: 1981, p. 51.

22. Deepak Nayyar, comments on Part I of *ibid.*, p. 82.

23. Wolfgang Schöller, " 'Komparativer Nachteil' und 'wechselseitiger Nutzen': Zur Kooperation zwischen COMECON und Entwicklungsländern am Beispiel Mosambiks," in: *Deutschland Archiv*, Vol. 17, December 1983, p. 1309.

24. Ralf Schaarschmidt, "Traditionelle und neue Formen der wirtschaftlichen Zusammenarbeit," in: *Horizont*, Nr. 7, 1984, p. 23.

25. Henrik Bischof, *Ost-West Wirtschaftskooperation in Drittländern*, Bonn: Forschungsinstitut der Friedrich-Ebert-Stiftung, 1985, p. 11.

26. Carl H. McMillan, *The Political Economy of Tripartiate (East-West-South) Industrial Cooperation*, Ottawa, 1980, pp. 10–11.

27. Jan and Grazyna Monkiewicz, two Polish economists, actually go so far as to call these reservations "ideological superstition," in their chapter of this volume.

28. Gerhard Scharschmidt, "Stellung und Perspektiven der Ost-West-Zusammenarbeit auf Drittmärkten aus der Sicht der DDR," in: *IPW Berichte*, July 1984, p. 12.

29. For a fuller discussion of these cases, see Bischof, *Ost-West-Wirtschaftskooperation* . . . , pp. 7–28.

30. Information included in talk delivered by Egon Overbeck, former chairman of the board of Mannesmann AG (an important West German multinational) at an international symposium on "Economic Cooperation between Socialist and Capitalist Industrialized Countries on Third Markets" in Berlin (GDR) from 15–17 May 1984.

31. Bischof, *Ost-West-Wirtschaftskooperation* . . . , p. 4.

32. *Neuer Weg*, Nr. 1, 1987, p. 30.

33. Gerhard Scharschmidt, "Economic co-operation . . . ," p. 8.

34. *Ibid.*, p. 8.

35. Interview with officials at the *Institut für berufliche Entwicklung* (ibe) on 7 March 1984. This organization is responsible for coordinating the vocational training of all foreigners in the GDR.

36. Gerhard Scharschmidt, "Economic Cooperation . . . ," p. 12.

37. *Ibid.*

38. *Ibid.*

39. *Neues Deutschland,* 13 August 1986, p. 2.

40. *Horizont,* No. 30, 1982.

41. See *ibe's* brochure entitled "Imparting of vocational-technical knowledge and skills to foreign citizens by vocational-technical training establishments of the German Democratic Republic," Berlin, no date, for detailed information concerning these programs inside the GDR.

42. Interview at the *ibe,* 7 March 1984.

43. *Neues Deutschland,* 13 August 1986.

44. For a detailed account of the GDR's perspective on agricultural production, see Klaus-Joachim Michalski, *Ökonomik der Landwirtschaft der Entwicklungsländer,* Parts I and II, Leipzig: Karl Marx University, 1982. This is the text book used in the Institute for Tropical Agriculture at the University and written by the foremost tropical agricultural expert in the GDR.

45. For an excellent analysis of the experience of China, North Korea, Albania, and Cuba in building their versions of socialism, see "Sozialismus und autozentrierte Entwicklung: Zur Korrektur eines entwicklungspolitischen Modells anhand der Beispiele China, Nordkorea, Albanien und Kuba," in: *Hilfe + Handel = Frieden? Die Bundesrepublik in der Dritten Welt,* Frankfurt am Main, 1982, pp. 307–358.

46. For the seminal work on the role of African women in agriculture, see Esther Boserup, *Women's Role in Economic Development,* New York: 1970.

47. The Soviet third world expert G. Mirski basically admits as much in a recent article "Zur Wahl des Weges der Entwicklungsländer," which appeared in a German translation in: *Sowjetwissenschaft: Gesellschaftswissenschaftliche Beiträge,* Nr. 1, 1988, pp. 64–75. Although Mirski does not single out women per se, he does discuss the fact that policy prescriptions of the East in the past have not paid enough attention to different sociological factors and have been too "eurocentric" in their approach.

48. For detailed analyses, see Joseph Hanlon, *Mozambique: Revolution under Fire,* London: 1984; John Saul, ed., *A Difficult Road: The Transition to Socialism in Mozambique,* New York: 1985.

49. Halina Araszkiewicz and Pavel Apostol, *Osteuropa und Afrika: Ökonomische und soziokulturelle Aspekte des Technologietransfers zwischen Ost und Süd,* Munich: Wilhelm Fink Verlag, 1986, p. 82.

50. During the author's various research trips to the GDR, she heard over and over that the East simply cannot afford "more Cubas and Vietnams." The feeling very clearly was that support for these two countries has already reached the limits of available means.

51. Gerhard Scharschmidt and Manfred Stelter, "Bedingungen und Tendenzen der ökonomischen und wissenschaftlich-technischen Zusammenarbeit zwischen Mitgliedsländern des RGW und Ländern Asiens, Afrikas und Lateinamerikas mit sozialistischem Entwicklungsweg," in: *Asien, Afrika, Lateinamerika*, Vol. 12, Nr. 5, 1984, p. 807.

52. Marie Lavigne, a noted Western expert on the socialist economies, argues that the case it not as simple as that, although in the end she too is forced to admit that in economic terms the Eastern bloc's interests are "linked to those of the developed market economies in an objective collusion." See "East-South Trade in Primary Products: A Model Borrowed from the North-South Pattern?" in: *Journal für Entwicklungspolitik*, Vol. 2, Nr. 2, Vienna, Summer 1986.

53. Michael Barratt Brown, *Models in Political Economy: A Guide to the Arguments*, Boulder: Lynne Rienner Publishers, 1985, p. 142.

54. See, for example, a doctoral dissertation written for the Academy of Social Sciences at the SED Central Committee. Ilona Schulz, *Voraussetzungen, Entwicklungsrichtungen und Hauptformen stabiler und gegenseitig vorteilhafter ökonomischer Beziehungen zwischen europäischen Mitgliedsländern des RGW (insbesondere der DDR) und Ländern Asiens und Afrikas, die einen sozialistischen Entwicklungsweg beschreiten (untersucht am Beispiel der Wirtschaftsbeziehungen mit der VR Angola, dem Sozialistischen Äthiopien, der VR Mocambique und der VDR Jemen*, May 1982. This dissertation outlines all of the main arguments advanced by the GDR for the claimed superiority of its relations with developing countries, particularly those with "socialist orientation."

55. For an example of this type of claim, see the GDR's report to the United Nations on its "aid" activities in the Third World, the first such report it ever submitted. *Communication from the Minister of Foreign Trade and Head of Delegation of the German Democratic Republic*, T5D/304, 14 June 1983.

56. See *Trade and Economic Co-operation between African Countries and Socialist Countries of Eastern Europe*, UNCTAD/ST/TSC/7, p. 24.

57. For an interesting analysis of the agricultural policy pursued by the Ethiopian government, see Keith B. Griffin, "The Economic Crisis in Ethiopia," in: W. Ladd Hollist and F. Lamond Tullis, eds., *Pursuing Food Security: Strategies and Obstacles in Africa, Asia, Latin America, and the Middle East*, Boulder: Lynne Rienner Publishers, 1987, pp. 121–136.

58. For an excellent overview of the problems associated with this "dual" agricultural system, see Michael F. Lofchie, "The External Determinants of Africa's Agrarian Crisis," in *ibid.*, pp. 98–120.

59. President Dos Santos of Angola even travelled to Davos, Switzerland in early 1988 to participate in the famous International Management Symposium in the hopes of attracting foreign investors to his country. *Der Spiegel*, Nr. 4, Vol. 42, 1988, p. 72.

60. Michael Barrett Brown, *Models in Political Economy . . .* , pp. 145 and 227.

About the Contributors

Istvan Dobozi is the Director of the Center for Development Studies at the Institute of World Economics of the Hungarian Academy of Sciences in Budapest. He has written extensively on East-South relations and is the Editor of the journal *Development and Peace*.

Helmut Faulwetter is a Professor of Economics at the Institute for the Economy of Developing Countries at the College of Economics (Hochschule für ökonomie) in Berlin (East). He is considered one of the most renowned experts in the GDR on Third World development issues. His two most recent books are *Entwicklungsländer am Scheideweg* and *Entwicklungsländer und Neue Wirtschaftsordnung*.

André Gunder Frank is a Professor of Economics at the University of Amsterdam as well as the author of many books and articles on history, international political economy, and development issues. His most famous work is the seminally influential *Capitalism and Underdevelopment in Latin America*.

William D. Graf is Professor of Government at the University of Guelph (Ontario). He has published many articles on African and European politics. Among his several books are *The German Left since 1945* and *Canada and the South*.

Patrick Gutman is an Economist at the University of Paris I (Pantheon-Sorbonne), Institute for the Study of Economic and Social Development (Institut d'Etude du Developpement Economique et Social). He is one of the world's leading authorities on tripartite economic cooperation and has published widely in Europe as well as the United States.

William W. Hansen is a Lecturer of Political Science at the University of Maryland, European Division. He has published articles in *Africa Today, The Journal of Modern African Studies,* and *Monthly Review*. He is currently doing research on the South African labor movement.

Winrich Kühne is a Research Analyst at the Institute for Science and Politics (Stiftung Wissenschaft und Politik) in Ebenhausen bei München. His latest book is *Die Politik der Sowjetunion in Afrika*.

Grazyna Monkiewicz is a Lecturer in Economics at the Institute of Economic and Social Sciences at Warsaw Technical University in Poland.

Jan Monkiewicz is an Associate Professor of Economics at the Institute of Economic and Social Science at Warsaw Technical University with an extensive publication record. His most recent book is *Technology Export from the Socialist Countries*.

Kunibert Raffer is a Professor of Economics at the Institute for Economic Science (Institut für Wirtschaftswissenschaften) at the University of Vienna. He

238

is the editor of the *Journal für Entwicklungspolitik* and has published widely on development issues. His latest book is *Unequal Exchange and the Evolution of the World System*.

Robin Alison Remington is Chair of the Department of Political Science at the University of Missouri (Columbia). She is author of *The Warsaw Pact* and editor of *Winter in Prague: Documents on Czecholovak Communism in Crisis*, as well as numerous articles.

Brigitte H. Schulz is a political scientist teaching at Trinity College, Hartford, Connecticut. Her articles have appeared in books and journals published in several countries. She is currently completing a book comparing the development aid strategies pursued by the East and the West in the South, using the two German states in Africa as empirical examples.

Peter W. Schulze is Senior Research Fellow of the Research Institute of the Friedrich Ebert Stiftung in Bonn. In addition to his numerous articles on East European politics and international economic and political relations, he is the author of several books, including *Herrschaft und Klassen in der Sojwetgesellschaft: Die historischen Bedingungen des Stalinismus*.

Index